The Book of the Greyhound

Sue LeMieux

To Pepi and Cindy,
an incredible team,
and
to Jody,
"Mama" to all the Gaia Greyhounds

ACKNOWLEDGMENTS

As with any endeavor of this kind, the compilation of a breed book cannot be accomplished without the assistance and support of many people and organizations. The author would like to take this opportunity to thank all of the Greyhound owners and breeders from around the world who have so graciously contributed their photos, artwork, knowledge, and information. This work would not have been possible without them.

Special recognition should go to Greyhound authors of the past, from whose material much of the historical information in this book was drawn; to guest authors Linda Colflesh, Sue Cassem, and Dani Edgerton; to the professional photographers for their skill and tireless effort to preserve our breed in photos; to Drs. Don and Judy Sanders and the staff at the Urbana Veterinary Clinic for proofing the Greyhound health chapters; to Jan Casto, for her moral support and many, many hours of typing to bring this work to fruition; to Bo Bengtson for having made suggestions; to Connie Isbell for bringing it all together; and to Jody Spires for keeping the home fires burning during these long months.

The author wishes to acknowledge that several important kennels are not mentioned in this publication. An invitation to be a part of this book was extended to all breeders, and *The Book of the Greyhound* includes those breeders who responded.

The following list includes, but does not encompass, all of these Greyhound kennels who have contributed to the breed in so many ways. The author would like to take this opportunity to acknowledge these kennels and the great Greyhounds they have produced.

Aroi	Kingsmark
Another Episode	Lochinvar
Cyrano	Lulworth
Gallant	Seamair
Heathero	Solstrand
Holmby Hills	Talos

CONTENTS

About the Author

Dogs have been an important part of Sue LeMieux's life since her childhood, when she taught the family pet every trick Lassie could do on television and every obedience exercise she could find in training manuals at the library. She and "Bootsie" performed at neighborhood talent shows and put on demonstrations at school. Ms. LeMieux even had a puppy in college, though she had to keep the dog at a friend's fraternity house once he was caught in her dormitory room.

Greyhound Club of America National Specialty, September 12, 1957. *Photo by William Brown*

In 1965 Ms. LeMieux began showing Collies and was quite active in the breed for several years. She started an obedience club, was co-founder of the humane society in her county, and held several offices in her local breed and all-breed clubs. She was also a regular contributor to Collie breed publications.

Soon after the birth of her second child, Ms. LeMieux found that the demands of motherhood and her teaching career did not permit enough time to devote to her dogs, so she reluctantly left the dog show world for almost 20 years. In the interim, she was never without a dog, owning two Golden Retrievers, a Labrador Retriever, and an Irish Setter.

During her career as a science educator, Ms. LeMieux wrote extensively in the curriculum field, and developed many innovative techniques for teaching science in the elementary classroom.

When Ms. LeMieux's career finally cleared enough to permit her return to her first love of showing dogs, she did so with alacrity and much success. Her first Greyhound, Ch. Sundridge So Be It, JC, was a Greyhound Club of America National Specialty and All Breed Best in Show winner and was ranked as the number one Greyhound in all-breed competition in 1995. Ms. LeMieux has bred and/or owned a number of Greyhound champions, including several ranked number one in Canada, a BIS and multi BIS Int. multi champion from one litter, and several Greyhounds with lure coursing titles.

Ms. LeMieux is the recording secretary for the Greyhound Club of America, a member of two regional Greyhound clubs, the Irish Water Spaniel Club of America, the Columbus All Breed Training Club, the Greater Columbus Sighthound Coursing Association, the Champaign County Humane Society, the Champaign County Arts Council, and the Phi Delta Kappa Honorary Society.

The Greyhound has graced the cover of many magazines, including this 1931 issue of *Woman's Home Companion. Courtesy Annie Fitt*

History of the Greyhound

The Greyhound is an ancient, majestic canine that has been a helpmate and companion of the human race for thousands of years.

"But I always thought Greyhounds were gray," is a comment I hear quite often when I am out with my dogs. Despite their ever-growing popularity, many people have never actually seen a Greyhound. I explain that Greyhounds come in many colors, and that the gray color, which breeders refer to as blue, is, in fact, not a very common color.

No one seems to know for certain the actual derivation of the Greyhound name. At least one historian of the breed, in agreement with those mentioned above, attributed the name to what apparently was the prevalent color of the day. Others have attributed the name to a corruption of "Greek-hound," or *Canis graecus*, stating the belief that the Greeks were among the first to course Greyhounds. According to Hugh Dalziel, writing in *The Greyhound* in 1887, Dr. Caius, cofounder of Granville and Caius College in Cambridge, believed the name "to have been given on account of the high rank or degree the dog was held among his fellows."

'The Grehound hath his name of this word *gre*, which word soundeth gradus in Latin, in English degree, because amoung all dogges, these are the most principall, occupying the chiefest place, and being simply and absolutely the best of the gentle kinde of Houndes.'"

Many spellings of Greyhound have appeared in writings throughout the ages. Ovid, in his *Metamorphoses*, written nearly 2,000 years ago, used Grewnde:

"And even as when the greedy Grewnde doth course the sillic hare

Amiddes the plain and champion fielde without all covert bare."

The poet Chaucer referred to the "greihounde," while old Norse writings referred to the Greyhundr. The Old English word for Greyhound was Grighund. The Middle English spelling was Grihunde or Grechound. Other spellings included Graehund and Grehound.

The exact date that the present spelling was first used is unknown, but by the time Shakespeare was writing, the modern spelling was already in use. In *Merry Wives of Windsor*, Master Slender asks, "how does your fallow greyhound? I heard he was outrun on Cotsale." In *King Henry V*, Shakespeare's King states, "I see you stand like greyhounds in the slips, straining upon the start, the games afoot."

Despite the variations in the spelling of Greyhound, it seems the pronunciation has remained fairly uniform and similar to today's English pronunciation.

ORIGIN OF THE BREED

The origin of the Greyhound as a breed is as steeped in mystery and conjecture as is its name. One

Hunt scene from the Palazzo Medici Ricardi, 15ᵗʰ century.

thing is certain, though, the Greyhound type of domestic canine can be traced back at least 5,000 years. Archeologists have uncovered many artifacts, coins, and paintings that depict dogs resembling present-day sighthound breeds, but we cannot know for certain whether any of these were actually selectively bred animals. Mary E. Thurston, in her article "The Dogs of Ancient Egypt," in the August 1993 issue of the *AKC Gazette,* states that "no archeological evidence linking modern dogs to ancient ones has been uncovered to date, so all we know for sure is that today's sighthounds are descendants of progenitors imported from the Middle East." She goes on to say, "It is plausible that with time genetic researchers may be able to determine whether modern sighthounds are indeed heirs to ancient pedigreed. But the wait may be a long one."

Eventually, the Greyhound-type dog was selectively bred, probably by nomadic people who prized its speed, endurance, and ability to hunt by sight. Connie Miller, in the fourth part of her series of articles that appeared in the March-April 1977 issue of *Gazehound,* corroborated this belief with her statement: "Here I tend to fall into line with the suspicions that the same genius that bred horses with such skill as to lead to the Arabian was also able to appreciate the budding gazehound." She goes on to say that "writers speak of the nomad's greyhounds reverently, becoming curiously oblivious to the useful but mongrel-appearing swarm of camp dogs." The gazehounds were the only dogs these nomads brought into their tents to live. According to Ms. Miller, "An irrational faith in the holy purity of the gazehound developed as it became the 'hot-blooded dog,' taking a universally admired place next to (or riding on) the 'hot-blooded horse' credited to the Arabs. Words, more than a little exaggerated, of the gazehounds' wondrous abilities and high-flown nature blanketed the civilized and not-so-civilized nations. By reputation, the gazehound became a precious trading commodity."

The smooth-coated, long-limbed dogs of ancient times were developed to hunt in a specific geographical location. One of these locations, often alluded to in discussions of the origin of various sighthound breeds, is ancient Egypt. Several breed histories trace their origins back to Anubis, the jackal-like dog depicted on tomb walls and religious iconography of this early culture. In the fifth part of her series of 1977 articles in the *Gazehound*, Connie Miller has this to say about Anubis: "Although his collar marks him as 'domesticated,' he so puzzled archeologists that they called him jackal-dog for lack of conviction either way. Despite some obvious resemblance to the erect eared Ibizan Hounds (and Pharaoh Hounds), the fact is that the genderless Anubis was not a hunting dog! From Old through New Kingdom he is unwaveringly presented as

Roman redware plate fragment depicting early hound.
Courtesy Ancient World Arts, Ltd.

Guardian of the Royal Dead. Aside from Anubis, there are a number of other long legged dogs on various dynastic tombs that do appear to be hunting dogs. All sighthound (and many non-sighthound) histories claim these dynastic dogs as forerunners of their breeds."

It is likely that Greyhound-type dogs were carried into Egypt and to countries north and east of the Mediterranean by nomadic tribesman, explorers, and those returning from wars. No doubt people of these different cultures quickly came to appreciate the keen hunting skill and beauty of these streamlined dogs.

The ancient Greeks, great lovers of beauty, embraced the Greyhound. They

Early sighthounds, including a Greyhound.

used them to course hare and included them in much of their artwork. In the 1930s Edward C. Ash wrote in *The Practical Dog Book* that "Certain areas of the Grecian Empire were known as dog-breeding centres, and the Greyhound type of dog was the important variety of dog in Greece. Coins and gems bore the effigy of the Greyhound." The coins Mr. Ash refers to were found on Aegean Islands off the coast of Greece and date from 500 B.C. to 200 B.C. In the *New Book of the Dog,* published in London in 1912, Fred Gresham told readers that the Greyhound "was recognized very early by the Greeks, whose artists were fond of introducing this graceful animal as an ornament in their decorative workmanship. In their metal work, their carvings in ivory and stones, and more particularly in the designs on their terra cotta oil bottles, wine coolers, and other vases, the Greyhound is frequently to be seen, sometimes following the hare, and usually in remarkably characteristic attitudes. Usually these Greek Greyhounds are represented with prick ears, but occasionally the true rose ear is shown, and in the British Museum there is a bronze lamp of the fourth century B.C., made in the form of a Greyhound's head. The lip of the lamp is fashioned in the form of a hare, held in the hound's mouth, thus proving that the hare was the recognized quarry." The Greek poet, Homer, mentioned the Greyhound in the *Odyssey,* composed circa 800 B.C. Odysseus, returning home from adventures lasting 20 years, was recognized only by his aged Greyhound, Argus.

According to the King James Version of the Bible, the Greyhound was mentioned in the Old Testament Book of Proverbs 30:29-31, written by Agur, son of Jakeh.

"There be three things which go well, yea,

Four are comely in going:

A lion, which is strongest among beasts and

Turneth not away for any;

A Greyhound;

And he-goat also;

And a King against whom there is no rising up."

There is some discrepancy as to whether the Hebrew word *zarziyr* means Greyhound, as translated by English scholars in 1611. According to *Strong's Exhaustive Concordance,* zarziyr means "Tightly girt, i.e., probably a racer, or some fleet animal (as being slender in the waist): Greyhound." However, when we find Greyhound in *Unger's Bible Dictionary,* we find the following: Greyhound—translation of Hebrew zarziyr mathnayim "well-girt or well-knit in the loins" (Proverbs 30:31).

As with all research into ancient cultures, histories, and writings, there is much room for conjecture. It may never be answered whether the Old Testament author of Proverbs Book 30 honored the Greyhound by including it as the only canine mentioned in the Bible.

Whether the Greyhound is a part of Biblical lore or not, we know that fleet hounds that hunted by sight existed during the time of the Old Testament and traveled with Semitic peoples.

Like the Greeks, the Romans kept and coursed Greyhounds; the breed also appeared frequently in Roman artwork. There is a Roman statue of two Greyhounds from the first century B.C. in the British Museum. This statue depicts a male and a female Greyhound, with the male appearing to chew on the female's ear. Two marble Greyhound statues were

Greyhounds Mr. W. Long's "David" and Mr. C. Randell's "Riot," by L. Wells, Delaware.

also found in the ruins of the villa of the Roman Emperor Antonius.

As the Arabs and their hounds migrated northward and eastward, these Greyhound-types were crossed with local dogs and developed into early forms of the sighthounds we recognize today. Size and coat type were largely determined by local climate, game, and terrain over which the dogs hunted. Gaelic tribesmen hunted with gazehounds and prized them highly. It is likely that these dogs accompanied the Galls when they moved into the British Isles. Greyhounds rose in popularity among the people of England and Ireland. They were highly valued by both peasants and kings. Early Irish records mention two types of Greyhounds, one referred to simply as the Greyhound, and the other, the hunting Greyhound. The Greyhound was more valued than the hunting dog, but no explanation was given as to the differences between the two.

GREYHOUNDS IN ENGLAND

The history of the Greyhound in England has been a long and colorful one. A 1959 excavation of the Avebury Stone Circle, a large prehistoric monument, revealed a 3,500-year-old skeleton of a Greyhound-like dog. When early progenitors of the breed arrived in the British Isles, we can assume that their elegance, speed, and agility attracted the attention of the local people. In *The Practical Dog Book,* Edward Ash suggests, "The value of such a dog to catch game would be realized at once. Indeed, the ownership

of a Greyhound meant, in rural districts, the end of starvation, for the owner of such a dog would be well-supplied with rabbits, hares, and an occasional duck or other animal. It explains the reason that legislation as to game of earlier times constantly refers to Greyhounds, and subjects this breed to restrictions, for the owners of game were anxious that those who had not right should not obtain it."

In *The Greyhound,* Hugh Dalziel also mentions the high value placed on the Greyhound and the restrictions concerning the ownership of a member of the breed. "That his possession was so restricted is shown by the Forest Laws of King Canute, which prohibited anyone under the degree of a gentleman from keeping a Greyhound." And "an old Welsh proverb says, 'You may know a gentleman by his horse, his hawk, and his Greyhound.' In the Welsh laws of Howel Dda (who died in 948), the King's Buckhound, or Covert-hound, is valued at a pound, and his Greyhound at six-score pence. In the Code of 1080 and the Dimetain Code of 1180, the Greyhound is valued at half that of Buckhound."

In Ireland, the Greyhound was also highly valued. The King's adult Greyhound was worth one pound, if trained, but only ten shillings if not trained. Even the King's Greyhound puppies, while still nursing, were worth 30 pence.

The Forest Laws of King Canute, who became King of England in 1014, established that "no mean" man could own a Greyhound, and no free man living within ten miles of a Royal Forest could keep a Greyhound on his property. The Royal House did not want the peasants interfering with their coursing of game.

Commoners who used Greyhounds to hunt hare and other small game for food were not willing to give up their dogs, and so England, for a period of over 100 years, experienced what have been called the Greyhound Wars. Local Courts were held every 40 days to try rural folk who broke the Forest Laws. Any Greyhound owners who were caught had to pay a fine to the King. Often their Greyhounds were mutilated or put to death. Fines consisted of produce or livestock, as the peasants had no money. Officers of the Court were appointed to identify those who broke the Forest Laws and could use most any means to find information leading to the conviction of these Greyhound-owning criminals.

To avoid being caught, the commoners hunted at night, and so preferred dark-colored dogs. White Greyhounds, on the other hand, were favored by the Court. White dogs became symbols of nobility and class, and until quite recent times, have been associated with and preferred by people of wealth and position. White or mostly white Greyhounds were considered to be of royal color.

When, because of continuous and widespread persecutions, the number of Greyhounds dwindled, the Royal House granted special privileges to farmers and clergymen who would breed and keep Greyhounds for the Court; these dogs could then be used for coursing by the King. Greyhounds were also imported from Ireland during this time to help increase their numbers.

When Edward became King (1272 to 1307), he enacted new laws to protect Greyhounds and required that any Greyhounds that were discovered hunting in the Royal Forests should be brought to him rather than killed. Eventually, though, the old laws were reenacted.

During the time of the Great Plague (1345 to 1348), Greyhounds were kept by peasants and farmers with little or no interference from the Court. However, during the reign of Richard II (1377 to

Lord Orford, who was instrumental in the early development of the sport of coursing. *Courtesy of The Greyhound Hall of Fame*

1399), the Greyhound Wars resumed. They continued into the 1600s when the old game laws were finally put to rest by Queen Elizabeth I (1558 to 1603). Queen Elizabeth, a great lover of Greyhounds, ordered Thomas Mowbray, the Duke of Norfolk, to develop an official set of rules for coursing. Those rules are much the same as the ones in use today. It was the British interest in coursing that shaped the Greyhound into the dog we know today.

The end of the Forest Laws and the increased means and leisure of the average English citizen led to a growing interest in the sport of coursing. Although coursing had existed for close to 2,000 years, it was an English Lord, the Earl of Orford, who was instrumental in developing the modern sport we know today. In 1776 he formed the Swaffham Club in Norfolk. This was the first coursing club in England. Membership was limited to 26. This is the number of letters in the English alphabet, which allowed each member to have a letter to use when naming his dogs.

Through his interest in coursing Lord Orford played an important part in the development of the modern Greyhound. Fra Vero Shaw, speaking of Lord Orford, quoted from "The Sportsman's Cabinet" in the *Illustrated Book of the Dog*, saying "There were times when he was known to have fifty brace of Greyhounds; and as it was a fixed rule never to part with a single whelp till he had a fair and substantial trial of his speed, he had evident chances (beyond almost any other individual) of having, amongst so great a number, a collection of very superior dogs; but so intent was he upon this peculiar object of attainment, that he went further in every possible direction to obtain perfection, and introduced every experimental cross, from the English Lurcher to the Italian Greyhound.

Maesydd Michael, the 1946 winner of the Waterloo Cup, a tradition since 1836.

He had strongly indulged an idea of a successful cross with the Bulldog, which he could never be divested of; and having persevered (in opposition to every opinion) most patiently for seven removes, he found himself in the possession of the best Greyhound yet known, giving the small ear, the rat tail, and skin almost without hair, together with the innate courage which the high-bred Greyhound should possess, retaining which instinctively, he would rather die than relinquish the chase."

It would seem that the eccentric Lord Orford also possessed an overwhelmingly keen interest in the chase, an interest that resulted in his own demise. According to Edward Ash, again in *The Practical Dog Book:* "Lord Orford's eccentricities had occasionally suggested insanity. A day came when he no longer attended coursing meetings. Well may it be imagined how anxiously he listened to the shouting and how deep were the longings that assailed him. On the last day of his life, for so it proved to be, Lord Orford's favourite Greyhound, Czarina, was to run a match against a well-known dog. The meet took place on Lord Orford's estate. It was a cold winter's day; the crowd was awaiting the match to start. All at once over the turf, as fast as the little short-legged, piebald pony could gallop, came Lord Orford. He wore neither coat nor hat. Friends hurried toward him. Their attempts to persuade him to return to the house (from which, evidently, he had escaped) were unavailing. Czarina and her opponent were on the hare. Lord Orford was galloping by their side. After an exciting course, Czarina won. Lord Orford had fallen off the pony. When the crowd reached him he was dying."

Czarina and others of Lord Orford's strain were purchased by Colonel

The Honorable Mrs. W. V. Beatty with her favorite pets on the grounds of their home in 1930.

Thornton. Czarina was to become the foundation bitch for some of the greatest coursing dogs in Britain. Claret, a dog from her first litter, sired the famous dog Snowball, who was owned by Major Topham of the Malton Coursing Club, founded in Yorkshire in 1781. The Malton Club's 20 members included some of the most famous names in English coursing history. Snowball won 30 courses and four cups during his career.

Another famous dog, who some think may be a descendant of Lord Orford's Bulldog cross, was King Cob. He was the first coursing Greyhound to be offered at public stud. Many pedigrees, if traced back far enough, contain King Cob blood.

Another early coursing club, the Ashdon Park Club, was formed in 1780 by Lord Craven. Edward Ash wrote of the Ashdon Club that "Each member wore a uniform selected by the patroness. If a steward appointed for a meeting, or his deputy, failed to attend, he was fined a dozen bottles of port, and a member criticizing the judging was immersed in a gallon of wine!"

Public interest in Greyhounds and the sport of coursing continued to increase, and new clubs and registries were established. In 1825 the Altcar Club was formed. Its founders were Viscount Molyreux and the Earl of Sefton. The first meeting was held in Liverpool, at the Waterloo Hotel. In 1836, William Lynn, the owner of the hotel, inaugurated the Waterloo Cup. This eight-dog stake was to become the most famous and prestigious coursing event in the world.

In 1858 the National Coursing Club (NCC) was formed. On July 15, 1883, all Greyhounds participating in meetings in England had to be registered with the NCC. On that date, almost 1,000 Greyhounds were entered into the registry. The first Greyhound Stud Book had already been published in 1882. Of the dogs listed, 35 were black or black and white, and 68 were brindle in color. In 1894 it was ruled by the NCC that all litters had to be registered by the time they were two months old. All markings on every puppy had to be listed, including the color of the eyes and of each toenail. In 1915 the Irish Coursing Club (ICC) was founded, with a registry similar to that of the NCC.

A natural outgrowth of the competitive spirit of Greyhound owners was the desire to compare their dogs, not just on coursing ability, but on beauty and conformation as well. These Greyhound owners were responsible, in part, for the formation of the Kennel Club of England in 1873. Fra Vero Shaw discusses the exhibition of some early Greyhounds: "It is a somewhat remarkable fact that Greyhound classes rarely fill well in the south of England, throughout several northern shows—Darlington, for instance—they are one of the chief features of the exhibition. This may be accounted for by the fact that coursing men do not come to show their dogs as a rule, and that the best performers, on their withdrawal from training, are valuable for stud purposes, and so never get into the possession of exhibitors who are not coursing men. There are, however, some grandly shaped Greyhounds shown in various parts of the country, and the only regret is that their number is so limited.

"By far the most successful show dog from the years 1873 to 1880 has been Lauderdale, who is the property of Mr. Tom Sharples. Mr. Tom Swinbrune's Marigold, too, is a bitch who has done her owner good service on the bench, and Mr. Fawdry's Ada is another who is near the top of the tree. Sister Mary, Dreaded Falcon, Mr. Waddington's Doctor, Mr. Bearpark's Game Cock, Mr. Sharple's Queen Bertha, and Mr. J.H. Salter's Amethyst and Fair Rosa have each and all of them made a reputation."

In 1926, Greyhound racing was introduced into England. Mr. Charles Munn from America and England's Brigadier-General A.C. Critchley were responsible for the Manchester track, in Bellevue, where on July 24, 1926, the first Greyhound race using a mechanical hare was held. Mistley, a Greyhound with only half a tail, was the winner of that first race. In 1928, the National Greyhound Racing Club (NGRC) was formed. Its responsibilities included licensing meetings, registering racing dogs, and running the races.

Greyhounds have experienced a long, varied, and interesting history in England. They continue to be quite popular as show dogs, coursers, racers, and beloved pets.

DEVELOPMENT OF THE BREED IN THE UNITED STATES

Greyhounds were some of the earliest dogs to accompany immigrants to the United States. Records indicate that the breed was brought to America as early as the 1500s by Spanish explorers and was present during the Revolutionary War. As the population grew and moved westward, it was discovered that Greyhounds were the perfect choice to help control the large jackrabbit population that was destroying farmers' crops. Many Greyhounds were imported from England and Ireland in the 1800s for this purpose. The competitive spirits of the owners of these magnificent animals soon came to the fore, and the sport of coursing live game grew out of their dogs' natural hunting abilities.

Soon coursing meets were being scheduled on weekends when the dogs were not working. The first coursing meet was held in Kansas in 1886, and Greyhound coursing become quite popular in the Midwest and West. In that same year, a gentleman by the name of Charles Frederick Holden began to assemble a pack of Greyhounds. Their hunting and coursing abilities were much appreciated by this English fox hunting gentleman. In 1888 Holden helped to organize the Valley Hunt Club in Pasadena, California, and in 1889, his Greyhound pack was presented along with other hounds at a festival and parade that became known in subsequent years as the Orange Parade, timed to coincide with the ripening of the oranges in the valley. This original celebration has changed over the years and is now known as the Rose Parade.

The National Coursing Association (NCA) was founded in 1896, a natural outgrowth of this country's growing interest in the sport of coursing Greyhounds. The history of coursing and racing Greyhounds is covered in later chapters. Here we will concentrate on the development of the Greyhound as a companion and show dog.

One of the most well-known owners of Greyhounds in the 1800s was General George A. Custer, who kept a pack of coursing and hunting dogs—including Greyhounds, Staghounds, and Foxhounds. These dogs accompanied him on

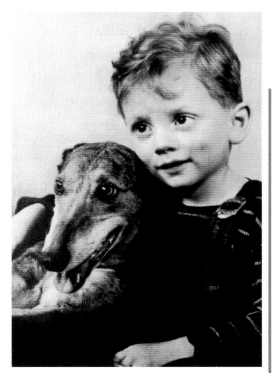

The famous Greenglen Greyhound "Meg" in 1944, with Willard Wright's son, Richard.

his marches, and he and his men were known to break rank and follow the hounds in pursuit of game when the occasion allowed.

We have several written accounts of General Custer's hounds, thanks largely to his wife Elizabeth. She kept diaries and letters that were compiled into three volumes describing army life on the frontier. Elizabeth made quite a few references to Custer's hounds, including a Greyhound named Byron. In the book *Tenting on the Plains*, Elizabeth talks about Byron. "We had a superb Greyhound called Byron, that was devoted to the General, and after a successful chase it was rewarded with many a demonstration of affection. He was the most lordly dog, I think, I ever saw; powerful, with deep chest, and carrying his head in a royal way. When he started for a run, with

Running a coyote with hounds in Southern California. Drawing by Frederic Remington appeared in an 1890 issue of *Harper's Weekly*.

French and American Ch. Canyon Crest's Coronation with Stanley Petter, Jr., and Ch. I. B. Reve D'Or Du Moyer Age with Contesse F. DeRobiano, in Deauville, France, 1958.

nostrils distended and his delicate ears laid back on his noble head, each bound sent him flying through the air. He hardly touched the elastic cushions of his feet to earth before he again was spread out like a dark, straight thread. This gathering and leaping must be seen, to realize how marvelous is the rapidity and how the motion seems flying, almost, as the ground is scorned except as a sort of springboard. He trotted back to the General, if he happened to be in advance, with the rabbit in his mouth, and holding back his proud head, delivered the game only to his Chief. The tribute that a woman pays to beauty in any form, I gave to Byron; but I never cared much for him."

Apparently this last sentence referred to Elizabeth's frustration with Byron over his typical Greyhound habits, such as pushing her from General Custer's bed and stealing food at mealtimes.

Surprisingly, we are also able to learn something of Greyhounds as pets and companions from two children's books published in the United States in the early 1900s. *Master St. Elmo: The Autobiography of a Celebrated Dog* (1904),

and *Greyhound Fanny* (1912) were written in the first person (or first hound, as may be more correct here), and both give us glimpses of daily life with a Greyhound during the first years of the 20th century.

In the first, St. Elmo humorously describes his experiences growing up in his new home with its highly polished staircase, so difficult for a gangly Greyhound puppy to negotiate. Apparently he had noticed an enticingly soft couch in a room downstairs and decided he would prefer it to his bed on the floor outside his master and mistress's bedroom. St. Elmo had been given a lesson in stair climbing earlier that evening, when his mistress had carefully placed one foot, then another, on the stair treads. St. Elmo relates his experience as follows:

"Then I thought, I can surely get down without assistance, so I put one trembling foot down, just on the first step, when—somebody pulled a string and those stairs seemed to close up, and the next thing I knew I landed in a heap on the first landing below, with such a bang that I woke the entire household, each one running to the head of the stairs and looking over the banister at poor me."

St. Elmo decided that he would rather try a bed upstairs. "I had noticed that all the family had high beds to sleep upon, with white coverlets, and I often rested my nose on them and knew they were nice and soft. I wondered if they were good enough for the family, why wouldn't they be just the thing for me, and save them making an extra bed up for me on the floor. So, one morning I quietly got up on that unoccupied bed, and found solid comfort at last—that is, for a dog. What a dandy sleep I was enjoying when my master discovered me, and I landed in a hurry on the floor." Like all persistent Greyhounds, St. Elmo did end up with a bed of his own and a place on the couch next to his mistress.

St. Elmo's first summer in his new home also saw the demise of the backyard full of beautiful flowers. He admits: "I dug tunnels in the velvety lawn as large as my body, and I would get right down in them and be almost out of sight."

"What surprised me the most was that after I had romped around for a day or so, the grass disappeared as if by magic, and not a blade of grass could be seen. That December when the flowers died—I felt a curious desire to see where they came from, so I dug way down into the ground and pulled up the bulbs and roots, and spaded the garden up in fine shape. At this time my master decided to turn the garden over to me, so he quit."

Any Greyhound owner who has raised a curious, rambunctious puppy can easily visualize the scenes described above. Greyhound youngsters have changed little in the past 90 years.

In *Greyhound Fanny,* Fanny lived a contented, love-filled life for 12 years with her mistress, known to her as "My Beautiful Lady." When her mistress grew quite ill, Fanny's master decided she should go to live with another family. She spent a long, lonely year in which she knew pain and some kindness, but she never forgot her Beautiful Lady. Christmas that next year found Fanny's original family living in a new house, and her mistress recovered from her illness. The Beautiful Lady's son, Harry, knowing how much his mother still grieved for Fanny, set out to reclaim the old dog for her. He was able to convince her new owners to part with Fanny, and he joyously took her home to his mother. In her own words, Fanny describes the reunion:

"When we reached my Master's home, a maid opened the door. We went

Ch. Seagift Parcancady Bluebell and Ch. Canyon Crest's Coronation with Stanley Petter, Jr. in June 1959.

Ch. Rudel's Jonny Come Lately, handled by Jean Millet.

Owned by Drs. Rudolph and Elsie Neustadt.

Photo by Gunderson

in and Harry unclasped my collar. Nothing was familiar to me, and feeling strange, I sank upon the floor. 'You will have to show her the way,' said my master. Then Harry bade me follow him again which I did, up a long stairway into a room where the glow of a soft red light fell shadowy everywhere. Then I heard that long-loved voice exclaim: 'Oh, Fanny, Fanny! My precious Fanny!' My delight was so great it seemed that I would tear up every rug as I ran back and forth, kissing my Beautiful Lady's hands at each turn, talking to her as I used to do in my dog fashion, listening to her words of welcome and praise, and watching the pleasure of my master and Harry as they witnessed this most joyful meeting between My Beautiful Lady and her dear dog."

All of those who have loved and been loved by a Greyhound can empathize with the feelings in the hearts of the Beautiful Lady and Fanny at the moment of the reunion some 80 years ago.

As interest in purebred dogs increased in this country, so of course did the number of breeders and owners.

Once again, America's competitive spirit asserted itself and inspired owners of Greyhounds and other purebred dogs to compare their pets and breeding stock in order to determine which animals were of the highest quality. Breed standards of excellence were developed, and breed clubs were formed to support the different breeds. The American Kennel Club (AKC) was instituted in 1884 to serve as a registry for purebred dogs in this country. Dog shows, both all-breed and specialties, were held by the various clubs and became quite popular sporting events, especially among the wealthy who had the leisure time and money to devote to large, well-staffed kennels.

The Greyhound Club of America was formed in 1907, but Greyhounds were exhibited at shows for many years prior to this. In 1909 the Greyhound Club of America (GCA) was officially recognized by the AKC. Originally the club was limited to 100 members, although there were only 23 members in 1909. Most of these original members belonged to New York society.

The first recorded Greyhound specialty was held in October 1923, in conjunction with the Whippet Club of America Specialty. There were 29 Greyhounds entered, including 2 braces, 5 teams, and 2 English imports. The show was held on the estate of J. S. Phipps, Esq. in Westbury, Long Island. Joseph Z. Batten served as judge. A coursing meet was held after the show, running live hare. The exhibitors were transported to the coursing field by a horse-drawn coach. A men-only, black-tie dinner was held the evening following the show, hosted by Mr. Ambrose Clark.

The American Kennel Club began keeping official records of Greyhound specialties beginning in 1936. The specialty that year was held at the Morris and Essex Kennel Club Show in May.

Dr. Elsie Neustadt with Ch. Argus of Greywitch in August 1969.

No specialty shows were held from 1937 to 1939. The Greyhound Club did hold specialties in 1940 and 1941, but did not try to host another show until after the war in 1945. An Eastern Specialty Show has been held every year since 1945, except for 1965, when the show was canceled.

Ch. Rudel's Solitaire with Tom Gately. Owned by Drs. Neustadt.

By 1968, the population of show Greyhounds in the West had grown to the point where a Western Specialty could be held. The Western Specialty has become an annual event, held in July as a part of the Western Sighthound Combined Specialties in Lompoc, California.

In recent years, obedience competition and lure coursing have been included as a part of each specialty show. Greyhound breeders and owners are regaining a sense of their breed as a performance animal as well as a show dog and pet.

Today, the Greyhound Club of America has just under 200 members, perhaps a small group by some comparison, but an extremely hard-working, conscientious, dedicated organization of breeders and owners who continually seek to preserve the very best of the breed.

History of the Greyhound Club of America

The Greyhound was one of the earliest breeds recognized by the American Kennel Club in the United States; records indicate that they were being shown as early as 1880, when 16 of them appeared at the Westminster Dog Show. The Greyhound Club of America (GCA), the parent club for the breed, was formed in 1907 and was officially recognized by the American Kennel Club (AKC) in 1909. Other national clubs preceded the GCA, but were mainly oriented toward the sport of coursing.

The Greyhound Club of America has always been the guardian of the breed. Many of the earliest members, such as Joseph Z. Batten, a founding member who remained active until his death at age 94, Mr. and Mrs. George West, Mr. and Mrs. James A. Farrell, Jr., Mr. and Mrs. Robert Forsyth, and Mrs. Susan Mason, to name a few, became pillars of the breed. It is thanks to them that AKC Greyhounds have developed into the exquisite animals they are today. The stock these early members imported from England has left an indelible mark on the breed.

Throughout the years the GCA has continued to increase and improve its membership services. As part of its mission, the club has made contributions to various veterinary schools, including Cornell University, the University of Pennsylvania, the Morris Animal Foundation, and others. The club's specialties—the eastern and western—have been major venues for AKC Greyhounds, and two new subsidiary clubs have been recognized; the Northern California Greyhound Club has held specialties since 1992, and the Texas Greyhound Club held its first in 1998.

In 1974, the club newsletter, first called *Greyhound Gleanings,* was begun. It was well received by the membership and slowly developed into the quality

Greyhound Club of America National Specialty, September 12, 1957. *Photo by William Brown*

publication that exists today. The first efforts of the club to sell old specialty catalogs and window decals have developed into the "Greyhound Boutique," which offers a variety of Greyhound-related items.

The club has also expanded its work to include a full-fledged rescue effort, which is funded by donations and auctions held at the specialty banquets, particularly the western. There is a code of ethics to which all members must subscribe, a video published by the American Kennel Club to help guide newcomers to the breed, and an out-of-print but classic book, *Greyhounds In America*. Finally, after many years the club formed an official archive in order to preserve the records of both the club and of the Greyhound in the United States.

—LAUREL E. DREW, ARCHIVIST

WHAT IS A GREYHOUND?

Dame Juliana Berners, in the *Boke of St. Albans*, printed in England in 1481, states:

"A Greyhound should be headed like a snake,

Necked like a drake,

Backed like a beam,

Sided like a bream,*

Footed like a cat,

Tailed like a rat!"

This modernized version of the oft-quoted classic detailing of breed characteristics is still descriptive of today's Greyhounds. Few breeds can boast a lineage as ancient as that of the Greyhound. And fewer still can claim that the dogs of today so closely resemble their ancient ancestors.

According to the British breed standard, the general appearance of the Greyhound is that of a dog who is "Strongly built, upstanding, of generous proportions, muscular power and symmetrical proportions, with long head and neck, clean well laid shoulders, deep chest, capacious body, arched loin, pow-

A bream is a type of flat-sided fish.

erful quarters, sound legs and feet, and a suppleness of limb which emphasize in a marked degree its distinctive type and quality."

The smooth-coated, sleek, well-muscled Greyhound is possibly the most aesthetically appealing member of the dog world. His elegance and form appeal to the artist in everyone. His regal bearing reminds us that he has long been the companion of kings and queens.

The Greyhound is built for speed. His entire outline is that of a well-honed, powerful running machine—symmetrical, graceful, and balanced. The purpose of a Greyhound is to run—run fast and with enough endurance and agility to catch the hare or other game it pursues. The Greyhound has always been a sporting dog, bred to work as a team with others of its kind to catch live game.

In *The Greyhound*, Hugh Dalziel writes of the Greyhound of the late 1800s. He states that the Greyhound "possesses an inherent right to occupy the highest place in the group of dogs hunting by keenness of sight and fleetness of foot....the modern Greyhound [is] the most elegant of the canine race, the highest achievement of man's skill in manipulating the plastic nature of the dog, and forming it to his special requirements. In all his beauty of outline and wonderful development, not only of muscle, but of the hidden fire which gives dash, energy, and daring, stands revealed a manufactured article, the acme of perfection in beauty of outline and fitness of purpose. He is a combination of Art and Nature that challenges the world, unequaled in speed, spirit, and perseverance, and in elegance and beauty of form as far removed from many of his clumsy ancestors as an English thoroughbred from a coarse dray horse."

Such accolades! It is obvious that Mr. Dalziel held the Greyhound in high regard. He continues: "It is clear...that our ancestors had, two thousand years ago, developed his form, swiftness, and wind, so as to enable him to run down the deer and hare at speed. Speed is the first and greatest quality a Greyhound can pos-

An attempt to draw a Greyhound from Dame Berner's (1486) description. Reprinted from *The Practical Dog Book,* Hutchinson & Co. Ltd., London, 1932.

sess, and his whole being which is so strikingly elegant, is designed to allow for this speed. In addition to speed, the dog must have strength to last out a severe course, nimbleness in turning, the capacity to catch and bear the hare in his stride, good killing powers, and vital force to give him dash, staunchness, and endurance."

What exactly does the Greyhound, this powerful and regal dog, look like? A later section takes an in-depth, comparative look at Greyhound standards and development over the years. The following description of the ideal Greyhound, penned by Major Harding-Cox in 1905 in *Dogs by Well-Known Authorities,* provides an example of one early standard and is quite comprehensive in its scope.

Head—The head itself should be long and tapering. The eyes are of moderate size—a light eye in a dog of dark color should be avoided. The cheek should be very muscular, so as to lend additional strength to the striking and holding power of the jaw. The neck of the Greyhound is peculiarly graceful, and its length, symmetry, and set-on are of vital importance. It must be of sufficient length and flexibility to enable him to strike his hare without losing stride. A long, graceful, and well-set neck adds to that vague—but to experts well-understood—term "quality."

Chest and Shoulders—The chest of the Greyhound is somewhat flat, but deep and roomy, giving plenty of space for lungs and heart to bear the extra strain put on them. The shoulders are long, well laid back working smoothly on the flat surface of the ribs, the latter being well separated and more convex as they approach the quarters. The back is arched and very powerful and supple, it is broad and shows enormous muscular development. These muscles should

BIS, BISS Ch. Gerico's Chasing the Wind captures the regal demeanor of the Greyhound. Owned by Geri Ann Hendrick.
Photo by Gay Glazbrook

Ch. Ryal Parisian, F.Ch. Owned by Sue Cassem.

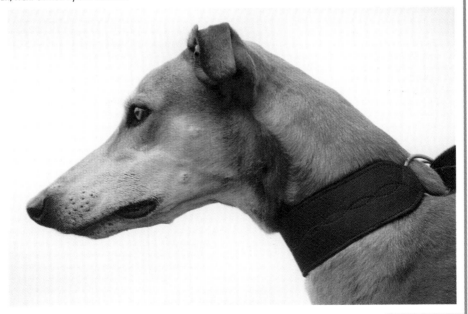

Greyhounds are built for speed. Gaia Summer Solstice JSC stretches out. Owned by Heather Minnich. *Photo by Shot on Sight Photography*

lie forward, setting the back well into the shoulder blades.

The quarters—The general impression is one of great power. The thighs are well breeched and full of muscle. The stifle long and well bent.

The second thighs—exceedingly muscular, and far more developed than in any other animal. The hocks let down, strong.

The tail—long and slightly curled at the extremity.

The forelegs should be straight and the bone carried well down, muscular on the outer surface, but flat on the inner. The pasterns long, but very strong and springy.

The feet of moderate size; the middle toes being slightly longer, makes them appear more oval than round. A flat foot is very bad and a splay one horrible. The knuckles should be strong, close, and well arched; but it is a bad sign to see a dog too much "on his toes."

Quality—It is difficult to define this point; but, as we previously hinted, it is easily discerned and appreciated by all "doggy" critics. It consists in a coup d'oeil glance, blink of an eye, which precludes analysis, but which embraces symmetry, blood, life, grace, movement, condition, and freedom from all coarseness.

Colour—There is really no rule in this respect, and no allowance should be made in a scale of points. "A good horse cannot be a bad colour" is a saying as true when applied to a Greyhound.

Scale of points of the Greyhound

General Symmetry and Quality	10
Head and Neck	20
Chest and Shoulders	20
Back	10
Quarters	20
Legs and Feet	20

Opposite: Am. Can. Ch. Gaia Dee's No Plain Jayne. Owner Lindsay Strutt. *Photo by Alex Smith*

Ch. Taikatassun Mamba takes a break from exercise. Owned by Sari Rantanen, Finland.

Greyhounds of all ages love their stuffed toys. Ch. Windborne Avion Zephyr at five months. *Photo by Brad Wood*

Athlete in an elegant body, Ch. Andarab Magic Raven, with owner Lois Bires.

Opposite: Seamair Fiesta Fandango–waiting patiently. Owned by Cheryl Reynolds

Friends of the Wind

THERE'S true kinship with the wind in every flowing line of the new '41 Lincoln-Continental. Completely streamlined from the inside out, it cleaves the rushing currents of air cleanly and quietly in its smooth, effortless gliding flight. You seem to ride on the wings of the wind!

SKILLED craftsmen in the great Lincoln precision plant have created for the staunch, power-charged, 12-cylinder heart of the Lincoln-Continental a long, luxurious, low-slung body that surpasses all previous conceptions of automotive beauty. Here is a car almost daringly young—so decidedly *different* in design and construction you know at a glance it's styled for you who want unstinted luxury tempered with good taste . . .

IN PERFECT keeping with such sheer splendor—such unusual performance—is the comfort of billowy seats cradled amidships on liquid-like, slow-motion springs. And the Lincoln-Continental is triple-cushioned in rubber to block out noise and vibration . . . give you a ride as smooth and quiet as a glider's flight!

BEFORE you buy any car make a date with your dealer and go for a ride in the new Lincoln-Continental. See how it hugs the curves, holds snugly to the road and cuts the air like a bullet. Delight in the brilliant performance and lithe streamlining that make it truly a "friend of the wind." You'll discover, at last, the thrill of driving a car that's altogether *new* and *unusual!*

LINCOLN *Continental*

Suave, sleek masterpiece in steel and luxury, the Lincoln-Continental Coupe shown above combines a host of unusual automotive comforts, conveniences and betterments: Exclusive Lincoln V-12 engine . . . push-button door openers . . . unit body-and-frame construction. (White sidewall tires extra.) C Interiors are custom-tailored. You choose from a wide range of fabrics and leathers. C Smart Convertible Cabriolet also available. Every feature of the dynamic *new-and-different* Lincoln-Continental will convince you that here, indeed, is a limited edition of a fine motor car!

LINCOLN MOTOR CAR DIVISION, FORD MOTOR COMPANY, BUILDERS ALSO OF THE LINCOLN-ZEPHYR V-12, SEDAN, COUPE, CLUB COUPE, CONVERTIBLE COUPE; THE LINCOLN-CUSTOM, SEDAN AND LIMOUSINE

1941 print advertisement for the Lincoln Continental draws comparisons between the car's streamlined grace and power and that of the Greyhound.

Greyhounds love the company of other Greyhounds. Notice the many different colors and markings in this group. Owned by Hanne Böckhaus.

In *The Complete Dog Book,* printed in 1922 before the AKC published its first all-breed book, William Bruette had this to say about Greyhounds: "The Greyhound is probably the oldest member of his race. From time immemorial they have been popular as companions at home and in the hunting field. As a result of the time and care that have been spent upon them, they are the most highly developed domestic animal in existence.

"In elegance of form, dignity, and cleanliness Greyhounds are worthy of their long descent. They are much more affectionate and intelligent than is usually believed, and in point of speed, courage, fortitude, endurance, and sagacity, they are the equals of any dog that lives."

Although the Greyhound's beauty may precipitate the initial attraction of fanciers, Greyhound lovers readily admit that it is the breed's incredible personality that captures hearts and en-sures pampered pets a place on the couch and a bed in front of the fire.

Apparently, the Greyhound's temperament has changed little through the ages. Arrian, a second-century Greek, wrote of a hound he owned with his friend Megillus. "He is...most gentle and kindly affectioned. While I am at home he remains by my side; accompanies me on going abroad; follows me to the gymnasium and whilst I am taking exercise,

Most Greyhounds get along with other animals. Ch. Another Episode Partylite and friend. Owned by Cindy Bellis-Jones.

37

sits down by me. If he has not seen us for only a short time, he jumps up repeatedly by way of salutation and barks with joy as a greeting to us. At meals he pats us first with one foot, then with another, to put us in mind that he is to have a share of our food." Arrian was in agreement with most of today's owners in his belief that Greyhounds seem to be almost human.

C. F. Holder, in his article "Coursing with Greyhounds in Southern California," which appeared in the November 1889 issue of *St. Nicholas*, shares a moment spent with one of his Greyhounds named Mouse: "As I write, a hound, faithful and true, is looking up into my face, her long slender muzzle resting on my arm, her eyes beaming with intelligence. She is blinking, puffing out her lips, whining, in fact, laughing and talking after her fashion."

Greyhound faces convey every thought and feeling. Their eyes seem to reflect the wisdom of the ages. Bright intelligence shines from those eyes and captures your soul. They are soft, yet piercing, and reflect great intuitiveness and understanding. But they can convey other messages as well. At different times they express sympathy, sensitivity, amusement, keenness, anticipation, mischievousness, and sometimes, just plain stubbornness. "Just watch me!" is a challenge many owners have met in their Greyhound's eyes. And Greyhounds seem to wink. At appropriate times they let you know by these winks that they see the humor in a situation, that they are fine with the status quo, that they are ready for some fun, that they love you.

Greyhound ears are extremely mobile. Whether carried high on their heads as puppies, folded back, or held alert, they enhance every expression.

Many Greyhounds smile, curling up their lips in closed or open-mouthed joy when greeting their families, when friends come calling, or when their dinner is being prepared. The Greyhounds' habit of puffing out their lips, as mentioned by Mr. Holder, is a common sight to Greyhound owners.

In spite of their regal bearing, Greyhounds are considered by many to be the clowns of the sighthound family. They are full of curiosity. As young dogs they always seem to be looking for some sort of mischief in which to indulge, a trait some hounds never outgrow. Our Greyhounds proved to be the best incentive my children had to keep their clothes and toys picked up, out of reach of those four-legged thieves who never tired of carrying off their belongings. Greyhounds grab dishtowels from hands, sandwiches from counters, stuffed bears from baby cribs, pillows from sofas. It is not unusual to walk into a room and see your young Greyhound lying in the middle of a pile of snow-white toilet paper, a strip still hanging from his mouth. Inevitably, his look is one of amazement and disbelief. "Now how do you suppose all of this paper got here?" he seems to ask, his tail wafting stray pieces around the room.

Greyhounds are very people-oriented dogs and extremely devoted to their human companions. They never forget a friend, and they will greet someone they have not seen for years as though they had played with them yesterday. They wait patiently for you to complete daily tasks and then cajole you into all kinds of creative games. These unique, trusting, intelligent creatures make the very best of canine pets, perfect companions with whom to share our lives.

THE STANDARD

In 1973 Dr. Braxton B. Sawyer wrote a series of four articles in the *Gazehound* discussing the development of the Greyhound standard. Much of the information contained in this chapter is taken from this series. Several early standards are reproduced in their entirety to give present-day breeders, owners, exhibitors, and judges the opportunity to read how the breed has developed over the past 150 years. It is interesting to note that some of the characteristics that we consider faults in the conformation of our Greyhounds today were actually desirable qualities in the past. It is also satisfying to see how little the breed has changed over the years.

Written descriptions of the Greyhound have appeared in print for close to 2,000 years. An early description, penned by Arrian (circa 100 CE), was included in *Hounds and Hunting in Ancient Greece.*

Edward, Duke of York, Master of Game of King Henry IV, wrote a book called *Master of Game* in the early 1400s. In it he described several different breeds, including the Greyhound. The Greyhound of his day had "right courage" and was "of good nature." According to Edward, "the best hue is red fallow with a black muzzle. The Greyhound should be of middle size, neither too big nor too little," have a "long head and somewhat large

made," with eyes "red or black as those of a sparrow hawk," "ears small and high," a neck "great and long bowed like a swan's neck," and a chest "great and open." He also described the correct foot as being "round as a cat," and the preferred tail as "a cat's tail making a ring at the end." Apparently, the Greyhound's temperament has changed little over the last 600 years, because Edward writes, "He shall be good and kindly and clean, glad and joyful and playful, well willing and good by all manner of folks, save to wild beasts to whom he should be fierce, spiteful and eager." The Greyhounds of the early 1400s were true hunters.

In 1845, William Youatt wrote a book entitled *The Dog*, in which he describes desirable characteristics in the breed but explains why coursing Greyhounds should be built according to his specifications.

"The English Greyhound is distinguished by its peculiarly long and attenuated head and face, terminating in a singular sharpness of the nose, and length of the muzzle and mouth. There are two results from this: the length of the mouth gives a longer grasp and secures the prey, but as the nasal cavities and the cavity of the skull are proportionately diminished, there is not so much room for the expansion of the membrane of the nose, there is less power of scent, and less space for the development of the brain.

"There is little want of extraordinary acute hearing, and the ears of the greyhound are small compared with his bulk. Markham recommends the ears to be close, sharp and dropping, neither protruding by their bulk, nor tiring by their weight.

"The power of the eye is but of little consequence, for the game is rarely distant from the dog, and, therefore, easily seen.

"The neck is an important portion of the frame. It should be long, in order to correspond with the length of the legs, and thus enable the dog to seize and lift the game, as he rapidly pursues his course, without throwing any undue or dangerous weight on the fore extremities. In the act of seizing the hare the short-necked dog may lose the centre of gravity and fall.

"The chest is a very important part of the Greyhound, as well as of every other animal of speed. It must be capacious: this capacity must be obtained by depth rather than by width, in order that the shoulders may not be thrown so far apart as to impede progression.

"The form and situation of the shoulders are of material consequence, for on them depends the extent of the action which the animal is capable of exerting. The shoulders should be broad and deep, and obliquely placed. They are so in the horse, and the action depends entirely on this conformation.

"The forelegs should be set on square at the shoulder: bulging out at the elbow not only gives a clumsy appearance, but makes the dog slow. The legs should have plenty of bone, and be straight, and well set on the feet, and the toes neither turned out nor in. The forearm, that portion of the leg that is between the

Greyhounds by Louis Agassiz Fuertes, from a 1919 issue of *National Geographic*.

elbow and the knee, should be long, straight, and muscular. These are circumstances that cannot be dispensed with. The length of the forearm, and the low placing of the pastern, are of essential importance.

"With regard to the form of the back and sides of the Greyhound...it is the strength of the back which is brought into requisition, in particular, in running over hilly ground. Here may be said to rest the distinctions between long and short backs, supposing both to be strong. The more lengthy the back, and proportionately strong, the more the Greyhound is calculated to beat the shorter backed dog on the flat; but on hilly ground one with a shorter back will have the advantage.

"The ribs should also be well arched. We should perhaps avoid him with sides too decidedly outswelling, but still more would we avoid the direct flat-sided dog.

"Without really good haunches and muscular thighs, it has been remarked that the odds are against any dog, be his other points whatever they may. It is by the propulsatory efforts of the muscles of the loins and thighs that the race is won. The thighs should be large, and muscularly indented; the hocks broad, and, like the knee, low placed.

"The color of the Greyhound varies exceedingly. Some are perfectly dark and glossy. In strength and endurance, the brindled dog, or the brown or fawn-colored one, is best. The white Greyhound, although a beautiful animal and swift, is not, perhaps, quite so much to be depended upon."

Dr. John Henry Walsh, a noted dog show and field trial judge and promoter, wrote about Greyhounds under the pseudonym "Stonehenge." In 1853, he first published *The Greyhound: The Art of Breeding, Rearing, and Training Greyhounds for Public Running—Their Diseases and Treatment.* He was editor of the magazine *The Field* from 1858 to 1888.

In his book on the Greyhound, Dr. Walsh wrote an 18-page description of the breed. A later six-page condensation of this description became the first bench-show standard for the Greyhound. It is from this first standard that later ones were developed.

In large part due to the influence of Dr. John Henry Walsh, through his articles in *The Field* and a series of five editions of a book called *The Dogs of the British Isles,* the whole world of purebred dogs—

Ch. Barmaid, an early National Coursing Club Greyhound, from vintage Ardath Cork & State Express 333 Cigarette Card.

Champion Barmaid
GREYHOUND
owned by
Mr & Mrs. Marchetti

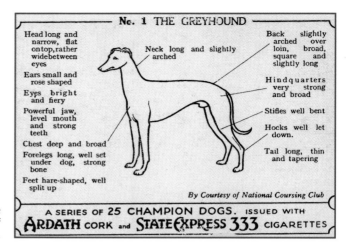

No. 1 THE GREYHOUND

Head long and narrow, flat on top, rather wide between eyes

Ears small and rose shaped

Eyes bright and fiery

Powerful jaw, level mouth and strong teeth

Chest deep and broad

Forelegs long, well set under dog, strong bone

Feet hare-shaped, well split up

Neck long and slightly arched

Back slightly arched over loin, broad, square and slightly long

Hindquarters very strong and broad

Stifles well bent

Hocks well let down.

Tail long, thin and tapering

By Courtesy of National Coursing Club

A SERIES OF 25 CHAMPION DOGS. ISSUED WITH **ARDATH** CORK and **STATE EXPRESS 333** CIGARETTES

Greyhound drawing and standard, from the National Coursing Club, printed on reverse of Ch. Barmaid cigarette card.

dog shows, kennel clubs, breed registries and standards, rules and methods for judging and handling—became popular.

An early standard for the Greyhound appeared in *The Illustrated Book of the Dog* (1879 to 1881), written by Fra Vero Shaw. It follows:

Head—Should be wide between the ears and flat at the top, with powerful jaws. The latter should not, however, be thick or coarse, but should, as regards appearance, seem light in substance, their strength depending on the muscles at the sides of the head.

Eyes—Dark and bright.

Ears—Small and fine.

Neck—Long and muscular, but not coarse, thick or clumsy.

Shoulders—Sloping and very muscular; loosely set on, so as to allow free play of the forelegs.

Chest—Deep, and rather wide.

Back—Square and "beam-like," and rather long.

Loins—Very powerful, with considerable muscular development.

Forelegs—Set well under the dog, and possessing plenty of bone.

Feet—Round, well split up, and with strong soles.

Hindlegs—Well bent at the hocks and very muscular.

Stern (Tail)—Fine, long, and curved.

Color—Almost any colour admissible in a Greyhound, but the most usual are black, white, brindle, fallow, fawn, blue, and the various mix of each.

In his book *The Greyhound*, published in 1887, Hugh Dalziel wrote a "Summary of Points of Modern Greyhound":

The Head—Long and lean, but wide between the ears, measuring in girth, just before or close in behind, about 15 in. in a dog 26 in. high, with a length from occiput to nose of about 10 in. to 10 $\frac{1}{2}$ in.

The Ears—Set on well back, small and fine in the slap, exposing the inner surface. Erect or prick ears are seldom seen, and are disliked.

The Eye—Varying in colour; must be bright, clear, and fiery.

The Teeth—Strong and white, the upper canines with the slight curve they possess, clipping those of the lower jaw. (Value 15)

The Neck—Length and suppleness are of great importance, to enable the dog to seize the hare as he runs at full speed. It is elegantly bent or arched

Greyhounds and head studies were featured on vintage cigarette cards from Will's Cigarettes and John Player's & Sons cigarettes. *Original paintings by Arthur Wardle*

above the windpipe, giving it a slightly protuberant form along the lower surface, the whole gradually swelling out to meet the shoulders. (Value 10)

The Chest and Forequarters (including shoulders and forelegs)—The chest must be capacious, and the room obtained more by depth than width, to give free action to the heart and lungs.

The Shoulders—The scapula, or shoulder blade, must be oblique, that the forelegs may be readily stretched well forward. The arm from shoulder to elbow, and forearm from elbow to knee, both of good length, and short from knee to the ground. The elbow must not turn either in or out, but be in a straight line, so that the action may be free. The

muscles for expansion and retraction of the several parts of the legs and shoulders must be large and well-developed. (Value 20)

Loins and Back Ribs—The back should be broad and square, or beam-like, slightly arched, but not approaching to the wheel back of the Italian Toy Greyhound. The loin wide, deep, and strong, the muscles well-developed throughout, so that, although the flank is cut up, it yet measures well round—and this is important, as showing strength. (Value 15)

Hindquarters—Strong, broad across, the stifles well bent; first and second thigh both big with muscle; the legs rather wide apart, and longer the fore-

Stanley Petter, Jr. with Fr. Am. Ch. Canyon Crest's Coronation and two French Greyhounds in Deauville, 1952.

legs, short from the hock to the ground. (Value 20)

Feet—Round, with the toes well sprung, the claws strong, and the pad, or sole, compact and hard. (Value 10)

Tail—Long, tapered, and nicely curved. (Value 5)

Coat and Colour—Coat fine, thick and close, and color clear. (Value 5)

In 1904, the Kennel Club published *The Dog Owner's Annual: The Dog Owner's Guide to Dogs and Dog Showing for 1904*, which contained a standard and picture of every recognized breed. These were the official standards by which the breeds included were to be judged. The short Greyhound standard reads as follows:

"Uses: Coursing. Origin: Lost in antiquity; the oldest breed of dogs extant. Colour: Various—black, brindle, red, fawn, blue, slate, and any of these colours mixed with white. Head: Long and lean, fairly large between the ears, jaws lean, but not weak. Eyes: Bright, full and penetrating. Ears: Small, folding down when at rest, but semi-pricked when animated. Body: Loins strong and broad, back powerful and slightly arched. Legs: Forelegs strong, good

length from elbow to knee, compared with that from knee to ground, hind legs, well turned and shapely. Feet: Hard and close, toes well defined and developed. Stern: Fine and nicely curved. Coat: Fine, thick and close."

The first American Greyhound standard was written by Brigadier General Roger D. Williams (1856–1925). General Williams founded the National Fox Hunters Association and was Master of the Iroquois Hunt of Lexington, Kentucky, for 30 years. His rather detailed descriptions of the Greyhound outlines a true coursing dog, relating several parts of the standard to the purpose or action utilized in coursing game. This standard appeared in 1891 in a book called *The American Book of the Dog*, edited by G. O. Shields.

The Complete Dog Book, by Dr. William A. Bruette, was published in the early 1920s and contained bench-show standards to be used in judging in the United States and other countries. This book predated the first American Kennel Club book by seven years. The introductory paragraph to the standard itself may bring a smile to the faces of those who feel that many of today's

Greyhounds come in many colors; pictured are Sunny, Zoe, and Baggie. Owner Cindy-Bellis Jones, Fox Run.

show dogs are not built for the coursing field:

"The following standard and scale of points is commonly used by bench-show judges, but, as previously stated, is given little consideration by practical coursing men:

Head—The head of the Greyhound should be long, lean, and tapering; narrow across the skull as compared with some breeds, but should have sufficient width to allow for brain room. The eyes should be full, clean, and bright; the ears should be small and folded back close to the head; the jaws strong and level, not pig-jawed; the teeth strong and sound, so as to be able to hold the hare. The furrow between the eyes should be slightly marked, with little or no stop; the eyebrows should not be prominent.

Neck—The neck should be long, lean, and arched, so as to enable the dog to catch up the hare without stooping. It should be set onto the head cleanly, and should widen gradually as it goes into the shoulders.

Coat and Color—The coat should be short, smooth, and glossy. The color is of slight importance.

Loin, Back, Ribs, and Hindquarters—There should be good length from shoulders to back ribs, which should be well-sprung to afford good attachment for the muscles of the loins. A slight arch is permissible, but not to such an extent as to form a roach or wheel-back. The hindquarters should be powerful and muscular and show great length by reason of well-bent stifles.

Shoulders and Forelegs—Shoulders should be oblique. Forearm of good length, in line with shoulders. Forelegs should be perfectly straight. The leg should be twice as long from the elbow to the fetlock joint or knee as from the latter to the ground.

Chest—Should be deep, but not so deep as to interfere with the irregularities of the ground when running at full speed. It should not be too wide nor too narrow; a happy medium.

Feet—The Greyhound may have either the cat foot or the hare-foot provided the toes are well together.

Tail—Fine, free from fringe, and nicely curved toward the end.

Scale of Points—Head, 10; neck, 10; chest and forequarters, 20; feet, 15; tail, 5; color and coat, 5. Total 100."

In 1929, the AKC published *Pure-Bred Dogs: The Breeds and Standards Recognized by the American Kennel Club*. The Greyhound standard contained in that book is exactly the same as the one still used today, save for the shifting of two important words.

These two words, "well arched," originally appeared under the description of the back of the Greyhound. The earlier standard read: "Back—Muscular and broad, well arched."

Later the two words were removed from the section describing the back and added to the description of the loins.

These sections now read:

"Back—Muscular and broad.

Loins—Good depth of muscle, well arched, well cut up in flanks."

The earlier version of the standard would have encouraged the breeding of Greyhounds with incorrect roach or wheel backs. A back of this nature does not have the flexibility needed when running.

Over the years, the Greyhound Club of America has voted to leave the standard unchanged. This very brief, succinct outline of the qualities desired in a correctly built Greyhound incorporates the ideals of the past and present hound. It, among all standards, has stood the test of time.

Ch. Tre Kronor Chelan. Owned by Sue Cassem, Ryal.
Photo by Lloyd W. Olson Studio

The American Kennel Club Official Standard for the Greyhound

Head—Long and narrow, fairly wide between the ears, scarcely perceptible stop, little or no development of nasal sinuses, good length of muzzle, which should be powerful without coarseness. Teeth very strong and even in front.

Ears—Small and fine in texture, thrown back and folded, except when excited, when they are semi-pricked.

Eyes—Dark, bright, intelligent, indicating spirit.

Neck—Long, muscular, without throatiness, slightly arched, and widening gradually into the shoulder.

Shoulders—placed as obliquely as possible, muscular without being loaded.

Forelegs—Perfectly straight, set well into the shoulder, neither turned in nor out, pasterns strong.

Chest—Deep, and as wide as consistent with speed, fairly well-sprung ribs.

Back—Muscular and broad.

Loins—Good depth of muscle, well arched, well cut up in the flanks.

Hindquarters—Long, very muscular and powerful, wide and well let down, well-bent stifles. Hocks well bent and rather close to the ground, but straight fore and aft.

Feet—Hard and close, rather more hare than cat-feet, well knuckled up with good strong claws.

Tail—Long, fine and tapering with a slight upward curve.

Coat—Short, smooth and firm in texture.

Color—Immaterial.

Weight—Dogs, 65 to 70 pounds; Bitches, 60 to 65 pounds.

Opposite: Aragon Autumn Storm. Owned by Helen Hamilton. *Photo by Rick Sara*

Scale of Points

General symmetry and quality 10
Head and neck 20
Chest and shoulders 20
Back 10
Quarters 20
Legs and feet 20
Total 100

THE KENNEL CLUB BREED STANDARD (UK)

Characteristics—The Greyhound possesses remarkable stamina and endurance. Its straight through, long-reaching movement enables it to cover ground at great speed.

General Appearance—The general appearance of the typical Greyhound is that of a strongly built, upstanding dog of generous proportions, muscular power and symmetrical formation, with a long head and neck, clean well-laid shoulders, deep chest, capacious body, arched loin, powerful quarters, sound legs and feet, and a suppleness of limb, which emphasize in a marked degree its distinctive type and quality.

Head and Skull—Long, moderate width, flat skull, slight stop. Jaws powerful and well chiseled.

Eyes—Bright and intelligent, dark in colour.

Ears—Small, rose-shape of fine texture.

Mouth—Teeth white and strong. The incisors of the upper jaw clipping those of the lower jaw.

Neck—Long and muscular, elegantly arched, well let into the shoulders.

Forequarters—Shoulders, oblique, well set back, muscular without being loaded, narrow and cleanly defined at the top. Forelegs, long and straight, bone of good substance and quality. Elbows, free

Ch. Hexham Mokan Rhythm 'n Blues, two-time Award of Merit Winner GCA Eastern Specialty.

Owned by Lynda and Dennis Meeuws.

Photo by Booth Photography

and well set under the shoulders. Pasterns, moderate length, slightly sprung.

Elbows, pasterns and toes should incline neither outwards nor inwards.

Body—Chest, deep and capacious, providing adequate heart room. Ribs, deep, well sprung, and carried well back. Flanks well cut up. Back, rather long, broad and square. Loin, powerful, slightly arched.

Hindquarters—Thighs and second thighs, wide and muscular, showing great propelling power. Stifles, well bent. Hocks, well let down, inclining neither outwards nor inwards. Body and hindquarters features should be of ample proportions and well coupled, enabling adequate ground to be covered when standing.

Feet—Moderate length, with compact well-knuckled toes, strong pads.

Tail—Long, set on rather low, strong at the root, tapering to the point, carried low, slightly curved.

Coat—Fine and close.

Colour—Black, white, red, blue, fawn, fallow, brindle, or any of the colors broken with white.

Height—Ideal Height: Dogs 71-76 cm (28"-30"); Bitches 68-71 cm (27"-28").

NOTE: Male animals should have two apparently normal testicles fully descended into the scrotum.

A COMPARISON

The American and British Greyhound breed standards have much in common, both describing the Greyhound familiar to all of us today. But there are a few readily observable differences between the two descriptions.

The first difference one notices when comparing the two standards is that the British standard begins with two paragraphs describing the characteristics and general appearance of the Grey-

Ch. Sunridge Solarius Gold Dust, a young champion is awarded BOB by Sighthound specialist Doris Wear.

Owned by Stanley Tyree and Cindy Kelly.

Photo by Ashbey Photography

hound. The first two sentences let the reader know right from the start that this is a breed built for running: "The Greyhound possesses remarkable stamina and endurance. Its straight through, long-reaching movement enables it to cover ground at great speed." The section on general appearance is quite good in giving the reader a concise, overall picture of the Greyhound. The type and quality of Greyhound presented is not a wispy, narrow-bodied, fine-boned dog, but one that exudes power, strength, muscle, balance, and presence.

Head

Both standards call for a long head that is wider in backskull than muzzle and has little stop. The American reference to "no development of sinus cavities" is comparable to the British "flat skull." The description of teeth that are even in front is not meant to imply that Greyhounds are to have an even bite. Actually, the accepted correct bite is a scissors bite, perhaps more aptly described in the Kennel Club's section on the mouth.

Eyes

It is interesting to note that both standards call for a dark eye that is bright and intelligent. No mention of a light-colored eye is made in either standard, although it is generally accepted in a dilute-colored dog.

Ears

The English description of a small rose-shaped ear is probably a better explanation of the correct ear than the American "semi-pricked." The latter seems to define the ear carriage of a Collie or Shetland Sheepdog rather than that of a Greyhound. The rose-shaped ear was probably the influence of the Bulldog crosses that occurred in England in the 1800s.

Ch. Andarab Wild Oats, Award of Merit at 1996 Eastern Specialty and multiple group placer.

Owned by Lois Bires.

Photo by B. Kernan

Neck

Both standards call for a long, muscular, arched neck that is well set into the shoulders.

Forequarters

Again, both standards are in agreement that the shoulders should be obliquely placed, muscular, but not loaded. Both describe straight forelegs that turn neither in nor out. The British standard goes into more detail about the pasterns, asking that they be "slightly sprung," thus cushioning impact when running.

Body

The chest is described in each standard as deep, with well-sprung ribs. Again we have a more detailed description of the body in the British standard—stating that not only should the back be broad, but long and square as well, a description that brings to mind Dame Berner's word picture "backed like a beam."

The flanks are to be "well cut up" as stated in each standard. It should be noted that the loin is only "slightly arched." This does not describe a Greyhound with more than a slight rise in the topline.

Hindquarters

Muscular, powerful hindquarters with wide, well-bent stifles are described in both standards, as are well-let-down, straight hocks. The British sentence stating, "Body and hindquarters features should be of ample proportions and well coupled, enabling adequate ground to be covered when standing," gives to the mind's eye a good image of how a Greyhound should appear when set up in the show ring.

Feet

Each standard calls for well-knuckled toes that are longer rather than

Am. Can. Ch. Gaia Sunridge Serenade, 1998 Number One Greyhound in Canada.

Owned by Sue LeMieux.

Photo by Bill Meyer

round. A round cat foot is not a desirable feature in a Greyhound.

Tail

The tail should be long, tapering, and have a slight upward curve. A ringed or severely skewed tail is not desired.

Coat and Color

The proper Greyhound coat should be short, and is described as fine in England and firm in the United States. Any coat color is permitted in the United States, while acceptable colors are delineated in the British standard. Nowhere in either standard is pigment mentioned.

Size

The two standards are at variance when describing the desirable size of a Greyhound. The Kennel Club describes the ideal height of dogs as 28 to 30 inches, and bitches, 27 to 28 inches. The weights given in the AKC standard would seem to be on the low end when viewing Greyhounds in the show ring today. A Greyhound that is 30 inches tall would be rather thin if he weighed only 70 pounds.

Scale of Points

A scale of points is included only in the American standard.

When assessing the qualities of your Greyhound, you might want to look at both of the standards discussed above. Taken together they present, in well-set-down terms, the ideal Greyhound of today.

An Illustrated Standard

The brevity of the American Greyhound standard often makes it difficult for newcomers to the breed to actually picture what a correct Greyhound is supposed to look like. Because of this dilemma, Sue Cassem, artist and longtime breeder and exhibitor of Greyhounds, has drawn and written an illustrated standard of the breed, with the hope of helping owners, breeders, exhibitors, and judges to better understand and visualize the desired structure of a Greyhound.

The extremely old AKC Greyhound standard has survived nearly intact (with only one minor change) throughout the decades. It was very adequate for its time, as the sportsmen of the day knew their dogs and horses well. For them, few words were needed to bring to mind the basics of a good coursing dog. Today, most of us are not raised amidst farms abundant with livestock, nor is our leisure time filled with sports centered around horses, dogs, and hunting wild game. For most of us bitten by the show bug, we must start from scratch learning form and function and how it applies to our breed's historical purpose. Our personal understanding of the breed's type and conformation may evolve and change over the years through education, observation, and trial and error.

For all of its short, deceiving simplicity, the Greyhound standard is, in fact, describing a very complex structure that is dependent upon every part being correct in order to create the ideal whole, perfectly functioning Grey-hound—solid, sound, powerful, and elegant of line.

Head—Long and narrow, fairly wide between the ears. Scarcely perceptible stop, little or no development of nasal sinuses, good length of muzzle, which should be powerful without coarseness. Teeth very strong and even in front. Although the Greyhound is not considered a head breed, a beautifully chiseled head is certainly an aerodynamic asset. There are varying "looks" in the breed, all well within the standard, but it must be remembered that a Greyhound should never be shown or bred on the basis of its possessing only a beautiful head, and ignoring all of its other functional parts. Having said that, a few points regarding the head may need some explanation.

Little or no development of nasal sinuses is asked for, producing a clean, flat backskull. However, this V-shaped bony area on the topskull is more prevalent in the very masculine heads, which may not smooth out until the dog is fully mature, sometimes at four or five years of age.

Teeth should be "very strong and even in front" (shown in the illustration). However, the bite position itself is not mentioned. "Even in front" means the teeth should be aligned (in a straight row; no wry teeth), it does not mean a level bite. Although the bite is not described, the Greyhound should have a scissors bite, the most punishing bite for a coursing dog.

Shoulders—Placed as obliquely as possible, muscular without being loaded. Obviously, the standard demands well-laid-back shoulders that are muscular, not bulging or over-done—but there are muscles. Bony, flat

shoulders with no overlying muscle are incorrect.

Forelegs—Perfectly straight, set well into the shoulders, neither turned in nor out. Pasterns—strong. From the front and side, the foreleg presents a straight column. Since the standard demands that they are well set into the shoulder, it therefore demands good upper arm return, placing the foreleg directly under the shoulder. You should be able to drop a line from the top of the shoulder where the neck and withers meet and hit the back of the elbow. Pasterns are slightly sloped, nicely boned and taut, but flexible.

Chest—deep, and as wide as consistent with speed, fairly well-sprung ribs. The chest reaches to the elbow, and from the front view the brisket is well filled. There is no hollow between the front legs. The ribs are sprung from the spine, but flatten on the sides. No barrel ribs. Check the angle of the last three visible ribs. From the spine they should angle from front to back. Upright ribs mean slab sides do not have the capability to rotate to meet full lung expansion. The dog should have width to it. A Greyhound is much more than a profile, as appealing as its profile is.

Back—Muscular and broad. Two words that again demand that the dog has width, substance, and muscle. Greyhounds are not paper dolls!

Loins—Good depth of muscle, well-arched, well cut up in the flanks. The correct topline is the most misunderstood, most asked about, and most difficult feature to breed in the Greyhound, for several reasons. First, because the topline is not level (level is a much easier concept to grasp), but rather, it contains curves. Second, because the correct placement of those curves depends on

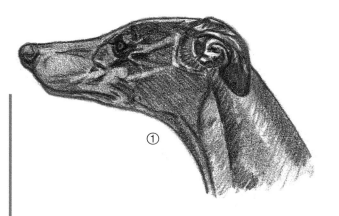

①

②

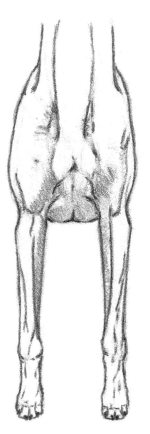

1. *Ears—Small and fine in texture, thrown back and folded, except when excited, when they are semi-pricked.*

2. *Eyes—Dark, bright, intelligent, indicating spirit.*

3. *Head—Long and narrow, fairly wide between the ears. Scarcely perceptible stop, little or no development of nasal sinuses, good length of muzzle, which should be powerful without coarseness. Teeth very strong and even in front.*

4. *Neck—Long, muscular, without throatiness, slightly arched, and widening gradually into the shoulder.*
   Shoulders—Placed as obliquely as possible, muscular without being loaded.

5. *Forelegs—Perfectly straight, set well into the shoulders, neither turned in nor out. Pasterns—strong.*
   Chest—deep, and as wide as consistent with speed, fairly well-sprung ribs.

6. *Tail—Long, fine, and tapering with a slight upward curve.*

7. *Feet—Hard and close, rather more hare than cat-feet, well knuckled up with good strong claws.*

⑦

Overview

Profile

Front

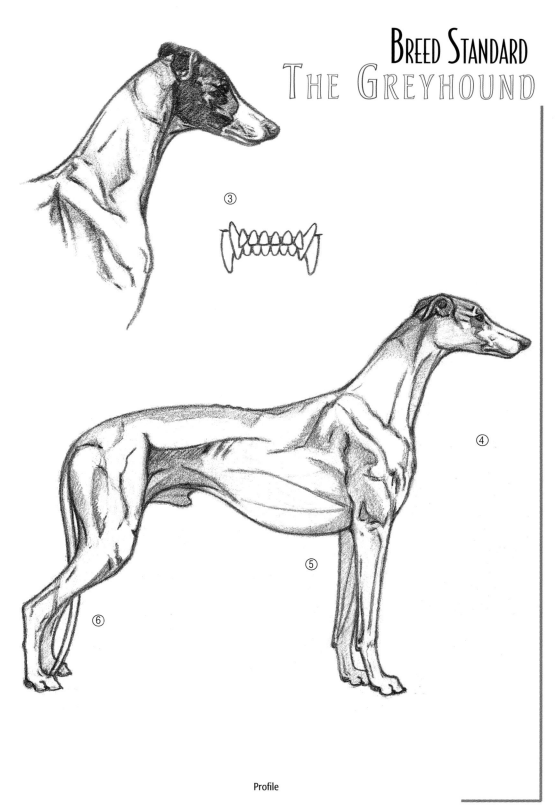

Profile

BREED STANDARD
THE GREYHOUND

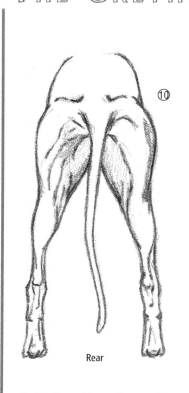

Rear

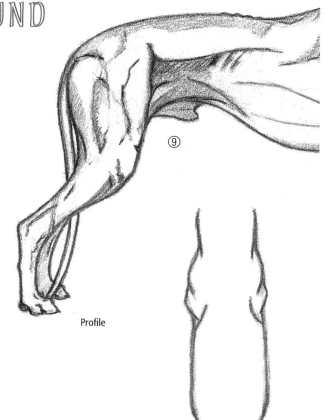

Profile

Overview

8. *Back* —*Muscular and broad.*

9. *Loins* —*Good depth of muscle, well-arched, well cut up in the flanks.*

10. *Hindquarters* —*Long, very muscular, and power ful. Wide and well let down, well-bent stifles.*

Coat —*Short, smooth and firm in texture.*

Color —*Immaterial.*

Weight —*Dogs, 65-70 pounds; Bitches, 60-65 pounds.*

Scale of Points

General symmetry and quality	... 10	Back	10
Head and neck	20	Quarters	20
Chest and shoulders	20	Legs and feet	20
		Total	100

every other connecting structure being correct.

Let's start at the withers. A long, well-laid-back shoulder produces a somewhat high wither with a smooth juncture to the neck. The withers slope down from the neck to the anticline (the low point of the topline where the vertebrae change direction). The arch starts here, right behind the anticline, with the next three or four vertebrae showing, each one just a bit higher than the previous one. Those third and fourth vertebrae are the highest part of the topline and are directly above the last two ribs. (There may or may not be a floating rib on one or both sides). No more than three or four vertebrae or ribs should be showing on a mature dog in correct condition and weight. This rise, consisting of these few vertebrae, is not extreme. It is gradual, not abrupt. It is flowing, not jarring.

Following this rise is the muscular loin, which is not only wide (as wide as the back), but also deep and moderately long. A too-long loin is weak, and one that is too short is rigid and restricts agility. The loin starts the descent of the arch and flows to the hip bones (which are level with the anticline) and through the croup, which is long and slightly sloping. The croup follows the flow of the gradual descent. It is not steep and does not appear to fall off.

The entire "topline" is muscular, long, and flexible. A "fixed" topline, (i.e., roached or camel-backed) is in direct opposition to the Greyhound's ability to flex—to totally extend and contract during the double suspension gallop.

The underline depends mostly on the formation of the ribcage. Ribs should be not only deep (to the elbow), but stay long and deep until almost under the anticline, when the ribs begin to shorten. If the upswing of the ribcage starts directly behind the elbow, it creates a "herring gut" and the appearance of no tuck-up. The ribs are also carried well back on the body. A too-short ribcage gives the Greyhound a Whippet-like look. The Greyhound is longer (measuring from sternum to buttocks) than it is tall (measuring from shoulder to ground).

Hindquarters—Long, very muscular, and powerful. Wide and well let down, well-bent stifles. Hocks, well bent and rather close to the ground, wide but straight fore and aft. The long, broad, slightly sloping croup is the foundation for the very muscular and powerful hindquarters. The long croup makes for the wide (in profile) hindquarters. The broad pelvic base makes for the wide (from the rear view) hindquarters. No croup equals no rear. The very long bones comprising the hindquarters are only possible with well-bent stifles and hocks. The long bones without adequate angulation would make the dog high in the rear. Short bones with poor angulation create a straight rear, and short bones with adequate angulation produce a dog low and short in the rear. The hocks are rather short and are straight from any angle—no hocking in, no hocking out, no sickle hocks.

Feet—Hard and close, rather more hare than cat-feet, well knuckled up with good strong claws. These are tough feet, with high toes and hard, thick pads. The outside toes are shorter and more upright, while the middle digits, although still high and well-knuckled, are longer and slope slightly to the ground.

Tail—Long, fine, and tapering with a slight upward curve. The tail is a smooth continuation of the croup. The tail root should be broad. A narrow tail base may

Faults In
A Greyhound

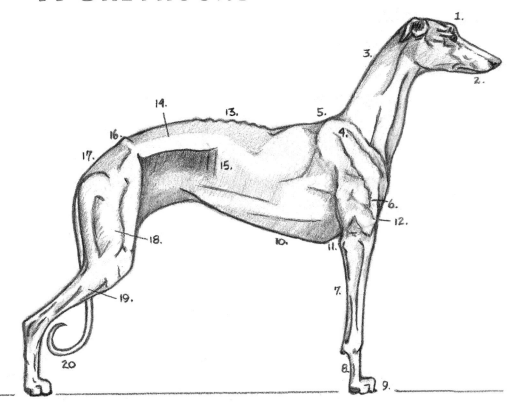

Listing of Faults

1. Prominent frontal bones (nasal sinuses)
2. Lacking underjaw
3. Ewe neck
4. Short, upright shoulder
5. Lumpy, short, low withers
6. Short, upright upper arm
7. Bowed foreleg
8. Upright pastern
9. Cat foot
10. Herring gut, poor underline
11. Shallow chest
12. No front fill
13. Arch starts too far forward; rise too extreme; too many visible vertebrae; roached
14. Shallow loin
15. Upright ribs; slab-sided
16. Hipbones set too low
17. Short, steep croup
18. Narrow hindquarters, inadequate muscling
19. Narrow, weak second thigh
20. Ringed tail

well indicate a narrow, fine-boned Greyhound. The tail tapers to a slight curve, never a ring, and in moving is carried low, never higher than the back.

Coat—Short, smooth, and firm in texture.

Color—Immaterial.

Weight—Dogs, 65-70 pounds; Bitches, 60-65 pounds. These were typical coursing weights nearly a century ago. Whether due to selective breeding or better nutrition, or both, these average weights no longer hold true. Greyhounds should be judged on quality and balance, rather than on size.

Lastly, a word about movement, which is not mentioned in the standard. Because it is not possible to assess the gallop in the show ring, we must depend on the trot to judge balance, ease of movement, flexibility, and control. The best we can do is ask for an easy trot—smooth, effortless, and totally balanced. Flexibility and power are shown in good front reach and rear drive. Control and strong ligamentation are demonstrated by coming and going cleanly (no elbows out or tied-in elbows, no hocks in or out, no joint rotation on impact) with both front and rear legs retaining a straight column of bones while tending to converge toward a centerline, but never single tracking.

Ch. Suntiger Christopher TD reflected. Owned by Gail Burnham, Suntiger.
Photo by Robert Pearcy

THE GREYHOUND IN MOTION

Watching a Greyhound gallop, trot, pivot, and leap is one of the greatest thrills an owner can experience. The beauty of a Greyhound in motion can only be compared to a well-choreographed ballet. Their gracefulness is unequaled by any other breed. Seeing the incredible speed of a Greyhound in top physical condition, limbs and muscles working together, is exhilarating.

The Double Suspension Gallop

The Greyhound's natural running gait is the double suspension gallop. Greyhounds run low and seldom raise their heads above their backs. During the double suspension gallop, the Greyhound has all four feet off of the ground two different times. McDowell Lyon, a well-known authority on canine movement, assesses the double suspension

The double suspension gallop. *Photo by Maggie Bryson*

gallop in his book *The Dog in Action* as follows:

"The leaping style or double suspension gallop of the gazehound has physical requirements not demanded by the normal gallop. One front leg, the leading leg, and the opposite back leg put the drive in the movement while the two other legs receive the concussion of landing. A good running gazehound shifts his lead from time to time either at turns or simply to alternate the work of the legs, reducing fatigue and preventing injury.

"The arched back is not a necessity and is actually a handicap to a good runner. The well-arched loin is an asset and is too often confused with an arched back."

At the take off of the double suspension gallop, one rear leg provides the support, which is then transferred to the other rear leg as the Greyhound stretches out, propelling himself forward. When the dog is fully extended, all four feet are off the ground. As the Greyhound lands, the front leg on the same side as the rear leg that provided the lift off of the extension period receives the impact. The Greyhound immediately transfers weight to the other front leg as the body contracts and the topline flexes. The pasterns of the Greyhound must be very strong to cushion this landing. At the same time that the body lifts off the ground again, this time in a fully contracted position, both front legs are extended backward between the rear legs, which are reaching forward to propel the dog on. When coming out of the contraction, first one rear leg and then the other hit the ground and the sequence is repeated.

Dual Ch. Godspeed Qui Tam SC ORC demonstrates the double suspension gallop. Owned by Terry Fletcher. *Photos by Steve Surfman*

Ch. Gaia Fox Run Reynard. Owned by Sue LeMieux and David Hintson. *Photo by DogAds*

BIS, BISS Ch. Sundridge So Be It JC.
Owned by Sue LeMieux, Gaia.

The Trot

Soundness and correct movement are judged in the show ring while the Greyhound is moving at a trot. A Greyhound with correct structure will move gracefully at a trot and will demonstrate great reach and drive. Balance is the key word in performing the trot. A Greyhound with a straight front and over-angulated rear cannot move correctly. Front and rear angulation must be comparable. Other structural factors that affect movement are length and angle of upper arm, body length, topline, shoulder placement, hocks and pasterns, depth of brisket, rib spring, slope of croup, as well as muscle, tendon, and ligament development. Proper nutrition, exercise, conditioning, and training will also affect your Greyhound's performance in the show ring.

Robert Cole, a noted Canadian Kennel Club–approved judge, describes the correct Greyhound trot in an article entitled "Trotting Greyhounds," which appeared in the May-June 1992 issue of *Sighthound Review:*

"At the correct trot: diagonal feet must relinquish support together; the opposite pair of diagonals must strike the ground together; and during the changeover of diagonals there must be a brief period where the body is airborne."

This period of suspension is a necessary part of the correct trot because it permits the dog to propel itself forward more easily and allows the hind foot to extend forward without interference from the front foot on the same side.

GREYHOUND ACTIVITIES

THE COURSING GREYHOUND

Tally Ho! With this call the chase begins! The words Greyhounds and coursing have been synonymous for thousands of years. A verse by the Roman poet Ovid, translated by Dryden, attests to the Greyhound's long history:

"As when the impatient Greyhound, slipped from far,

Bounds o'er the glade to course the fearful hare,

She in her speed does all her safety lie,

And he with double speed pursues his prey,

O'erruns her at the sitting turn; but licks

His chaps in vain; yet blows upon the flix,

She seeks the shelter which the neighboring covert gives,

And, gaining it, she doubts, if yet she lives."

The first organized coursing meet in the United States was held in 1886 in Cheyenne Bottoms, Kansas. In November 1889, C. F. Holder wrote about "Coursing with Greyhounds in Southern California" in *St. Nicholas,* Vol. XVII, No. 1. The following excerpts and drawings are taken from his detailed account of a hunt and are given to confirm the love of the chase that lies deep in the heart of all Greyhounds.

"Mouse...is but one of a number of dogs that constitute the pack of the Valley Hunt Club of Pasadena, Southern California. In the field together they present a fine appearance...long, slender forms, delicate limbs, powerful muscles, rat-like tails, deep chests, pointed muzzles, and feet like springy cushions.

"Suddenly there is a shout and horses and dogs are away. From under the very nose of Mouse a curious apparition springs up—a fluffy object of grayish tints. It is the jack-rabbit! For an instant he stands astonished, then dashes away like a rocket and is followed by the field. Nearly all the dogs see him; while those that do not, follow the others.

Ch. Lakilanni Broken Arrow. Owned by Laurie Soutar. *Photo by Daniel R. Gauss, Shot on Site Photography*

"They sweep on like the wind—a kaleidoscopic effect of grays and yellows passing and repassing. Now Silk leads, then in turn the blue dog is ahead. See! Mouse is in the air. Losing sight of the game, she leaps bodily three feet upward over the brush, looks quickly around, catches sight of the fleeing form, and is away again. The speed is marvelous!"

Mr. Holder goes on to describe the scene after a successful hunt. "Now one may see a thirsty dog drinking from a canteen which one of the huntsmen has unslung, while other dogs await their turn; others again are lying in the cool grass, panting like steam engines, yet very proud of their work....dogs and riders join the coaches and carriages at the hunt breakfast, spread on the slope among the wildflowers; and here, looking down on the lovely valley and the Pacific Ocean thirty miles away, the day's sport ends."

Mr. Holder's treatise discusses what has come to be called open field coursing. It differs from lure coursing in that live game is pursued, rather than an artificial lure.

Open Field Coursing

The National Open Field Coursing Association (NOFCA) and the more recent North American Coursing Association (NACA) are the regulating bodies of open field coursing competition in the United States. The NACA was formed in 1987, and most of its hunts take place near Medicine Bow, Wyoming. NACA offers two coursing titles, the NACC or North American Coursing Champion and the higher title, the NACM or North American Courser of Merit. To qualify for this title, a hound must score 100 points in breed competition.

In open field coursing, sighthounds pursue live game, usually hares or jackrabbits, in large open areas. Open field is the original form of coursing. The length and makeup of the course are determined by the pattern run by the rabbit as he flees the slipped hounds. The jackrabbit can be a formidable opponent. He is on his own territory, can attain speeds of up to 40 miles per hour, can

---

Opposite: From "Coursing in Southern California," *St. Nicholas* in 1889. Reprinted in *Gazehound* in 1974.

Seamair Sunrise Sirocca. Owned by Cheryl Reynolds.

make sharp turns, and can make quick starts and stops. The rabbit will normally run in a straight line, but will turn if forced by a fast hound. The hound in the lead performs the work of turning the jackrabbit. At the beginning of a run, the rabbit and hounds will be running close to 40 miles per hour. Eventually the pace slows, giving the hounds with superior endurance the opportunity to demonstrate their abilities to work the prey. Hounds are judged on their skill in forcing a turn (wrench), run ups, go-bys, takes, as well as their speed, technique, and enthusiasm.

Coursing Vocabulary

The following terms are commonly used when discussing coursing. A familiarity with their meanings is helpful in understanding the sport. Many of these terms refer exclusively to open field coursing.

AK—assisted kill.

Blanket Colors—a dog's coat worn in lure course competition, colors are pink, blue, and yellow.

Drop—attempt to catch quarry. Successful drop results in take or kill; unsuccessful drop, a trip.

Action shot of P's Call Bell CD FC. "Owen" was awarded Best in Field in 1997 in Lompoc, California.

Owned by Beth Levine.

Photo by Leaping Lizard's

Follow—staying with the quarry. Involves speed, agility, maintaining visual contact when turning, confronting obstacles or difficult terrain, and attempting to resight after visual contact is lost.

Gallery—spectators and competitors spread out in a horizontal line and walk behind hounds to help raise game.

Go-by—a hound who is at least one body length behind another hound, passes the hound and moves a clear length ahead.

Hedging—a hound runs alongside the chase by 5 to 20 yards in order to make a take during a turn. The hound must successfully anticipate the direction in which the quarry will be turned.

Huntmaster—the official of the hunt, the one who sounds the release.

Interference—the deliberate impeding of one hound by another during the course.

No Course—a course that terminates before the judges have a chance to evaluate a hound. The time may vary, but it is usually 25 seconds.

Preslip—a hound released or pulling away before sounding of the release, "Tally-Ho."

Pushing—forcing the quarry by pressure or threat.

Recall—the return of the hound to its handler following the course, hound may be penalized if it delays the start of the next course.

Running Cute—letting other hounds do most of the work, usually results in a poor score.

Run Up—the initial sprint from the slip to the quarry.

Take—kill.

Tally Ho—call given by huntmaster that game has been sighted and hounds may be slipped.

Trip—unsuccessful attempt to kill quarry.

Turn—the quarry is forced to change from its original direction at an angle of 90 degrees or more.

UK—unassisted kill.

Wrench—the quarry turns from its original direction at an angle of less then 90 degrees. Points are awarded for a forced wrench, but not if the game turns on its own with no pressure from the hounds.

The Greyhound in the Open Field

Steve Copold, in an article on open field coursing that appeared in the July-August 1975 issue of *The Gazehound,* compared "Running Techniques

Built for speed, Greyhounds excel at coursing.

Dual Ch. Godspeed Qui Tam SC, ORC.

Owned by Terry Fletcher.

Photo by Steve Surfman

Ch. El-Aur Shining Adventure.
Owned by Laurel Drew.

and Movement in the Sighthound Breeds." Copold had this to say about Greyhounds: "When discussing the Greyhound in the field, it must be kept in mind that although there are three distinct types of Greyhounds, the NGA, the AKC, and the NGA/AKC cross, they are all Greyhounds and as such must be evaluated as equals in the coursing field.

"Speed is the Greyhounds' strongest point in the field. No other breed of sighthound is capable of completely overpowering a jackrabbit as is the Greyhound. A Greyhound's acceleration is only a hair off that of the Whippet and when this is combined with their speed, the result is the ultimate in coursing hounds. Greyhounds are low runners that are ideally suited for picking up hares. They rarely raise their heads above the centerline of their backs, even when negotiating a turn! A Greyhound's enthusiasm is at best difficult to understand. He is far from lacking in this area, but seems to take a different approach to the entire situation than do the other breeds. Whippets are almost reckless and devil-may-care in their enthusiasm, and although the Greyhound is their equal in desire, it is a cold and calculating enthusiasm. Perhaps it would be best

to say that the coursing Greyhound is more dedicated than enthusiastic. While the other hounds are having good times, the Greyhounds take everything very seriously.

"The Greyhound's technique in the field is best described as a type of charge! His first love is pressing the quarry as hard as is possible...Greyhounds that hedge are few and far between. In competition, Greyhounds are very difficult to outscore unless the course becomes a contest of endurance. Endurance is the Greyhound's shortcoming.

"Greyhounds come highly recommended for the coursing enthusiast. They are gentle and tractable, while, although not perfect, highly efficient in the field."

Three Great Coursing Events

THE GRAND COURSE

The Grand Course is the grand finale of the NOFCA open field coursing season in the United States. It is an invitational event that takes place on a weekend in February. A hound must accumulate a certain number of points or be ranked as one of the top three coursers in the breed the previous year to be

Ch. Suntiger e.e. cummings is currently the only all-AKC Greyhound to hold the NOFCA CM title.

Owned by John and Beth Anne Gordon.

Photo by Baines Photo

issued an invitation. Each year the number of points required can differ.

All hounds entered in the Grand Course run a preliminary and final course in breed competition. Each of the breed hunt's competition is based on a random draw, and each is scored by a different judge. The scores are then added together to award breed points for the first five placements. The breed hunt competition takes place on the first day of the Grand Course and the mixed competition on day two. Each hound runs only once on the second day but is scored by two judges. The final day's score is then added to that of the previous day to get the total score.

The Grand Course offers non-regular stakes. The stakes offered are Champion, Field Champion, CD, CDX, UD, Novice, Veteran, Coursing Champion, Courser of Merit, Oval Race Champion, ARM/R. Ch., Breeder and Kennel. Based on a hound's Grand Course total points, the winner of the stake takes all.

The hounds that run the Grand Course are some of the very best coursing hounds in the country. To attain the top position at the end of the meet is a highly desirable and prestigious achievement.

THE WHITETAIL INVITATIONAL

David Skeldon and Karen Ackerman shared this information about the Whitetail Invitational (WI), which is held at the end of March each year. The NACA holds the Whitetail Invitational, its premier coursing event of the season. The WI is open to all sighthounds who have met the qualification requirement of participating in at least three NACA hunts during the coursing season. The WI is based on two days of competition, with a winner each day and an overall winner.

For Greyhounds only, the NACA offers the Ladybug Cup. This event is based on one day of Greyhound competition. The trophy features a running Greyhound mounted on a wooden base with a small ladybug affixed near the statue. The trophy was donated by Peter and Daphne Lowe in memory of their Greyhound, Ladybug FCh., CC, CM. Past winners of the cup have been Dutch Bahama Fleet, owned by Fern White; Point Breeze Darq

69

Adventure, owned by Susan Loop-Stanley; Free Sum, owned by Dana Olson; and Point Breeze Slate Gray, owned by David and Joyce Skeldon.

THE WATERLOO CUP

The Waterloo Cup, begun in England in 1836, has come to be recognized as the most competitive and prestigious event in the coursing world. The Waterloo Cup was originally an 8-dog stake, but now this early spring meet is run by 64 Greyhounds. Each dog must be nominated to participate. Nominations are given to longtime and well-established coursing owners. If an owner has nothing to run, the nomination is returned to the Waterloo Cup committee, which reissues it to another owner.

Points awarded at two- to three-day national events such as the Waterloo Cup are the same as those given at the smaller 8- to 16-dog one-day stakes. Points are awarded for the following six skills, as follows:

Speed—1, 2, or 3 points can be awarded
Go-Bye—2 points, 3 points if pass is on the outside
The Turn—1 point is awarded
The Wrench—$^1/_2$ point is awarded
The Kill—2 points or less, based on skill
The Trip—1 point is awarded

The Greyhound earning the most points during a course is declared the winner.

There are a number of interesting stories told about many of these dogs, one in particular about Master McGrath. Legend has it that he was found as a puppy by the tenant of an Irish nobleman who had heard the puppy crying. He had been tied in a sack that had caught on a root in a stream that ran through the estate. That poor puppy, who almost drowned, grew up to be the most well-known coursing Greyhound of all time. Master McGrath was defeated only once in his career, when he fell through the ice of a frozen river.

In the 1930s another Greyhound, named Jamie, became the most well-

Winners of past Waterloo Cup competitions include:

Milanie—red bitch, was the first winner, 1836
Cerito—bitch who weighed 50 pounds, 1850, and twice later
Lobelia—bitch who weighed 44 pounds, 1867
Master McGrath—1869
Fullerton—brindle dog, 1889 to 1892
Fabulous Fortune—bitch who had been purchased for a few shillings, 1896
Laato—owned by Lord Lonsdale, 1923
White Collar—owned by Mrs. Whitburn, the first woman to receive a nomination, 1928
Rotten Row—black dog owned by Mr. Rowland Rank, 1937
Maesydd Michael—black dog owned by Mr. D.K. Steadman
Life Line—black dog owned by Mr. L. Lucas, 1949
Old Kentucky Minstrel—Irish fawn dog owned by Mr. B. Dolphin, 1957
Mutual Friend—bred, raised, and owned by Mr. Forsyth, 1959

known coursing dog in England. Although he never won the Waterloo Cup, he is famous as the sire of Mutton Cutlet, whose progeny became many of the top-winning racing and coursing Greyhounds in England. Mutton Cutlet, who died in 1934, sired more than 500 track and field winners.

ASFA and AKC Lure Coursing

The idea of lure coursing traces back to the 1960s. Open field coursing, which was so popular in the West, was not readily adaptable on a nationwide basis. Many people objected to the hunting and killing of live game. Plus, large open spaces containing jackrabbits were not available everywhere in the country. Lyle Gillette, who was active in open field coursing in California, wanted AKC recognition for the sport of coursing. He realized that a different type of coursing would have to be developed to be accepted and practiced nationally.

Mr. Gillette worked with others to develop an artificial lure system that could be laid out in different patterns. These patterns were intended to simulate the running of a rabbit in an open field.

AOK Speed Chic F.Ch. "Brandy" began lure coursing at age five. She is a winner of six Bests of Breed and three Bests in Field.

Owned by John Parker.

Photo by Pam Ross/Pet Portraits

Thus, the American Sighthound Field Association (ASFA) was established in 1972, and rules and regulations for holding lure trials were set forth. In 1976 the original lure system was improved by making it a continuous loop, eliminating the need to restring after every course, saving much time.

Although Gillette and others continued to seek AKC recognition of lure coursing, it was not until 1991 that the AKC sanctioned lure coursing trials. At the present time, 11 breeds of dogs are considered sighthounds and are permitted to compete in ASFA and AKC lure trials. The breeds are Afghan Hounds, Basenjis, Borzois, Greyhounds, Ibizan Hounds, Irish Wolfhounds, Pharaoh Hounds, Rhodesian Ridgebacks, Salukis, Scottish Deerhounds, and Whippets.

The ASFA and AKC lure trials are very similar. The ASFA requires a course to be a minimum of 500 yards; the AKC, 400, but some courses may be as long as 1,000 yards. Each course must contain several turns and straight runs. Sighthounds run with members of their own breed to compete for breed titles, then compete against other breeds for Best in Field. Hounds usually run in trios and are selected by random drawing. Each dog wears a yellow, pink, or blue blanket.

A perfect example of power, speed, and control. *Photo courtesy Laurie Soutar*

Dogs are slipped when the Huntmaster gives the "Tally Ho!" signal. The call is sounded after the lure has been started and is several yards away from the dogs.

The lure operator's job is a very important one, as operators actually control the dogs and their running. It helps to be able to anticipate movements of the dogs and know where they are likely to turn, cut corners, or overrun. This means an operator should be familiar with the running styles of the different sighthounds. The job requires quick reflexes and the ability to make snap decisions. The lure must always be kept 10 to 30 yards in front of the lead hound and should be stopped 20 yards before the lure machine on the return. An operator has to be constantly aware of the location of each dog and make certain that they are all safe. The lure operator must stop the lure immediately if a dog gets tangled in the line or some other potentially dangerous situation occurs.

Hounds are scored by at least one, preferably two, judges in both ASFA and AKC lure trials. Points are awarded as follows:

In ASFA trials, a hound that has never been coursed must twice run with a similar type of hound before competing for points in an Open Stake. The number of points awarded toward an ASFA title is

The slip. *Photo by Gail Burnham*

Quality	ASFA	AKC
Enthusiasm/Overall Ability	15	10
Follow	15	10
Speed	25	10
Agility	25	10
Endurance	2	10
Total Possible Score	10	50
Penalties		
Preslip	-1 to -10	-1 to -5
Course Delay	-1 to -10	-1 to -5

based on the number of dogs entered in that breed. The first place winner in Open is awarded 4 points for each dog defeated, up to a total of 40 points. The second hound receives 3 points, up to a total of 30; the third place winner 2 points, up to 20 points; and the fourth place, 1 point, up to 10 points. To obtain the ASFA title of Field Champion (FCh.) a hound must earn 100 points, which includes two first-place wins in breed competition, or one first-place and two second-place wins in breed competition.

A sighthound that is a field champion can be entered in Field Champion Stakes and compete for a Lure Courser of Merit (LCM) title. Three hundred points and four first-place finishes are needed to attain this title. Field Champion and Open Stakes winners compete for Best of Breed. Best of Breed winners compete for the Best in Field award.

Ch. Aragon Darkwind CDX, TDX, SC. Owned by Helen Hamilton.

The American Kennel Club requires that a hound prove that it can successfully run a course before qualifying for the Open Breed Stake. A dog runs twice by itself to earn a Junior Courser (JC) title. Then, after a few practice runs with other hounds (not required, but strongly recommended), a dog competes in Open Stake to earn a Senior Courser (SC) title. A hound must receive four qualifying scores to be awarded an SC title. At the same time a sighthound is competing for a Senior Courser title, the dog is also accumulating points toward a Field Champion (FC) title. A hound needs 15 points and two majors to earn an FC title. First through third places in each breed receive points. The number of points awarded is determined by the number of dogs entered in competition in that breed. Winners of Open and Special (FC titled hounds) stakes in each breed compete for Best of Breed. Best of Breed winners then compete to determine Best in Field.

To be allowed to participate in ASFA trials, a sighthound must be registered with the AKC, NGA, an AKC-recognized foreign registry, or, in the case of Salukis, possess a critique case number from the Saluki Club of America. To run in AKC trials, a hound must be registered with the AKC, any AKC-recognized foreign registry, or hold an AKC ILP (Indefinite Listing Privilege) number. National Greyhound Association Greyhounds can be registered with the AKC and do not need to use the ILP number if they are cross-registered.

Spayed or neutered hounds may run in both ASFA and AKC trials, but dogs that exhibit any breed disqualifications may not participate.

This list of Top Ten ASFA Lure Coursing Greyhounds for 1995 was printed in the May-June 1996 issue of *Sighthound Review,* taken from information sent by Sue Sefscik and printed in the Field Advisory News.

1. SecondWind Sportster, LCM
2. Point Breeze Southern Siren, FCh.
3. Beeline B Quick, LCM
4. Vintage Moments, LCM
5. Laura Lindberg, FCh.
6. Soloist Kelly
7. Winner The Pooh, LCM
8. Blue Marble
9. Kilmarney Micki, FCh.
10. Oh Clare, LCM

Point Breeze Slate Gray, the 1996 Ladybug Cup winner.

Owned by David and Joyce Skeldon.

Sighthounds are hunting dogs and born athletes. Giving your Greyhounds the opportunity to participate in coursing events permits them to use ancient natural instincts and have a good time doing so. For more information about open field or lure coursing, contact the NOFCA, NACA, ASFA, or AKC. You will be able to obtain copies of rules and regulations as well as lists of clubs holding trials.

If you have never coursed your Greyhound but think you and your dog may enjoy the sport, try it. If you have the good fortune of owning a Greyhound that loves the chase, then you are in for a rare treat. If a Greyhound loves to run, this love is stronger than just about anything else. Coursing affords an opportunity for your Greyhound to exercise his mind and body, utilize his working gait and the double suspension gallop, prove himself a capable competitor, and have great fun.

Greyhounds with Open Field and ASFA Coursing titles are too numerous to mention in this chapter, but some interesting stats from the American Kennel Club (March 1999) list the Lifetime Top Lure Coursing Greyhounds as follows:

1.	M's K Lofton SC	K. Lorenzo
2.	FC Second Wind Black Comet SC	M. Lorenzo
3.	FC Second Wind Sporster SC	K. Lorenzo
4.	FC Wild Abbey Leigh SC	R. Tierney/G. Bothner
5.	FC Lindsey Party SC	R. J. and M. E. Summerhill
6.	FC Second Wind Sunbeam SC	K. and M. Lorenzo
7.	FC Madison SC	J. P. Henderson
8.	DC Artesia Flash Dance CD SC	N. Woodward
9.	FC Regal Ruler	M. Houghton
10.	FC Point Breeze Ruler SC	B. and J. Bulman
11.	Tem Tex Megan	J. Arabas/S. Fried
12.	K Zoe Oldenbourg SC	P. Burlingham
13.	DC Tova's Apollo SC	C. Colbert
14.	FC Little Tina	J. and K. Steeves

THE OBEDIENCE GREYHOUND

Training Greyhounds, or any sighthound for that matter, can be a challenge. Many people have tried to do obedience work with Greyhounds and have given up when they felt they were making no progress. But quite a few owners have successfully trained Greyhounds in obedience. Possibly the first Greyhound to earn a CD (Companion Dog) title was Ch. On-Da-Way Skipper, CD, bred and owned by Ivy Dolan. Skipper was awarded the title in 1937. One of these successful trainers is Linda Colflesh. Linda trains dogs professionally and is the author of the book *Making Friends*, a training manual for dogs and people. Linda's main emphasis in her training classes and in her books is "building better understanding between people and dogs." She accomplishes this with much patience and love, as well as

Sisters BISS Ch. Heathero Silver Daphne UD and Ch. Heathero Really a Rita CD. Owned by Marjorie Leider.

a willingness to get to know each person and dog and how they learn best.

Linda has written the following section in which she discusses, with considerable insight, the challenges specifically associated with training Greyhounds in obedience. She offers many good suggestions that may encourage Greyhound owners to try their hand at obedience training.

Basic Training

Training your Greyhound benefits you, your dog, and your relationship. It can save your dog's life as well as allow him more freedom. It provides him with mental stimulation. Your relationship with your dog is improved by communicating what you want, rather than restraining or punishing your dog to prevent him from doing undesirable behaviors. Training allows you to more fully enjoy your Greyhound.

Whether your plans for your Greyhound include breed or obedience showing, therapy dog work, agility, or simply life as a special companion, basic good manners are a necessity. Every Greyhound owner is happier if his dog is trained to lie down, stand, stay, come, walk on leash, and accept restraint.

You will get the best results from training if you start before 12 weeks of age; even 7 weeks is not too soon to begin at home. Your Greyhound will be learning at that age, and you have a choice about what he learns. Puppy kindergarten classes are a good way to start training, and they provide an excellent opportunity for important socialization.

Ch. Windborne's Avion Zephyr, sitting in heel position, is owned and trained by Linda Colflesh.

Photo by Brad Wood

Sitting is commonly one of the first things taught in basic obedience classes. However, Greyhound owners should be aware that teaching a Greyhound to sit presents special difficulties. Because of their build, Greyhounds are less comfortable in a sitting position than other non-sighthound breeds. They rarely assume a sitting position on their own without being given a command.

To begin training with sitting can be frustrating for both the Greyhound and his owner. It causes some Greyhound owners to give up before they have really even started. Making an issue of sitting at the beginning of a training class can ruin a Greyhound's attitude toward training. The stress of being in the new environment of a training class may cause your Greyhound to tense his thigh muscles, making it almost impossible to guide him into a sitting position. If your obedience instructor has little experience with sighthounds, he or she may not be aware of the difficulty with sitting.

In my basic obedience classes, Greyhounds are given the option to use a sitting or standing position when the other dogs are required to sit. While other dogs usually master a sit first and progress to a stand/stay, Greyhounds do just the reverse. They learn the stand/stay first. Usually by the end of an 8- to 12-week class, the Greyhound has relaxed and become accustomed to being guided into positions. This makes training the sit much easier.

In fact, it is not necessary for your Greyhound to learn to sit at all to be a well-mannered companion. A stand/stay or down/stay is all that is necessary for control.

Another challenge for the Greyhound owner is teaching a dog to come when called. Just because you are trying to train a dog that operates like a Corvette with no brakes is no reason to skip this train-

"Zephyr" heeling; Zephyr is a recipient of the Greyhound Club of America's Versatility Dog Award.

Photo by Brad Wood

"Zephyr" fronting as part of the recall exercise.

Photo by Brad Wood

"Zephyr" going over the broad jump. *Photo by Brad Wood*

ing. Even if your dog never learns to come when outdoors, it is a useful command in the house. Make liberal use of treats and long lines. You will be more successful if you start training early (before 12 weeks), never allow your dog to become frustrated by lack of freedom, keep your dog well exercised, and don't give up!

Because of their sensitivity to anesthesia, teaching a Greyhound to accept restraint could save his life. A well-trained Greyhound will not need to be chemically restrained for many veterinary procedures.

A good basic obedience goal for all dogs, including Greyhounds, is the AKC Canine Good Citizen award. The CGC test requires a dog to sit only once to pass, a relief for most Greyhound owners. There is no come exercise in this test. The whole test is on leash. Greyhounds adopted from the track do not need to be registered with the AKC to obtain this title.

Choosing a Training Method

Training can be a positive or negative experience, depending on how well suited the training method is to you and your dog. There are a number of training methods used across the country, some of which utilize food rewards and some that do not. Some rely on choke-collar corrections and others do not. Your choice of method should be based on you and your dog's personalities.

The personality of a Greyhound varies from dog to dog, but generally he is intelligent and independent, with low energy (except for sprinting) and low defense drives. What does this mean for training? As an independent dog, the Greyhound is less eager to please. This makes him more difficult to motivate to obey your commands.

Your Greyhound's low energy level presents another motivational problem. He will not like repetitious training, so your training sessions should not be too long. Training sessions must be pre-planned so time can be used effectively. Several short sessions are better than one long one. Train when he is most energetic, such as before a meal.

Their low defense drive makes Greyhounds less able to recover from forceful corrections than other breeds. A

Effective training requires a good deal of concentration on your Greyhound's part. "Fielding" and "Julia," owned by Maggie Bryson, have what it takes.

Greyhound's reaction to stress tends toward flight or freezing, and that is sometimes their reaction to correction. They cannot learn in this state.

Because motivation and correction are a problem for Greyhounds, training methods that rely mainly on positive reinforcement using food rewards work well. Good rewards keep the attention of an easily bored dog that would rather be sleeping, and they reduce the number of corrections that are necessary. Praise is usually not a strong motivator for Greyhounds because of their independence. While they may enjoy the sound of a happy voice, it may not be enough to motivate them to get off the bed and work on heeling. They want to be paid for their work!

The less-than-voracious appetite of some Greyhounds may force you to be creative in your choice of rewards. If yours turns up his nose at the usual dog treats, be inventive. Here are some sug-

gestions: cheese, hot dogs, liverwurst, pepperoni, garlic bologna, animal crackers (for those with a sweet tooth), bacon, garlic bread, and turkey. It will also help to keep his interest if you use different treats each time.

Be careful when choosing a collar for training. A Greyhound's neck is sensitive. Look for something soft and wide. Use small bolt snaps on the leash that will not swing and hit your dog's eye.

Training an Adopted Greyhound

Training an adult dog that spent the first part of his life in a racing kennel presents special problems. First, training is much easier if started as a puppy. Even if all you do is teach your puppy to sit for a treat, your dog has learned to respond to a command. Dogs that do not learn before the age of four months about being given a verbal command, respond-

Greyhounds come with their own set of abilities and limitations. Keep these in mind when working on training exercises.

Photo by Isabelle Francais

ing, and then receiving a consequence, have a hard time understanding the concept later. It is difficult for them to attach a specific meaning to our words. The acquisition of this knowledge can initially be frustratingly slow, but if you persist in teaching one command, all subsequent training will go faster.

Second, the sit training will be especially difficult with an adopted Greyhound. Sitting is strongly discouraged in the starting box at the racetrack, so train the rest of the commands first. Trying to physically guide the dog into a sit will be met with resistance. It will be easier for both of you to use a food lure to move your dog's head up and back until his back legs start to fold. Break the

sit into parts, rewarding at the beginning for just a slight bending of the legs.

Competition Training

Showing a Greyhound in obedience is definitely a challenge. Their bodies are not built for quick sits, and their lack of hair makes it easy to see a crooked sit. As mentioned before, Greyhounds find repetition boring and are hard to motivate. They find the idea of doing a down/stay on a hard surface appalling. Even lower on their list are cold or wet surfaces. They are cold when other dogs are comfortable. And at any given moment, they would rather be sleeping in bed.

On the plus side, you'll be admired for showing such an unusual breed in obedience, and it's a lot easier to make the top ten obedience Greyhound list than the top ten Golden list. Nonetheless, Greyhounds can win in all-breed obedience trials, as I can personally attest.

If you intend to show in obedience, you should teach your dog a tuck sit rather than a rock-back sit. In the tuck sit, the dog plants his front legs and brings his back legs up toward his front feet, often hopping his rear underneath him. In the rock-back sit, the dog rocks back as he folds his rear legs and steps back with his front feet. The problem with this type of sit is that it moves the Greyhound back out of proper position for a sit while heeling or in front.

The sit/stay is also a problem. As an example, I started teaching my Greyhound Zephyr to sit at eight weeks of age. She was well over a year old before she could hold the sit position for a one-minute stay without her legs starting to tremble from the effort. She achieved high scores and placings in obedience competition even though she almost always missed one sit during the heeling. Obedience titles are not made by sits alone!

Teaching a Greyhound to retrieve can be a major stumbling block to advanced competition, but it does not need to be. There are different ways to do it, many using food rewards. In addition to reading books and attending classes or seminars, there are videotapes available to teach retrieving.

Jumping can be a breeze for a Grey-

Gail Burnham's Suntiger Star Traveler CD was High in Trial at the 1994 Western Specialty. *Photo by Kitten*

hound in the advanced classes, but be careful not to teach your dog to use speed to get over the jumps. A fast, flat jump is unsafe within the confines of a ring. It is preferable for a dog to jump in an arc.

Greyhounds sometimes exhibit a frustrating behavior when in the obedience ring. They slow down, sometimes freeze, and stare off into space. The poor dogs look as if they are drugged or having an out-of-body experience. This behavior doesn't mean that the dog hates obedience, nor does it mean the dog was harshly handled. It is just a typical Greyhound reaction to stress. This stress can be caused by the show environment or by incomplete training. For instance, handlers often talk to their dogs a lot while training, then their dogs become confused in the ring when the handler is mostly silent and seems angry.

Again, the right training method and an instructor that has experience or at least an open mind toward training sighthounds will make all the difference as you pursue an obedience title. Most important of all is having a positive attitude yourself.

Ch. Sundridge Sagitta. Owned by Sue LeMieux.
Photo by P. Gail Burnham

Conformation and Obedience Together

Training in obedience can improve your performance in the breed ring, and vice versa. Obedience skills useful in the breed ring are gaiting on a loose lead, a reliable stand/stay, and paying attention. Showing in the breed ring will provide a good introduction to being in the ring for obedience. You get to have food in the breed ring and practice your stand for exam. The Greyhound breed has many dogs with both obedience and breed titles. Obedience training does not ruin a dog for conformation. Only poor obedience training ruins a dog for the breed ring, but it also ruins him for obedience showing as well.

If you are going to show your dog in conformation and obedience, it is best to start the training at the same time, preferably when your Greyhound is a puppy. The reason for this is that neither the behaviors required for breed nor obedience will be stronger than the other. Your body language and commands will tell your Greyhound whether or not you are heeling or gaiting him. They will also tell him whether to sit or stand when you stop. This is not difficult for a Greyhound to understand; his only limitation is his handler.

83

A Well-Trained Owner

As Linda Colflesh has illustrated, training is communicating, a way of teaching your Greyhound your language. English is a foreign language to him, just as his language of body motions and facial expressions is foreign to you. In the process of teaching him your language, you will learn a lot about his. You can learn to tell the difference between when he is not obeying because he is confused or when he is just choosing not to obey. You'll learn the subtle signals he gives you when he is stressed. By working on this mutual communication, you will develop trust, respect, and understanding. Training is love in action.

Most Greyhound owners guiltily admit that when you share your life with a Greyhound, you are the one who receives the training. You learn to share when you can no longer stretch out on the sofa to watch television, or when you lose all but a three-inch edge of your bed. You learn patience as you wait while your Greyhound stretches and yawns after a nap, then walks slowly, stiff-legged, arching his back to stretch some more, before trotting to the door to go outside. You learn tidiness when

P's Call Bell CD, JC, awarded High in Trial at the 1997 Western Specialty. Owned by Beth Levine. *Photo by Rich Bergman*

you make certain that the dishtowel is always hung inside the cupboard, your shoes are put into the closet, and the evening paper is gathered up from the floor before you go to bed. After many months of hard work, you may find that your Greyhound has been as successful at training you as you have him. Good luck!

If you are seriously interested in obedience competition, write to the American Kennel Club for a current copy of the Obedience Rules and Regulations. Find a trainer and group with which to practice. Try to locate someone who is familiar with sighthounds or is willing to try different training approaches, and one who is willing to work with you on an individual basis if necessary.

The AKC awards four obedience titles: Companion Dog (CD), Companion Dog Excellent (CDX), Utility Dog (UD), and Obedience Trial Champion (OTCh.). The first three titles are earned by scoring at least 170 points out of a possible 200 at three obedience trials under three different judges. In order to earn points toward the OTCh. title, dogs must place first or second in open and utility classes.

Frolic of Aroi, an early CD Greyhound. El-Aur Greyhounds.

To obtain a Novice Obedience degree, CD, a dog must successfully complete the following exercises.

EXERCISE	MAXIMUM POINTS
1. Heel on Leash and Figure Eight	40
2. Stand for Examination	30
3. Heel Free	40
4. Recall	30
5. Long Sit	30
6. Long Down	30
Maximum Total Score	200

To obtain an Open Obedience degree, CDX, a dog must successfully complete the following exercises.

EXERCISE	MAXIMUM POINTS
1. Heel on Leash and Figure Eight	40
2. Drop on Recall	30
3. Retrieve on Flat	20
4. Retrieve over High Jump	30
5. Broad Jump	20
6. Long Sit	30
7. Long Down	30
Maximum Total Score	200

To obtain a Utility Obedience degree, UD, a dog must successfully complete the following exercises.

EXERCISE	MAXIMUM POINTS
1. Signal Exercise	40
2. Scent Discrimination Article No. 1	30
3. Scent Discrimination Article No. 2	30
4. Directed Retrieve	30
5. Moving Stand and Examination	30
6. Directed Jumping	40
Maximum Total Score	200

Tracking Dog (TD) and Tracking Dog Excellent (TDX) titles are also awarded by AKC. To earn either title, a dog must complete a single track judged on a pass/fail basis.

According to *Sighthound Review* statistics, the following are the top ten placing Greyhounds in obedience for 1996.

1. OTCh. The Merry Prankster TD
2. Midnight Rendevous CD, HIT
3. Shot in the Dark CD
4. Koni Lambchop UD
5. Silly Sophie CD
6. Marnics Hug-A-Blue Ashley CD
7. CKS Benjamin P. Bounce CD
8. Silk CD
9. Double C's Ron Jon CDX
10. Ch. Aragon Darkwind CDX, TDX, HIT

No obedience stats are available from *Sighthound Review* for 1997 and 1998. However, the following is a list of Greyhounds acquiring obedience titles in 1997 and 1998.

COMPANION DOG

Companions Seka
Ch. Wilrick's Lucky Shamrock
Jim Cruz
Ch. Golightly Blueberry Hill, JC, NA
Skiddy Geisha
I.B.A. Happ'nin Dude
Treppie
Desert Sage
Golightly Kiss of Chaos
DM's Nelson Bet
Tigger Too
CB's Gold Star
Impress Tiger Lilli
Delight's El Aur Summer Smoke
P's Call Bell
Dal Pal Ricochet
Rhewllyd Sleeping Beauty
Krueger's Czar Nicholas

Michelle's Egypt
KC
Whirlwind's Sun Runners Fire
Clonbrin Mick
Aladdin
Hot Pursuit

COMPANION DOG EXCELLENT

Ch. Aragon Silver Cloud CD TDX
Dal Pal Ricochet CD
Cleo CD
Nutmegan of Tachevah CD
MML's Bo Zed CD
Ch. Arborcrest Danae CD SC
Cherish CD

TRACKING DOG

Tigger Too CD

THE VERSATILE GREYHOUND

The Greyhound was originally a coursing dog, helping his human companions to find food for the family. When coursing meets became popular, the skill of the chase began to be regarded more importantly than the kill. As time passed, showing and racing became popular. Dogs were bred specifically for one of three purposes: coursing, racing, or showing. Many top-winning coursing dogs were bred by mixing AKC and NGA bloodlines, but the NGA dogs used for racing and the AKC dogs that entered the show ring became separate entities. There have always been some show Greyhound breeders that have trained in obedience and run their dogs in ASFA lure coursing trials, but it has only been in the past several years,

Greyhounds can do wonders for anyone's spirit; here, one works the crowd at a nursing home.

Photo by Brad Wood

since the AKC has begun to put more emphasis on retaining performance aspects of the different breeds, that more people with AKC Greyhounds have become involved in performance activities. In the chapter devoted to AKC breeders, almost everyone mentions that their goal is to produce Greyhounds that have the ability to do the job for which they were bred, and more and more Greyhounds that are being campaigned regularly have obedience and coursing titles. The Greyhound is becoming a truly versatile dog—a family pet and companion, a keen courser, a successful obedience competitor, a beautiful show animal, a therapy dog, an oval track runner, an agility contender, and a canine good citizen.

Versatility Dog Award

In 1993, the Greyhound Club of America began recognizing Greyhounds that hold multiple titles. The Versatility Certificate is awarded to any Greyhound that has a title in conformation, coursing, and either obedience or tracking.

Scent discrimination is another talent possessed by Greyhounds. *Photo by Brad Wood*

The following titles will qualify a Greyhound for a VC award:

Conformation—AKC Champion (Ch.)

Coursing—one of the following: ASFA Field Champion (FCh.), AKC Field Champion (FC), NOFCA Coursing Champion (CC)

Obedience/Tracking—one of the following: Companion Dog (CD), Tracking Degree (TD)

The Versatility Certificate Excellent is awarded to a Greyhound that has met the above criteria and also has one of the following: Conformation—Group I win, Best in Show (BIS), or Specialty BIS; Coursing—ASFA Lure Courser of Merit (LCM), NOFCA Courser of Merit (CM); Obedience/Tracking—AKC Utility Dog (UD), AKC Tracking Dog Excellent (TDX).

According to the March 1993 *GCA Newsletter,* these certificates, which were retroactive, have been awarded to the following Greyhounds:

VERSATILITY CERTIFICATE

Ch. Windwood Sweet Arriba FCh. TD, "Arriba," owned by Sheila Grant:
Ch.—September 1986
FCh. (ASFA)—October 1983
TD—April 1988

Ch. El Aur Aztec CDX TD FCh., "Parker," owned by Laurel Drew:
Ch.—November 1979
FCh. (ASFA)—June 1979
CD—September 1976
TD—September 1977

Ch. Zanzibar's Flash Dancer CD FCh., owned by Joy Bidmead-Brown:
Ch.—1985
FCh. (ASFA)—1987
CD

Ch. Suntiger True Love FCh. CD, "Sonny," owned by Gail Burnham:
Ch.—August 1991
FCh.—July 1992
CD—April 1994

VERSATILITY CERTIFICATE EXCELLENT

Ch. Morley's Sue LCM CD, "Tiger," owned by Stacy Pober:
  Ch.—October 1988
  LCM—November 1983
  CD

Ch. Midnight Shadow Traveler FCh. UDT, "Tiger," owned by Gail Burnham:
  Ch.—December 1975
  FCh. (ASFA)—April 1976
  UD—August 1975
  TDX—March 1981

Ch. Suntiger No Greater Love FCh. TDX, "Love," owned by Gail Burnham:
  Ch.—September 1982
  FCh. (ASFA)—July 1987
  TDX—April 1985

Am. Can. Ch. Golightly Really Rosie FCh. CD, "Rosie," owned by Stacy Pober:
  Ch.—May 1988
  FCh. (ASFA)—September 1989
  CD—February 1989

Ch. Windborne's Avion Zephyr CDX SC FCh., "Zephyr," owned by Linda
    Colflesh:
  Ch.—October 1989
  FCh. (ASFA)—June 1990
  CD—November 1989

Ch. Iveragh Suleima Penny Lane CD FCh., "Charter," owned by Betsy Marvel
    and Jay Hoge:
  Ch.—August 1984
  FCh. (ASFA)—September 1985

Ch. Suntiger the Ridge Runner SC FCh. CD, "Julia," owned by Maggie
    Bryson and Gail Burnham:
  Ch.—November 1991
  FCh. (ASFA)—October 1994
  CD—June 1994

Ch. Ekohils Cinnamon Life CD CCTDX "Shattab," owned by Helen Hamilton:
  Ch.—November 1985
  CC—October 1990
  CD—March 1987
  TDX—February 1992

Ch. California Sunshine Traveler FCh. UDT, "Sunny," owned by Gail Burnham:
  Ch.—December 1983
  LCM—March 1978
  UD—August 1975
  TD—1984

Ch. and F.Ch. Suntiger No Greater Love, the first TDX Greyhound bitch.

Owned by P. Gail Burnham, Suntiger.

Ch. Southwestern Episode Holly, five-time Best in Show winner, and Ch. Southwestern Silver Moon, Group winner and 1994 Westminster Kennel Club Best of Breed.

Owned by Greg Davis, Roger Owens, and Marsha Wartell.

Photo by Rich Bergman

Ch. El-Aur Aztec CDX, TD, F.Ch. (left), a Versatility Certificate Winner, and Ch. El-Aur Midsummer Moonwind F.Ch. (right).

Owned by Laurel Drew.

Photo by Wayne Cott.

Ch. Suntiger the Ridge Runner SC, F.Ch., CD. Owned by Maggie Bryson and P. Gail Burnham. *Photo by Luc Allen*

AKC Dual Ch., Can. Ch. Golightly Really Rosie CD, SC, F.Ch. CGC. Owned by Stacy Pober, Golightly.

Agility

Greyhounds and agility are a winning combination. Agility competition originated in England in 1977, developed by John Varley, a member of the Crufts Dog Show committee, and Peter Meanwell, a dog trainer, judge, and competitor in working trials. The first demonstration and competition took place at Crufts in February 1978.

Agility competition became so popular that the Kennel Club recognized this new kind of event in 1980 and developed regulations for agility tests. The first sanctioned agility competition was held at Crufts in 1980.

Agility found its way to the United States in the early 1980s, and the United States Agility Association was formed in 1986. Its goal was to promote and standardize competition, agility clubs, and obstacle courses. The American Kennel Club licensed agil-

ity competition in 1994, and the first agility trial was held on August 11 of that year at the Astro World Series of Dog Shows, in Houston, Texas. Wherever agility trials are held, they draw huge, enthusiastic crowds that applaud and cheer on the dogs and their handlers. Agility has great spectator appeal, and it is a sport that is fun for both dog and handler.

Agility dogs jump through hoops, crawl through tunnels, scale an A-frame, walk a dog walk, weave through poles, clear hurdles, and traverse a seesaw. This rigorous obstacle course requires dogs and handlers who are in good physical condition. The agility course is never arranged the same way twice. At every trial, the handler and dog may have to use a different strategy. Both have to think quickly as they race through the course, competing with other teams for the fastest time and fewest mistakes. The handler uses ver-

"Zephyr" emerges from open tunnel in agility competition.

Owned by Linda Colflesh.

Photo by Brad Wood

bal and hand signals to direct the dog through the course.

There are three levels of competition: novice, open, and excellent. At each level, the number of obstacles and their complexity increases, as does the speed required to complete the course. A perfect score is 100. A qualifying score is 85 points or better, with no disqualifying faults. Agility judges score competitors with hand signals and a whistle. There are four agility titles that can be earned: Novice Agility Dog (NAD), Open Agility Dog (OAD), Agility Dog Excellent (ADE), and Master Agility Excellent (MX).

Disqualifications in agility include failure to perform obstacles in accordance with established performance regulations (missing a contact zone, knocking a bar off a jump, or touching a board on the broad jump). Other elimination faults occur when a handler or dog knocks over an obstacle, a handler touches the dog when giving directions, excessive handling, (example, using bait), crossing the finish line before correcting a course fault, exiting the course area, accruing three course faults. Faults are indicated to the scribe who tallies the scores by the judge, who uses different hand signals to indicate faults.

Ch. Heartaway's Crimson 'n' Clover TD, SC, NA, CGC. "Brielle" was the first Greyhound to earn points toward her flyball dog title.

Kim Hamm, owner and trainer.

"Brielle" was the first Greyhound to win an agility title. Kim Hamm, owner and trainer.

Agility can definitely be considered an athletic event. It requires skills that Greyhounds can easily perform, but begin training your "couch potato" slowly to build up stamina and muscle tone. If you decide to get involved in agility, you will probably want to join a training group. Many obedience clubs now hold agility classes, and members often compete as a group at local shows. Some competitors build their own obstacles and set up an agility course in their yard. They can practice by themselves or with other handlers and dogs between regular classes.

Agility training, whether competitive or otherwise, provides fun and exercise and is a great way to spend time with your Greyhound. The successful completion of agility obstacles will increase your dog's confidence and condition, provide a positive outlet for an active dog, and strengthen the bond that already exists between you and your Greyhound.

The whistle is used to signal an elimination with excusal from the ring. Causes for elimination with excusal include the use of bait or toys, a collar other than the flat buckle type, fouling in the ring, or a dog that is totally out of control, stops performing (completely), or runs the course so slowly that its speed doubles or exceeds twice the established course time.

Agility is quickly becoming one of the fastest-growing performance activities. Many Greyhound owners are finding this a wonderful outlet for all of the exuberance inherent in their pets.

Ch. Windborne's Avion Zephyr CDX, SC, ASFA, F.Ch., CGC, TT Versatility Certificate Excellent.

Owned by Linda Colflesh.

Photo by Brad Wood

The following is a list of agility titled Greyhounds through 1998:

NOVICE AGILITY

OTCH The Merry Prankster UDX TD
Cleo
Ch. Golightly Blueberry Hill JC
KL's Idgie Lou
BB's Silly Lily Girl
KC
Companions Seka

OPEN AGILITY

KL's Mandoid From Marze CDX NA
BB's Silly Lily Girl NA
KL's Idgie Lou NA
Ch. Golightly Blueberry Hill CD JC NA
OTCH The Merry Prankster UDX TD NA
Companions Seka NA

EXCELLENT AGILITY

KL's Mandoid From Marze CDX OA

MASTER AGILITY EXCELLENT

KL's Mandoid From Marz CDX AX

Mandoid From Marz, owned by Kate Crawford, is the first Greyhound to earn an MX (Master Agility Excellent) title. She won this title in September 1998.

Canine Good Citizen

In September 1989, the AKC introduced the Canine Good Citizen test. This test is open not only to AKC-registered dogs, but to non-AKC-registered and mixed-breed dogs as well. Dogs are evaluated on ten on-lead exercises. These exercises are judged simply as pass/fail and are non-competitive. According to the AKC, the CGC test "seeks to identify and recognize officially those dogs that possess the attributes that enable them to serve effectively as personal companions and as members in good standing with the community." The ten tests that the CGC consists of are as follows:

Test 1. Appearance and Grooming.

The dog permits the evaluator to examine ears, coat, and feet without a struggle. The dog must be clean and neat and have a rabies certificate and license.

Test 2. Accepting a Stranger.

The dog shows no shyness or aggression when the evaluator walks up to the handler, shakes hands, and exchanges a few words.

Test 3. Sitting Politely for Petting.

Dog sits by owner's side and permits a friendly stranger to pet its head and body.

Test 4. Walk on a Loose Lead/Out for a Walk.

The handler and dog walk a course with a left turn, right turnabout turn, and halt commands given by the evaluator. This test demonstrates that the handler is in charge of the dog.

Test 5. Walk Through a Crowd.

The dog and handler walk close to at least three people. The dog shows no resentment, fear, or shyness.

Test 6. Sit, Down, and Stay on Command.

The dog demonstrates that it has received some formal training and will sit and down on command. The dog assumes a sit or down position as directed by the handler. The handler walks 20 feet away, then returns to the dog. The dog stays in position until released.

Test 7. Praise and Interaction.

After dog is released from the stay, the handler plays with the dog. After ten seconds, the handler must calm the dog.

Test 8. Reaction to Another Dog.

The dog and handler are approached by another dog and handler. The dog should demonstrate no more than casual interest in the other dog.

F.Ch. and Ch. California Sunshine Traveler UDT, LCM and Ch. Midnight Shadow Traveler UDTX have both earned their Versatility Excellent Certificate. Owned by P. Gail Burnham, Suntiger.

Versatility stars Ch. Golightly Runaround Sue, Golightly Really Rosie, and Ch. Morley's Sue.

Owned by Stacy Pober, Golightly.

Test 9. Reaction to Distractions.

The dog shows confidence at all times when faced with distractions. Two distractions, one visual and one auditory are used; a person in a wheelchair or using a walker, a loud noise, people pushing and shoving each other, someone riding a bike. Dog may show interest but should not panic.

Test 10. Supervised Isolation.

The dog is left with the evaluator when the handler is out of sight for three minutes. The dog may show mild agitation but should not whine, howl, or pace.

Proposed Test 11. Come When Called. Dog should come on command when called.

This test can be passed fairly easily. Obviously, obedience and show training will help, as trained dogs are used to crowds and being handled and are familiar with many of the commands.

Canine Good Citizen tests can be given by any kennel or training club. The evaluator does not have to be licensed by the AKC, but should be experienced in showing, training, and handling dogs. A certificate is awarded to the dog and owner on the day of the test if the dog passes.

THE RACING GREYHOUND

By the mid-1800s, many Greyhounds had found their way to the United States. Most of these dogs came from England and Ireland and were brought over by farmers in the West and Midwest to help them rid their land of animals that were destroying crops. These new owners discovered that their Greyhounds were great sporting dogs and they began holding coursing matches. The wide open spaces provided the perfect venue for these coursing meets, and they became quite popular with the local farmers.

Some owners desired a more controlled environment for the running of their dogs, and the idea of track racing evolved. Early races were held in Salt Lake City, Utah. In 1919, Owen Patrick Smith, an engineer from Memphis, Tennessee, perfected the mechanical lure. This invention was destined to create a Greyhound racing industry that would grow into a multi-million dollar venture and spread to many countries around the world.

The mechanical lure was first demonstrated on a regulation oval track in Emeryville, California. Oval track racing became popular for two reasons: 1) many people had objected to the hunting of live game, and 2) spectators were able to watch Greyhounds run on the oval tracks, instead of trying to follow the dogs over open country. In 1922, the first night races on a lighted track were held in Chicago, Illinois. Greyhound racing quickly grew from an interesting form of entertainment to big business. In 1926, Charles Munn introduced Greyhound racing in England. It has grown in popularity there as well as in Ireland, Australia, Spain, Italy, and Mexico.

But nowhere did Greyhound racing become as popular as it did in the United States, growing to become the nation's sixth largest spectator sport. There are 18 states that sanction pari-mutuel Greyhound racing. The states that have legalized dog racing are listed below. The number of tracks in each state at present are in parentheses.

Alabama (4)
Arizona (3)
Arkansas (1)
Colorado (4)
Connecticut (2)
Florida (17)
Idaho (1)
Iowa (2)
Kansas (2)
Massachusetts (2)
New Mexico (1)
New Hampshire (3)
Oregon (1)
Rhode Island (1)
Texas (2)
West Virginia (2)
Wisconsin (3)

National Greyhound Association

The first Greyhound registry in the United States was the American Coursing Board, established in 1894. In 1906, the National Coursing Association (NCA) began keeping track of pedigrees and other records, publishing the annual studbook and a quarterly magazine called *The Coursing News*.

The NCA moved from its original home in Nebraska to Abilene, Kansas, in 1945; its present offices were acquired in 1961. In 1972, the association's name

Derby Lane Greyhound Race Track, the oldest track in the world, located in St. Petersburg, Florida.

Photo by St. Petersburg News Bureau

The greeting from this 1950 Florida postcard reads: "Paul, the dogs are slow, the women are fast, send money. Steve."

was changed to the National Greyhound Association (NGA). *The Coursing News* became the current monthly magazine, *The Greyhound Review.* NGA membership is composed of more than 5,000 owners and breeders of racing Greyhounds.

The NGA is an associate member of the World Greyhound Racing Federation. It is a charter member and founder of the World Alliance of Greyhound Registries and the American Greyhound Council.

The NGA maintains a rigid identification system of their Greyhounds, a method that other animal registries have emulated. Information about all breedings, litters, individual registrations, transfers, and leases are recorded at the national headquarters in Abilene.

For purposes of identification, each Greyhound is registered according to precise color and markings. A pictorial record is made of coat color pattern as viewed from the front, rear, and both sides, as well as the color of each toe, and even of each toe nail. Both ears of

an NGA registered Greyhound are tattooed. The tattoo in the right ear shows the month and year the Greyhound was whelped and its position in the litter. For example, if the tattoo read 65A, it would mean that the Greyhound was whelped in the sixth month, June, of 1995, and was the first pup tattooed in the litter. The numbers tattooed in the left ear are the same as those that appear in the upper right-hand corner of the breeding acknowledgment form.

American Greyhound Council, Inc.

The American Greyhound Council (AGC) is a nonprofit organization that was founded by the NGA in 1987. Its eight-member board is made up of representatives from the American Greyhound Track Operator's Association (AGTOA) and the National Greyhound Association. The AGC's task is to oversee the welfare of racing Greyhounds and work toward the betterment of the racing industry. The AGC considers proposals requesting funds for Greyhound adoption programs as well as research and other activities that would improve Greyhound racing.

The AGC has established a Greyhound Adoption Fund, which is overseen by the American Society for the Prevention of Cruelty to Animals (ASPCA) and is used to assist groups in placing Greyhounds in homes on an emergency basis. It has funded a toll-free number to help with Greyhound adoption, provided $1,000 annual grants to nonprofit adoption agencies, developed a computerized electronic bulletin board to facilitate Greyhound adoptions, and supported Canine Working Companions in a pilot project to determine if Greyhounds would make good companions for physically challenged persons.

A Greyhound Farm Inspection Program has been created to inspect Greyhound farms for poor conditions. One full-time and 75 part-time inspectors are employed to help ensure humane treatment of Greyhounds. As AGC promotional literature states, "The Greyhound racing industry will not tolerate mistreatment of Greyhounds. Anyone found to be treating Greyhounds inhumanely is subject to disciplinary action, including expulsion from the NGA registry."

The AGC has also published *Care of the Racing Greyhound,* the most comprehensive book to date written about the care of Greyhounds. The authors of this textbook are Dr. James R. Gannon, Dr. Linda L. Blythe, and Dr. A. Morrie Craig.

The AGC also funds, maintains, and prints the *International Greyhound Research Database Catalog.* This valuable resource is compiled at Oregon State University by the College of Veterinary Medicine.

The Council is opposed to any use of live lures to train Greyhounds. It funds programs and distributes a video to demonstrate successful training methods using artificial lures.

The AGTOA developed a model of an on-site Greyhound adoption program that was made available to all member tracks. Quite a few AGTOA tracks have implemented adoption programs or affiliated themselves with outside adoption agencies. The NGA board also passed a resolution to encourage membership to reduce the number of Greyhounds being bred.

1952 postcard from Daytona Beach, Florida.

Racing Facts

According to the National Greyhound Association, most Greyhound track programs consist of 12 races, occasionally 13 or 14. Eight Greyhounds run in each race, and each Greyhound runs only once every three to five days. The distances usually run are $\frac{5}{16}$, $\frac{3}{8}$, $\frac{7}{16}$, and $\frac{9}{16}$ of a mile. Greyhounds can run a $\frac{5}{16}$-mile course in close to 31 seconds and have been clocked at speeds as high as 45 miles per hour. Greyhounds are muzzled during races to keep them from injuring one another during the excitement of the race and to assist in determining the winner in photo finishes.

Greyhounds begin their racing careers when they are about one and a half years old, and they may continue racing until they are five. Before a Greyhound's first race, known as its maiden race, he receives much training and conditioning. Racing Greyhounds are housed in climate-controlled kennels, which are often located on the grounds of a racetrack. Many kennels are located at each track. Greyhounds are kept in double-deck rows of crates, on bedding usually made of shredded paper.

At the Greyhound farms, puppies are weaned at eight to nine weeks of age and are tattooed at this time. Most littermates are housed together for the next several months and are turned out in long runs for exercise. Informal training begins with six-month-old puppies, when they are taught to run after an artificial lure. Training on live lures is now illegal in most states and is discouraged by the NGA. A resolution was passed in 1992 stating that any kennel found to be using a live lure will be banned from racing.

Greyhound puppies are first trained to chase a lure dragged on the ground. As they mature and gain more skill, they train on a small circular track, chasing a suspended lure. Eventually they graduate to the larger oval tracks, learn to use the starting boxes, and begin to run more often with other Greyhounds.

In order to be a successful racing dog, a Greyhound needs to have speed, endurance, and most of all "heart." Obviously, not every Greyhound bred to race will be successful. A Greyhound must place first, second, or third in a maiden race before moving on to other races. A young Greyhound has six chances to win or place in a maiden race before being retired from the racing life. This is the time when many of the younger Greyhounds become available for adoption.

Marching Mike, a famous racing Greyhound.

Greyhounds are graded according to their placement in races run. When Greyhounds win their maiden race they are placed in Grade J. A dog is graded A, B, C, or D according to how he places in each race; the Grade A dogs having done the most winning, and Grade D, the least.

The Greyhound Hall of Fame

The Greyhound Hall of Fame, located in Abilene, Kansas, functions as a nonprofit museum devoted to the racing Greyhound. One or two retired racers are always on hand to greet visitors as they enter the lobby of the Hall of Fame. Many displays are found inside the museum, including videos, interactive computer activities, and pictures that depict the history of the Greyhound and the development of Greyhound racing. Top-winning racers from the past and present are featured.

Forty-nine Greyhounds from the United States, Australia, England, and Ireland have been inducted into the Hall of Fame since 1963. They include such greats as Rural Rube, Chief Havoc (Aus), Mutton Cutlet (Ir), Mick the Miller (Eng), Julius Caesar (Eng), Unruly, and more recent winners, Dutch Bahama, Kunta Kinte, and P's Rambling. Twenty influential members of the racing industry have also been honored with induction into the Hall of Fame.

The following is a list of Greyhounds and people who have had the honor of being inducted into the Greyhound Hall of Fame since its inception. These are the past greats of the racing world. This information is graciously shared, courtesy of the Greyhound Hall of Fame.

Dual Ch. Godspeed Qui Tam SC ORC.

Owned by Terry Fletcher.

Photo by Ashbey Photography

The Greyhound Hall of Famers

1963
1. Rural Rube   R. B. Carroll, Owner
2. Flashy Sir   Ohlinger-Blair, Owners
3. Real Huntsman   Gene Randle, Owner

1964
4. Traffic Officer   Art Wilson, Owner
5. Lucky Pilot   Ray Holmes, Owner
6. Indy Ann   Ed Willard, Owner
7. Gangster, Imp.   John Pesek, Owner

1965
8. My Laddie   F. W. Jones, Owner
9. Lucky Roll   J. A. Austin, Owner
10. Golden Sahara   Arch DeGeer, Owner
11. Fern Nature   R. B. Carroll, Owner

1966
12. Upsidedown, Imp.   Vernie Mikels, Owner
13. Kitty Dunn   Ralph McMimmy, Owner
14. Beach Comber   Paul Sutherland, Owner

1967
15. Sunny Concern   Frank Lawman, Owner

1968
16. Never Roll   H. A. Alderson, Owner

1970
17. Mixed Harmony   J. R. Hodges, Owner

1971
18. Rocker Mac, Imp.   R. H. Stevenson, Owner

1973
19. O. P. Smith
20. Denis Calaghan

1974
21. Fieldcrest   Orville Moses, Owner
22. Chief Havoc (Aus.)   Jack Millerd, Owner
23. Mutton Cutlet (Irish)   T. A. Morris, Owner

1975
24. Just Andrew, Imp.   John Pesek, Owner
25. Highley E. Alderson

The Greyhound Hall of Famers

1975
24. Just Andrew, Imp.   John Pesek, Owner
25. Highley E. Alderson

1978
26. On The Line   Aaron Kulchinsky, Owner
27. Tell You Why, Imp.   La Croix and Black, Owners
28. Johnny Leonard   Jack Roche, Owner
29. John Pesek

1979
30. Racing Ramp   Frank and Joe Loomis, Owners
31. More Taxes   L. C. LeTourneau, Owner
32. Kinto Nebo   George Nihart, Owner
33. Paul Hartwell

1980
34. Oklahoman   Tommy Lee, Owner
35. Rocking Ship, Imp.   David Cahill, Owner
36. Fred Whitehead

1981
37. Big Gossip   Red Ford Kennel, Owner
38. Mick The Miller (Eng.)   Arundel Kempton, Owner
39. Harold Shugart

1982
40. Miss Whirl   Ralph Ryan, Owner
41. Merrill Blair
42. Joseph Linsey

1983
43. Westy Whizzer   George Nihart, Owner
44. Keith Dillon
45. Murray Kemp

1984
46. Downing   Downing Syndicate Kennel, Owner

1985
47. Tumble Bug, Imp.   Harold Shugart, Owner
48. Edward Keelan, III

1986
49. G. A. "Sonny" Alderson
50. L. L.'s Doug   L. Franklin, Owner

The Greyhound Hall of Famers

1987
51. Onie Jones   Block and Thompson, Owners
52. K's Flack   Jack Kahn, Owner

1988
53. Julius Caesar (Eng.)   Gold Coast Kennels, Owner
54. Unruly   R. H. Walters, Owner

1989
55. J. W. Rocket One   Wilbert and Julia Hart, Owners

1990
56. Dutch Bahama   Herb "Dutch" Koerner, Owner
57. Perceive   Keith Dillon, Owner

1991
58. Kunta Kinte   Carol Paris, Owner
59. Marathon Hound   Dick Andrews, Owner
60. Ed Moses

1992
61. J. R.'s Ripper   Ruth Stags, Owner
62. Clyde Lemon
63. Norman McAsey

1993
64. Miss Gorgeous   Wayne Strong and Warren J. Wegert, Owners
65. Charles F. Horne

1994
66. Ken Guenther
67. P's Rambling   P's Rambling Syndicate

1995
68. Louis Derteen, Jr.
69. Al Ross

1996
70. Walt Collins
71. Isadore Hecht
72. C. N. "Chuck" Lambert

1997
(No inductions)

1998
73. Carroll Blair

Future of Greyhound Racing

The future of Greyhound racing in the United States is unsettled, if not uncertain. Eight tracks have closed since 1990, while only four new ones have opened. Three states have banned Greyhound racing, and efforts are underway in three others to do the same.

According to the Greyhound Protection League's fall 1995 figures, taken from data published in *The Greyhound Review* from 1990 to 1994, "Attendance at dog tracks nationwide has dropped 27 percent. Revenues provided to state governments have dropped 25 percent nationwide. The gross amount wagered on live racing at dog tracks nationwide has dropped 14 percent."

The report goes on to state, "According to *International Gaming and Wagering Business* (August 1995), the United States gaming industry grew by 15 percent in gross gaming revenues (less payouts/winnings) in 1994. By comparison, live dog racing declined by 17.2 percent. Even with the addition of simulcasting, inter-track wagering, and off-track betting, Greyhound racing dropped a total of 8.5 percent in 1994." Some tracks' "live handle" (money wagered) is down 50 percent. In order to boost revenues, many tracks around the country are bringing in other forms of gaming; video poker games, slot machines, and gaming tables are beginning to appear at tracks. Track operators are also considering interactive wagering, simulcasting, and in-home betting.

Greyhound breeders, in response to the previously mentioned declines, the resolution passed by the NGA board members to reduce the number of dogs being bred, and pressure put on them by the public and news media, are cutting back on the number of litters being bred. Almost 3,000 fewer litters were recorded by the NGA in 1995 than in 1991.

NATIONAL OVAL TRACK RACING

Some mention should be made of another kind of racing in the United States. The National Oval Track Racing Association (NOTRA) regulates a type of amateur racing competition for Whippets, Greyhounds, and other sighthounds where the hounds run on level grass or a dirt track. The track is equipped with a continuous loop device that propels the lure around. The dogs are muzzled and must use starting boxes. This is a test of speed, and a dog must be in top form to compete in this type of racing.

Dogs win points when they win heats. The number of points awarded depends on where a dog finishes, how many dogs were competing, and how many dogs are Oval Racing Championship (ORC) titled. The accumulation of points awarded following each race leads to an ORC title. Oval track racing, which is becoming more and more popular, gives Greyhounds a chance to run and gives their owners the excitement of competition. In many countries, families can take their pet Greyhounds to amateur tracks on an informal basis to compete with others pets or just to get some exercise. These outings are enjoyed more as family affairs than heated competitions and provide pleasure for dogs and owners alike. Oval track racing is gaining popularity in North America as more and more owners find ways to have fun with their Greyhounds.

There have been 373 Greyhounds—over a period of about ten years—registered in NOTRA. Nineteen Greyhounds have earned Oval Racing Championships, and two dogs (both from the same kennel and owner) have earned Supreme Oval Racing Championships (G-125 and G-910):

Rita, ORC
  Clarke, owner

Windwood Caermaerthon Silver, ORC
  E. Ann Webster, owner

T-Cee's Tommy, ORC
  Capacette, owner

Amazing Gracie, SORC
  Robert S. and Jane Bulman, owners

Point Breeze Skywalker, ORC
  Jane Bulman, owner

Vintage Moments, ORC
  Robert S. Bulman, owner

Char Coal Chieftain, ORC
  Regina Tierney and Bruce Czacherski,
    owners

Jungle Fire, ORC
  Robert S. Bulman, owner

Dighton Donna, ORC
  Allyson Godfroid, owner

Windwood's Heading out to Eden, ORC
  Mary Zabukobec, owner

Lakilanni Barbie Doll, ORC
  Dan Rycroft, owner

Godspeed Qui Tam, ORC
  Terry Fletcher, owner

Point Breeze Dark Victory, ORC
  Jane Bulman, owner

Zephyr Kandahar, ORC
  Lee and Seth Hayes, owners

Windyglen's Kansas, ORC
  Don Papin, owner

Oui Ouie Revenge, ORC
  Terry Fletcher, owner

Point Breeze Pacific Pride, SORC
  Jane Bulman, owner

Marble Moss, ORC
  Don Papin, owner

Windwood Obsidian, ORC
  E. Ann Webster, owner

Adopting a Racing Greyhound

More than 40 states now have Greyhound adoption groups. These dedicated people place hundreds to thousands of retired racers each year and represent the ever-growing movement in our country to save the lives of ex-racers. Greyhound Friends, founded by Louise Coleman more than ten years ago, is one such organization. As its literature attests: "Greyhound Friends, Inc., located in Hopkinton, Massachusetts, is a small nonprofit organization dedicated to saving racetrack greyhounds and placing them in responsible homes. Most of the dogs racing at the 51 tracks in the United States are killed when they can no longer win. The dogs passing through the shelter of Greyhound Friends are sweet dispositioned and make wonderful companions. Many are Irish imports. In the past few years Greyhound Friends has found homes for nearly 7,000 dogs.

"Greyhound Friends maintains a kennel for 20 Greyhounds. As soon as a dog is adopted another one comes in from a racing kennel. Dogs who come to us are groomed, treated medically, fed and walked, and are outfitted with a new collar and leash. They respond almost immediately to kind treatment and are often ready for adoption in just a few days."

More than 150 Greyhound adoption centers now exist in the United States. Some of these are small kennel operations similar to Greyhound Friends, others consist of well-organized networks of people across the country, but many are simply individuals who are willing to serve as foster homes for one or two Greyhounds at a time, as they make the transition from racing dog to household pet.

Why are there suddenly so many Greyhound adoption agencies? Why has this grassroots movement grown so rapidly and become such a widespread concern? The media has done much to champion the cause of the retired racing Greyhound. Local newspapers, magazines, and television have all carried stories about the plight of Greyhounds that are no longer needed or wanted by the racing industry.

But it is the Greyhounds themselves that have won the hearts of so many people. Every time an ex-racer success-

"Fast Eddie," an adopted ex-racer, is just one of many Greyhounds that have made the transition from track to household. *Photo by Jini Foster*

fully becomes a cherished house pet, word of the breed's lovable qualities spreads a little farther. Many Greyhound lives are saved as one friend tells another, who tells another, who tells another. In spite of all the optimism and hope of rescue organizations, the question remains, What can be done to ensure the well-being of all racing Greyhounds?

According to the Greyhound Protection League figures from the fall of 1995, the popularity of Greyhound racing in the United States is beginning to wane. This is due, in part, to all of the negative publicity the industry has received, but also to the increased use of technology. It is often more profitable to use simulcasts and run fewer races. But while interest in Greyhound racing in the United States declines, it is on the rise in several other countries. Although Greyhound racing has existed in England and Ireland for many years, it has now spread to Australia, Spain, Mexico, and Venezuela. Brazil, South Africa, and Turkey are seriously discussing opening tracks. In launching their programs, these countries will draw their racing stock from the United States, Ireland, and England. This is another concern occupying the attention of Louise Coleman and others who have dedicated themselves to the rescue and adoption of Greyhounds.

Ms. Coleman has made several trips abroad and is planning others. She is working to help establish rescue programs in Europe and to restrict or prohibit the export of Greyhounds for racing purposes.

Most Greyhound adoption groups try

to screen potential homes for their rescue dogs and usually require that you fill out an application. They may want you to visit their kennel, to bring your children, and even, sometimes, your other pets. Their goal is to find the Greyhound best suited to each individual family and the best family for each Greyhound. They usually ask that you pay a fee to cover expenses for the care the Greyhound receives after coming to the adoption center. If the Greyhound has not been neutered or spayed, you will be asked to do so within a reasonable amount of time and to send a statement from your veterinarian when the surgery is complete.

Greyhound adoption applications may ask for some of the following information:

1. What is your name, address, phone number?
2. What is your employer's name, address, phone number?
3. What are the ages of the adults and children in your household?
4. Why do you want to own a Greyhound?
5. What is your preference as to age, sex, color in a Greyhound?
6. What other pets do you own?

7. Is there someone home during the day? For part of the day?
8. How long will the dog be left alone?
9. What type of home do you have? City, suburb, country, apartment, condo, single dwelling?
10. Do you have a fenced yard?
11. If you have no fence, how do you plan to exercise your Greyhound?

You may also be asked to make the following commitments:

1. To keep your Greyhound only in your house;
2. To always exercise your Greyhound on leash or in a fenced area;
3. To keep vaccinations up-to-date;
4. To use heartworm preventative;
5. To not use your Greyhound for commercial racing or laboratory research;
6. To contact the adoption agency if you are unable to keep the dog.

Many people feel they have run the gauntlet by the time they reach this point in the adoption process. But be assured that each group's main concern is to correctly match Greyhounds with their new families. They want to be certain that

Children and Greyhounds are a winning combination; give your ex-racer extra time to become friendly with children.

Photo by Jini Foster

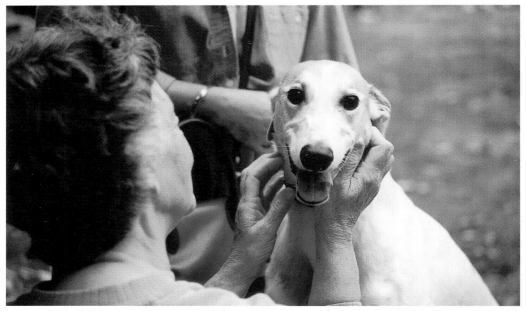

The bonding between an ex-racer and his new owner begins almost immediately. *Photo by Jini Foster*

each ex-racer will lead a safe, healthy, happy life, and will remain with his new family for the rest of his life.

The names, addresses, and phone numbers of many rescue organizations are available through The Greyhound Project, Inc. This organization is not affiliated with any rescue group but provides information about most of the adoption groups in the United States as well as several other countries. They publish a directory, an on-line service, a magazine, and a calendar (the group's address and phone number are listed in the appendix).

BRINGING YOUR EX-RACER HOME

Though Greyhound racing using mechanical lures has been in existence for 75 years, the concept of mak-

ing ex-racers available to the general public as house pets is a fairly new one. It has only been in the last 10 to 15 years that adoption groups have formed with the purpose of placing retired racing Greyhounds in loving homes. Prior to this time, many people believed that Greyhounds were high-strung, vicious dogs, hardly suited for the role of family pet. The fact that the racing dogs were always seen wearing muzzles was probably the reason for the belief that they were ill tempered.

But those who have lived and worked with Greyhounds have always known what sweet, gentle creatures they really are. Many owners, trainers, track vets, and others associated with the racing industry have taken a favorite Greyhound or two into their home. They know them to be highly adaptable to the soft life of a household, and that they make wonderful companions for everyone in a family. "A well-kept se-

Rebecca and "Knight" have found each other and couldn't be happier.

cret, these Greyhounds," one trainer told me. "It's about time they were appreciated by the general public. Greyhounds are smart dogs that love people and want to please. They are calm and quiet and make great house dogs."

Be Prepared

Before bringing an ex-racer home, you will need to make some preparations. Be certain that you are familiar with the precautions necessary when using pesticides, herbicides, anesthetics, and other chemicals. Greyhounds are sensitive to many different preparations that may not adversely affect other breeds.

Ask about your dog's racing history and any medical or health problems that may cause problems later in life. Ask for a copy of his inoculation record and learn when the Greyhound was spayed

"Goldie Fawn" has made herself right at home in her new surroundings. *Photo by Cheryl Reynolds*

or neutered. Give all of this information to your vet when you take your Greyhound in for the first examination.

Learn all you can about Greyhound temperament and behavior so that you are prepared when you get home. Be certain, in advance, that you really want a dog that will probably take possession of your favorite couch, poke his nose into everything, and try to steal dinner from the table. You will want to bring your children with you to the adoption center to meet the Greyhounds. Some Greyhounds will be much more affectionate toward children than others. If you have a small dog or cat at home, find out if the Greyhound of your choice has been exposed to small pets.

Become familiar with the daily life of a racing Greyhound. This knowledge may help you to understand some of your dog's reactions to new situations.

Typical Day at a Racing Kennel

During a normal day at one particular racing kennel, work begins very early. The Greyhounds, who live in crates in a heated and air conditioned kennel building, are turned out into large paddocks or yards to exercise. They wear muzzles while in the yards in case tempers flare during rough play. During this time crates are cleaned thoroughly and bedding is replaced. At the end of the exercise period, the Greyhounds are inspected for any injuries or other problems, petted and talked to, then returned to their crates to be fed and watered.

All of the Greyhounds are turned out four times each day and fed twice daily. Some mornings, several dogs at a time are taken for long walks. Other mornings, puppies and young dogs are trained by playing with them with pieces of cloth and floppy stuffed toys. Those Greyhounds that are a year old begin to receive some track practice. Generally, Greyhounds race only once every three to five days. Special attention is paid to diet, fluid intake, and physical condition of the dogs that are actually racing. More training sessions and walks take place in the afternoon.

The Greyhounds are well cared for, healthy, and free of parasites; they are also handled frequently, and they receive excellent veterinary attention. Many younger dogs who obviously are not go-

Those that have adopted ex-racers understand the importance of socialization and many make an extra effort to be active and to attend group functions.

Photo by Mel and Paula Hodder

ing to make the grade are neutered and placed directly into homes as pets. The Greyhounds at this kennel seem content. They do not know any other life. Because Greyhounds are so adaptable, they make the transition from the racing kennel to a home rather easily. This is the opportunity that adoption groups give to ex-racers.

Some adoption groups take time with each Greyhound after it retires from racing. These dogs spend time in foster homes learning daily household routine. The dogs learn to walk on slippery surfaces and go up and down stairs. They become accustomed to the everyday noises of vacuum cleaners, televisions, and telephones. They meet other dogs and cats and interact with unknown adults and children. This procedure helps the adoption group know more about

the dogs' temperaments before placing them in permanent homes. It also helps the dogs make the transition from kennel to home life.

When You Get Home

Whether you adopt a Greyhound who has gone from racing kennel to adoption kennel, or one who has spent time in a "halfway house," there will be a period of adjustment when you bring your ex-racer home. Your Greyhound may exhibit some signs of anxiety. He may pace nervously, hide under a table or in a corner, whine, not eat for a day or two. Be gentle and understanding. This is a big change in your Greyhound's life and routine. Many people who have taken ex-racers into their homes report no obvious signs of stress in their Greyhounds. They walk into the

Adopted Greyhounds at rest after a hard day of play. *Photo by Jini Foster*

house and after a short period of exploration, settle down in a soft place and go to sleep. "It's like she has always lived here," commented one new adopter.

If at all possible, especially if everyone in the household works, try to take a few days off following the homecoming. This will help with the bonding process and make the change much easier for your Greyhound. The more time you can spend together when you first come home, the more quickly that bond will form.

When you arrive home, walk your Greyhound on a leash so that he may relieve himself before coming into the house. Even if you have a fenced yard, now is not the time to allow free running. Allow time to explore the new home and get used to new surroundings. Point out the location of food and water bowls, and introduce the crate if you are using one. Gently present boundaries. Instruct your

children to sit quietly and let their new friend come to them, rather than overwhelming the dog with attention. You might ask them how they would feel if they were alone in a new place full of strangers. Remind them not to bother the Greyhound when the dog is sleeping, eating, or chewing on a bone.

Temporarily place several pieces of masking tape on glass doors, windows, and mirrors that are close to the ground. There have been instances when Greyhounds were injured when trying to run through the glass, not realizing it was there. Some household items that may bewilder your Greyhound need to be introduced slowly. The television, telephone, washer and dryer, vacuum cleaner, garbage disposal, dishwasher, and ceiling fan are common items in most homes, but totally unknown to your new family member.

New friends Nicholas and "Okie" share an afternoon snack.

Photo by Jini Foster

During these first few days, your Greyhound will probably need to be taught how to go up and down stairs. Coax gently, while on lead. You may even have to place each foot on a step. Go slowly. Do not push or pull the dog. The lesson will be learned quickly, and soon your Greyhound will follow behind you every time you go up or down the stairs.

Introduce other family pets slowly and do not leave the animals alone together until you are certain they will get along with each other.

Continue to walk your Greyhound on lead another time or two before giving him the freedom to run in the yard. For the first few days or even a week or two, you may want to accompany your dog outside. Watch closely for a time until you are absolutely certain there will be no attempts to escape.

If you do not have a fenced yard, you will have to walk your Greyhound at least four or five times each day. A long, brisk walk in the morning will burn off some energy early in the day and help calm an energetic Greyhound who has to spend several hours at home alone. Another long walk or run in the afternoon or evening will also be necessary. If possible, try to take your Greyhound to a large, safe fenced area to run once or twice each week. The ideal situation is a household where someone is home all day or where a couple works opposite shifts. But in many cases, a newly adopted Greyhound will have to learn to be alone for long periods. If this is your situation, see if you can work out a schedule that permits you to come home at lunch to exercise your dog and hand out some love and attention. Or find a neighbor, relative, or friend who

Like other Greyhounds, ex-racers require a great deal of exercise, which can come in all forms—even swimming. *Photo by Jini Foster*

will come on a regular basis to help break up the day. Greyhounds crave companionship. If your work schedule is such that you are away from home for long hours at a time, and you have no one to attend to your dog, you may want to wait to adopt a Greyhound until your circumstances change.

Crating and Housebreaking

A crate can be helpful in housebreaking your Greyhound and keeping him out of trouble when you are not at home. Many racing Greyhounds live in crates and identify them as safe havens. Others do not like the confinement, especially in their new surroundings, and will become agitated or try to escape. If you must use a crate, try it out at first

A retired racer sleeps with her new pals, a Shiba Inu and a Norfolk Terrier, owned by Barbara Parker.

to eliminate, and praise him for keeping the crate clean.

Gradually you will be able to leave your Greyhound loose in the house for longer periods of time when you are not at home, until eventually the use of the crate will not be necessary. It takes time to adjust to a new routine, but soon your dog will learn to let you know when it is time to go outside.

Bedding

Before you bring your Greyhound home, decide where you want him to sleep. Because Greyhounds have so little body fat and do so much "resting," they need and will insist on having a soft place to sleep. Of course, their first choice will be the couch or chair or your bed. If you do not want your Greyhound on the furniture, you will have to provide a soft bed, preferably several, as alternatives. These can be purchased in most discount and pet food stores. They are usually lightweight and can be moved from room to room if necessary. Because Greyhounds love to snuggle and believe themselves to be quite human, they will try to climb up on the couch with you every time you sit down. It will take much patience and praise to convince your Greyhound that his bed is the one on the floor. But be forewarned—even if your Greyhound appears to be perfectly happy with this arrangement, he will probably avail himself of the furniture the moment you leave him alone in the house.

If you have any questions at all about your new Greyhound companion, call the adoption center. They will be ready with answers to most of your questions or can direct you to someone who can help you.

Many adoption organizations hold reunions once or twice a year to celebrate

when you are home. Make the crate as inviting to your Greyhound as possible. Include soft bedding, a stuffed toy, something to chew on, and a small bucket of water. Start with 15 minutes at a time. Leave your Greyhound in the crate, reassure him that you will be back soon, and leave him alone. When you return, praise him lavishly when you open the crate door. Gradually increase the time in the crate until you know your Greyhound is content to nap and relax until you return. Be certain during part of this training that you actually leave the house, get in your car, and drive away. Greyhounds are intelligent and will know that even though you are out of sight, you are still close by in the house. Any time you leave your Greyhound in the crate for an extended period of time, let him outside

Naps are best when shared. A retired racer and her friend, an AKC Greyhound puppy named Cody, couldn't be cozier.

Owned by Barbara Parker.

the new lives of these special dogs. The reunions give owners a chance to compare experiences, share funny stories, and receive help with any adjustment problems they may be having. They also provide an opportunity for the Greyhounds to get together and to reconnect with other ex-racers.

THE NETWORK OF EX-RACER OWNERS

There are probably 75,000 retired racing Greyhounds in homes today, according to estimates of the Greyhound Project, Inc., of Milton, Massachusetts. In 1995 alone, more than 14,000 Greyhounds in the United States, Canada, Great Britain, and Europe found new homes. How have all of these ex-racers become much-loved family pets? Through the efforts of countless people around the world who have worked individually or have formed organized adoption agencies to rescue retired racers and give them a chance for a new beginning.

Quite a few of the adoption groups in the United States were formed by people who adopted a Greyhound, fell in love with the breed, then decided they would like to help other dogs find homes. Adoption groups have grown from such humble beginnings to place thousands of Greyhounds each year and have volunteers in many states. The Greyhound Project (listed in the appendix) publishes a Greyhound Adoption Resource Directory, which is updated each year. This is a complete listing of every group or individual who is doing Greyhound work in this country and abroad.

One of the best things about adopting a Greyhound, besides enjoying their companionship, is networking with others who have also adopted ex-racers. Many adoption groups hold reunions, parades, picnics, fun shows, fun runs, coursing meets, and obedience and agility classes. Volunteers and adopters are involved in therapy dog work and visit schools, hospitals, and nursing homes in their areas. All of these activities give the owners of adopted Greyhounds the opportunity to show off their pets, interact with other owners and their dogs,

Adopted Greyhounds and their families stay in touch by meeting at picnics, group walks, and other events.

Photo by Mel and Paula Hodder

and raise funds and other support for the organizations actively involved in saving the Greyhounds. People will often come forward who are willing to donate time at a kennel, help with placement in their area, or care for a dog in their home until it is placed.

These gatherings meet several other valuable objectives. They are a time for potential adopters to meet with owners of ex-racers and actually see how the dogs have adjusted to their new lives. Future adopters can ask questions, play with the Greyhounds, and decide if they truly want to make the commit-

ment to adopt a Greyhound. Many who attend these festivities begin adoption proceedings that day.

Another purpose served by these reunions is that of public education. The events are often attended by interested and sympathetic members of the media who interview the owners and members of the organization and film many dogs, adults, and children with smiling faces.

Picnics, open houses, and other social events sponsored by adoption groups serve as important fund-raisers. Almost all of the groups rely on donations to cover vet bills, dog food, housing, rent

Retired racers and their owners enjoy a day of companionship, sun, and sand at places such as Dewey Beach.

Photo by Heather Minnich

Greyhound reunions are an opportunity for socializing as well as raising awareness about ex-racers. *Photo by Mel and Paula Hodder*

and mortgage payments, utilities, brochures and public education, office work, and any medical care or emergencies. The sale of Greyhound-related items such as T-shirts, mugs, jewelry, wide collars and matching leads, coats, and toys helps replenish an ever-depleted money supply.

Public education is an important function of most adoption groups. They publish brochures, newsletters, pamphlets, calendars, and directories containing information about Greyhounds and the adoption process. They let people know about the fate of many of the ex-racing dogs. They gather and publish up-to-date statistics about the rac-

ing industry itself and report current news items related to Greyhound racing. They write letters and contact members of Congress and state legislators to protest the opening of new racetracks, and they work hard to convince states with legalized racing to abolish it.

It seems that everyone who adopts a retired racer becomes a spokesperson for the breed. "You couldn't hire better public relations people," commented one volunteer at an adoption center. Greyhounds attract attention wherever they go. Their owners are constantly approached by people asking questions about the dogs and the adoption process. These adopted racers and their proud owners find many new homes for other Greyhounds and continue to enlist new devotees.

Adopted racing Greyhounds live wonderful lives, learning obedience exercises, enjoying agility competition, beating other Greyhounds at lure coursing meets, or just lying around the house. One of the most rewarding activities that adopted Greyhounds and their owners participate in is therapy work. The Greyhound's calm, mannerly demeanor makes the breed excellent for use as therapy dogs. They are welcome guests in many retirement

A gathering of more than 200 Greyhounds creates quite a spectacle for onlookers at Dewey Beach.

Photo by Heather Minnich

homes, hospitals, hospices, schools, and recreation centers. Faces of the sick, elderly, or specially challenged light up when a Greyhound enters the room. They are their own best ambassadors.

There are a number of ways you can become actively involved in the network of people who help retired racing Greyhounds. If you are seriously interested in joining the ranks of those who rescue and place dogs from the tracks, contact an adoption group near you. They are always looking for volunteers to care for the Greyhounds awaiting adoption in their shelters or to serve as temporary foster homes for Greyhounds who may need a little extra care and acclimatization before going to a new home. Financial support is always welcomed, as are donations of food, bedding, and other supplies. You may know of a veterinarian who would be willing to vaccinate, treat injuries, and spay or neuter dogs at a reduced rate. If you belong to a kennel club, obedience club, or humane association, you may want to talk with your members about getting involved in the rescue effort. If you have already adopted a Greyhound, you may want to become involved in public education activities or volunteer to work with those doing therapy visits with their Greyhounds. The list of activities goes on.

THE GREYHOUND RESCUE NETWORK

If you are interested in becoming more directly involved, you may want to set up a local chapter for Greyhound rescue. You may choose to function as a satellite of a state or national

The rewards of living with an adopted Greyhound can be seen throughout a family. *Photo courtesy of Greyhound Friends, Inc.*

Those that wish to adopt ex-racers are carefully screened and evaluated, all in an effort to provide these deserving dogs with happy and safe homes.

Photo by Mel and Paula Hodder

organization already in existence or work independently of other groups. Whichever you choose, talk with as many people as possible who are already involved in rescue work. The advice and materials they can share with you will be invaluable and save you much wasted time, effort, and heartache.

Before you begin any actual rescue work, clearly define your goals and make certain you have the time, resources, and support necessary to make the commitment. Determine your policies and put them in writing. Develop a mission statement. Make up the essential paperwork: logo, business cards, letterhead, health forms, adoption applications, contracts. Produce pamphlets with information about Greyhounds, their care, and the adoption process.

Another area to investigate before undertaking a placement operation is the legal liability relating to rescue work. It is important to be aware of legal issues and to know how you and/or your organization could be at risk.

Use great care when handling rescue dogs. While a dog is in the keeping of an adoption agency, that group or individual is liable for any damage that dog may do.

You are legally responsible if the dog causes harm to another person or animal. To avoid the possibility of personal litigation, you may want to consider incorporating, probably as a nonprofit organization. Seek legal counsel for assistance in incorporating your rescue program.

To help make placements successful and reduce the number of Greyhounds returned to you, pay close attention to a number of details and learn as much about each dog as you can. From which track did it come? Was it a big winner? How does it get along with other animals? Does it require a lot of attention or is it content to climb up on the couch after dinner and sleep? Has the dog had any injuries that may affect its life as a family pet? Assess the temperament of each Greyhound before it is placed. Look for activity level and any aggressive, dominant, or overly submissive behaviors. Observe the Greyhound in a new environment. See if the dog will come to you if called or follow you when coaxed. See how the dog responds to affection and attention from adults and children. Use these observations to help you determine placement for each Greyhound.

Long walks and runs are essential for Greyhounds. They must, however, be leashed at all times, unless they are in a safe and enclosed area.

Photo by Heather Munnich

Screen potential owners closely. Talk with them at length. Find out what dogs they have owned and what happened to them. Determine if they have a suitable home environment for a Greyhound. You should even consider the age, health, and financial circumstances of a potential adopter before placing a dog. If you have any doubts about a person or their home, or wonder if they are being truthful, you may want to set up a home visit.

The use of a carefully prepared contract could be your best protection against the threat of litigation. Specifically outline all of your conditions and go over each one with the new owner. If your group is not going to take care of spaying and neutering, require that this be done. Spell out care and housing requirements. Include the right of the adoption agency to inspect the Greyhound and its living conditions and the right to take back the dog if the owner has not abided by the stipulations in the contract. Be certain to include a clause requiring the Greyhound's return to your agency if he can no longer be cared for by his new owners. The final section of the contract should specify that the new owners indemnify and hold harmless the adoption group from liability for any actions of the dog while in the possession of its new owner.

After all the preliminary work is done—you have a safe place to keep the retired racers until placement, you have a clear idea of your goals, and all paperwork is prepared—begin to let people know you exist and what you are about. Contact all shelters and pounds, racetracks, and dog clubs in your area. Get on the Internet. Advertise locally. Distribute business cards with your name, phone number, and a Greyhound logo to attract attention. Providing an adoption service is not a matter entered into lightly. You will have taken on an enormous responsibility. But every time you see a Greyhound leave with its new owners, you will know that all of your efforts have been worthwhile.

GREYHOUND PUPPIES

People love puppies. Their big eyes and silly antics touch us at the very core of our being. Sitting on the ground with a warm, wiggly six-week-old puppy is a better stress reliever than any pill a doctor can prescribe.

Puppies love people. Greyhound babies are no exception. From the time they are barely standing on wobbly legs they seek out and delight in human contact. The bond formed between you and your Greyhound will be a strong one and will last for many years. Greyhounds can live 11 to 14 years, some even longer. When you decide to buy a Greyhound puppy, you are making a commitment that will last for more than a decade. Be certain you are willing to honor this commitment before you bring a puppy home.

FINDING A GREYHOUND PUPPY

Locating a Greyhound puppy is not always an easy task. Less than 200 Greyhounds are registered with the American Kennel Club each year. The breeders of AKC Greyhounds are a small, very reputable group of people who love their dogs and strive always to produce the very best representatives of the breed. They meticulously plan each breeding, carefully weighing the strengths and weaknesses of the sire and dam, and identifying qualities they hope to produce in the offspring. These breeders are not in the business of making money, but of producing the finest hounds. They consider conformation, temperament, health, intelligence. They study genetics, pedigrees, photographs, and try to see and evaluate as many Greyhounds as they can.

Because their numbers are so few, many AKC Greyhound breeders and exhibitors know each other and are familiar with the different lines that have developed over the years. They can visualize most of the dogs in a four- or five-generation pedigree, and often the littermates of these dogs as well.

123

This kind of knowledge and dedication can be invaluable to a new Greyhound owner. Puppy buyers can be assured that they are getting a top-quality puppy and that they will receive expert guidance in raising and caring for him.

So how can a prospective buyer find a Greyhound puppy? One way is to attend a dog show in your area. Shows are held somewhere nearly every weekend of the year. Choose to go to a show within driving distance. Arrive early and ask where you may pick up a catalog. Go to the ring at the time Greyhounds are being exhibited. It's fun to watch the different dogs in the ring, and you will start to form an idea of what you like in the breed.

After the breed judging, approach the exhibitors and let them know that you are seriously interested in purchasing a Greyhound puppy. They will be happy to answer your questions if they are not too busy or will give you a card or a phone number where they can reached when they have the freedom to talk. Greyhound owners love to talk about Greyhounds. If, as may happen, no Greyhounds are being shown, speak with handlers of the other sighthound breeds. They may be able to put you in touch with a Greyhound breeder.

Another option is to call the AKC and ask for a contact person in the Greyhound Club of America. The national breed club has one person who serves in a breeder referral capacity. This person should know who has litters and adult dogs for sale. Local all-breed clubs may also be able to put you in touch with a Greyhound breeder.

PICKING A GREYHOUND PUPPY

If you are lucky you may find a Greyhound breeder close enough to visit, where you can see the puppies and their mother. Chances are, however, this may not happen. So few litters are whelped each year that it may be quite awhile before puppies will be available in your area. If at all possible, try to see the puppies. If not, you may have to rely on photographs, videos, and the breeder's recommendations.

Puppies are usually sold between the ages of 8 to 12 weeks. Some breeders may have older pups that they have kept for a few more months to see if they will develop into show- and breeding-quality dogs. Adult dogs and finished champions may sometimes also be available to good homes.

Greyhound breeders are very careful about placing puppies. Be prepared to answer questions about your work and play schedules and your home and yard. They will want to know if you have access to safe, fenced areas for exercise, space for a large dog, or experience owning and training dogs. They will ask the ages of your children and if you are willing to give your puppy plenty of socialization experiences. You may feel that you are being interviewed for a job or interrogated by the FBI, rather than questioned as a prospective puppy buyer. Do not take offense at the breeder's interest in proper placement of their Greyhound puppies. All of us have stories we can tell of puppies that, despite our best efforts, ended up in less

Greyhound puppies may be found through reputable breeders, or, occasionally, through ex-racer adoption groups.

Photo by Jini Foster

At six weeks, Greyhound puppies bear little resemblance to the large, lean, and graceful adults that they will someday be.

than ideal situations. Each Greyhound breeder's foremost concern is for the welfare of the pups.

You will probably have many questions to ask the breeder. You may want to know about the parents of the puppies, their personalities, their show careers, their health, their color. You will want to ask about any heredity problems and about specific needs of Greyhounds. It is important to determine if a Greyhound is the appropriate canine choice for your family.

Another important aspect to consider when purchasing a puppy is whether or not you want a pet or a pet that is also a show dog. If you are looking for a show-quality puppy, remember that the only way you can be absolutely certain what an adult Greyhound will look like is to buy an adult Greyhound. When buying a young puppy as a show prospect, you are always taking a risk. Greyhounds are such a large breed and have many stages to pass through as they grow to maturity. A lot can happen along the way.

This is the time to rely on the breeder's experience. After many years

A Greyhound litter at four weeks old. Bred by Chris Durance and Joy Bidnead. *Photo by Ann Cantrell*

of grading litters of puppies and studying the growth patterns in their line, they should be able to help you choose the best puppy for you. Look for a sound but typey puppy, with good bone and outgoing personality. The Greyhound has no coat to cover his faults, so everything about him is exposed in the ring.

Many breeders like to grade their puppies at six weeks of age, affirming that the overall picture at this stage of development is a good indicator of adult conformation. Some breeders swear that they can tell show-quality pups at one week of age, while others prefer to choose at 8 to 12 weeks, and still others wait until a pup is five or six months old. Whatever the age, start with a puppy that is structurally correct and balanced, even if he looks a little clunky. The alert, showy puppy will probably be a successful show dog. Color should not be a consideration when picking a puppy, as color is supposed to make no difference when judging Greyhounds. However, most people do have their preferences. Pick conformation, temperament, and style first, and then consider color.

Ch. Heathero Ariel of the Tempest CDX and her sister Ch. Heathero African Queen winning a Western Specialty Best Brace in Show at only six months old.

Photo by Vicky Cook

Am. Can. Ch. Ramachandra Windstorm Cebar at five months and as an adult.

Ch. Gaia Sunridge Sunrise, at nine and a half months, winning the Sweepstakes at the 1996 GCA National Specialty.

Breeder/owner Sue LeMieux.

Photo by Ashbey Photography

"Noel" and "Angel," two-week-old red brindle puppies, bred by **Helen Hamilton**. *Photo by Dianne D. Derrin*

PREPARING FOR A PUPPY

Be prepared before you bring your new Greyhound puppy home. Purchase all of the supplies you will need ahead of time to make the transition less stressful for you and the puppy. The items you will need include food, food and water dishes, a large crate, leash and collar, and safe toys.

Food

The basis of a good diet for your Greyhound puppy should be a high-quality kibble. There are many brands available, and no one brand seems to be better than another. Although all breeders swear by the brand they use, they each raise healthy, beautiful animals. If you intend to change the brand of food you will be feeding your puppy, be sure to ask the breeder for a small amount of food the pup is used to eating. Make the change by gradually increasing the amount of new food added to the old until the changeover is complete. This method helps reduce the chance of digestive upset. How often and what to feed will be discussed more fully in the chapter on nutrition.

Food And Water Dishes

Purchase large, two-quart bowls for feeding your puppy. This is a perfect size for feeding an adult Greyhound and will save the expense of purchasing two sets of bowls. Stainless steel bowls work well and last forever, or you may want to use a heavy plastic or ceramic type.

Four-month-old Seamair Looney Tune enjoys a day a the beach. Owned by Cheryl Reynolds. *Photo by Steve Eltinge*

Leash and Collar

The preferred collar for a Greyhound is a fairly wide nylon slip or choke collar that is easy on their long necks, but closes snugly when they strain or pull on the lead. Buckle collars can easily slip over the Greyhounds narrow head if they try to back out of them. Slip collars should not be left on when your Greyhound is unattended, however, as they may catch on something and choke the dog. If you want to leave a collar on your dog, choose a soft leather or nylon buckle collar and use the slip collar for walks.

Buy a good-quality, six-foot leather or nylon lead. This will last for many years. Another type of lead that has become very popular is the type that has a plastic handle into which a 26-foot lead retracts. This lead gives your Greyhound more room to run and play on walks. But be careful when using this type of lead and learn to control your dog's movements on it. More than one Greyhound has suddenly bolted at top speed, hit the end of the line, and been thrown to the ground, sometimes badly wrenching his neck.

Feeding time for a litter bred by Johnny and Marsha Wartell and Greg Davis and Roger Owens.

Crates

A large dog crate will probably be the most expensive but most important purchase you will make for your puppy. Purchase a crate that will be large enough for an adult Greyhound. The crate serves many purposes when raising a Greyhound puppy. It provides a haven or resting place when the puppy wants to be alone, and it serves as a great housebreaking aid. Greyhounds are very clean creatures and do not like to soil their sleeping area. It also serves as a safe place to keep the puppy when he cannot be supervised. He can come to no harm and neither can your best shoes or antique Oriental rug. Make the puppy's experiences in the crate positive ones, and do not abuse its use. Do not use the crate more than is absolutely necessary.

Nine-week-old puppies by Ch. Jet's Washington Post.

Bred by Hanne Böckhaus, Kennel Eikica, Denmark.

At nine weeks old, this Greyhound puppy knows enough to guard her toys against other Greyhounds.

Toys

Greyhound puppies love their toys and will amuse themselves for hours by inventing all kinds of games. They love stuffed animals. Find the kind that do not have plastic eyes and nose, as these can be chewed off and swallowed. Large, bleached natural bones available in groceries and pet food stores provide a satisfactory release for teething puppies. If you allow your puppy to chew on rawhide bones, choose large ones and do not permit him to have them unless you are around to supervise. There have been instances of dogs chewing off and swallowing large pieces, which may result in surgery. Puppies also love big latex toys and balls, but, again, be on the alert for missing pieces that may have been swallowed. Most Greyhounds have the utmost respect for their toys and take great care of them. Some toys will become their favorites and they will carry them around for years. Other Greyhounds view their toys as "prey" and attack and kill every new object that is given to them. Stuffing from a plush animal will be spread from one end of the house to the other. Latex toys are squeaked for a day or two and then appear in pieces, with sections scattered everywhere. Get to know your puppy and watch him with his toys.

Gaia No Plain Jane, owned by Lindsey Strutt, enjoys stuffed animals and toys. Be certain the toys you provide are safe for your puppy.

Opposite: Four-month-old puppies by Ch. Ramachandra Windstorm Cebar, full of personality and charm.

HOW DOES A PUPPY GROW?

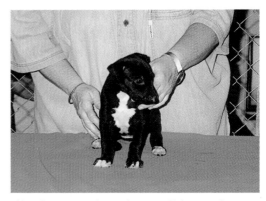

Although young puppies need contact with humans, they should remain with their litter for at least the first eight weeks.

The first two weeks of a puppy's life are spent nursing and sleeping. Motor skills are limited. The puppy is deaf and blind for most of this period. But even at this early stage, handling is important. Studies have shown that early, but not excessive, handling of these very young puppies can have a beneficial effect upon their relationship with people when they are grown.

From two to four weeks, puppies' eyes and ears open. They begin to walk and play with each other and with their mother. Continued attention from humans is also important throughout this period.

The time from four to eight weeks of age is extremely crucial to the social development of a Greyhound puppy. What occurs during this period has a tremendous impact on adult behavior. During this time puppies learn about the other members of their litter, their mother, and people. The time spent with their dam and littermates develops appropriate canine social interaction. As puppies run and jump, they are developing motor skills. As they chew on each other, they are learning to inhibit their biting, which is an extremely important lesson for a Greyhound that is a family member. The dam's response to her puppies teaches them much about social order. Puppies removed from a litter before six weeks of age often have problems relating to other dogs when they are adults. From birth to 12 weeks of age, Greyhound puppies need to have an abundance of contact with humans. Puppies raised in a kennel sometimes do not get enough exposure to people and may be frightened of them

Ryal Kalahari at eight weeks old. *Photo by Sue Cassem*

Puppy love. Lynda Meeuws and five-week-old blue fawn puppy.

Greyhound puppies from 3 to 12 months will grow and change rapidly. The early part of this period is a good time to teach basic obedience commands and housebreak your puppy. Use treats and make learning fun. Your puppy should be accustomed to being handled, to having teeth and ears examined, and to having nails trimmed. These procedures need to be well tolerated before the puppy has a chance to grow too large and decide that he just doesn't want to be bothered with such nonsense. This is the time to lay a strong foundation and be firmly consistent in a gentle way to establish who is boss.

As your puppy moves into adolescence, from 5 to 12 months, you may be in for some surprises. If you have raised teenage children, you will know what to expect. One day your adorable Greyhound puppy follows you everywhere, comes every time you call him, and flips over on his back for you to rub his tummy. The next day, you put him out in the yard, and when you call him

as adults. It is every breeder's responsibility to correctly and completely socialize each puppy. Experiences with many different people and with gentle children are extremely important. Once the puppies' immunity to disease is established, they can be exposed to many different situations, people, and animals. They should be played with, held, talked to, and gently directed into acceptable behaviors. They should be loved.

A litter of 12-week-old puppies by Ch. Shazams the Journey Begins. Breeder, Kim Fritzler.

Adolescence is a time of patience and humor for Greyhound owners. Understand that it is a natural part of growing up. Ch Ekohils Dust Storm CD. Owned by Helen Hamilton.

he refuses to come in. He forgets all of his manners. He howls and struggles when you try to trim his nails. Your sweet, adoring puppy is now arrogant and cocky, challenging your every wish and command. If you have laid a strong foundation in earlier months, you will manage this stage more effectively and emerge with a smile on your face. Realize that the behaviors of your adolescent canine are a normal part of the maturation process and not something you have done wrong.

Be prepared ahead of time to meet the challenges of canine adolescence with some strategies of your own. During this period, try to spend more time with your puppy. Go for long walks and runs. Arrange for him to play with other dogs in a safe fenced area. Go for rides in the car. Attend obedience classes. Visit the mall. Go to dog shows or puppy matches.

Your greatest allies during this independent stage in your Greyhound's life are a sense of humor, patience, and the ability to anticipate a situation before it arises.

Take heart. Most Greyhounds do settle down as they mature and often become such couch potatoes that they have to be pried off to go outside for exercise. They never do completely lose their clownish ways, however, and the years spent with your Greyhound will be filled with much laughter.

Physical Growth

Greyhounds are large dogs that do a tremendous amount of growing in the first 12 months of their lives. Greyhounds weigh about a pound at birth. Healthy puppies gain weight daily and by three months of age can weigh 25 to 30 pounds. For the first eight or nine weeks of their

Huzzah Wild At Heart exhibits early signs of show potential. Owned by J. Lovci.

Ch. Ryal Rumours JC at 11 months.
Photo by Ashbey Photography

Ch. Woodcreeks Jamaican Sunrise at seven months.

Owned by Marsha Wartell

"Willow" and puppies. Good development and growth begins at an early stage in a Greyhound's life.

Regular weighing of puppies is a good way to make certain they are receiving adequate nutrition.

lives, Greyhound babies are cute roly-poly little creatures. By three months everything starts to lengthen, and you can tell that these puppies truly are going to be Greyhounds. All of the body parts do not grow at the same rate, so there will be times when you think your puppy is all legs, as long as a Dachshund, or high in the rear.

From three to ten months, Greyhounds are in such a rapid growth stage that you wonder if your beautiful puppy has completely fallen apart. It is not unusual for puppies to toe out, hock in, or become narrow in front. They can go down in pasterns, their briskets become shallow, brows become high over the eyes, and their ears will go in every direction. My best advice during this period is to just close your eyes to all of the changes and "keep the faith." Most of these changes are temporary and will correct themselves as your puppy matures.

By 10 to 15 months, your puppy should be coming back together again, and will have fulfilled the promise he showed at 6 to 12 weeks. Adult height is usually attained by 15 months, but your Greyhound has a lot of filling out to do. Muscles will become more developed and defined. You will see more substance, briskets will drop below the elbows, heads will lengthen, and necks will strengthen.

The charts that follow trace the development of several Greyhound puppies. They are presented as a reference only. Every Greyhound is unique and will develop at his own individual rate.

HEIGHT-INCHES

MONTHS	3	4	5	6	7	8	9	10	11	12
Dog White/Red	$20\frac{1}{2}$	$24\frac{1}{2}$	$25\frac{7}{8}$	$26\frac{7}{8}$	$27\frac{1}{2}$	$28\frac{1}{2}$	29	$29\frac{7}{8}$	$30\frac{1}{4}$	$30\frac{1}{2}$
Dog Brindle	$19\frac{1}{2}$	$23\frac{7}{8}$	$25\frac{1}{4}$	$26\frac{1}{2}$	27	28	$28\frac{1}{2}$	29	29	$29\frac{1}{2}$
Bitch White/Black	18	$22\frac{3}{4}$	$24\frac{1}{2}$	$25\frac{3}{4}$	26	$27\frac{1}{4}$	$27\frac{1}{2}$	$27\frac{5}{8}$	28	28
Bitch Black	$17\frac{1}{2}$	22	$23\frac{3}{4}$	$24\frac{5}{8}$	$25\frac{7}{8}$	$26\frac{1}{2}$	$26\frac{3}{4}$	27	$27\frac{1}{2}$	$27\frac{1}{2}$

WEIGHT-POUNDS

MONTHS	1	2	3	4	5	6	7	8	9	10	11	12
Dog White/Red	9	18.6	33.8	47.5	58	65.4	72	75	78	80.8	82.6	85
Dog Brindle	8.7	17.8	31.4	46.1	56.5	63	70	73.4	76.1	78	79	80
Bitch White/Black	8.2	16.7	27.6	41.5	51	58.2	63	67	69	71	73.1	74
Bitch Black	7.8	15.3	25.4	38.7	49.1	56.2	61	63.4	65	66.3	68	69

LIVING WITH A GREYHOUND

Greyhounds make exceptional pets—a fact that has, until recently, remained a well-kept secret. Although fanciers have admired the breed for thousands of years, it has always ranked in the lower end of the American Kennel Club's registration scale. However, the Greyhound rescue and adoption movement has placed many Greyhounds into loving homes, where they are winning many new devotees.

Those who love Greyhounds and are familiar with their warm personalities, intelligence, playfulness, and charm maintain they could not imagine life without one of these gentle dogs. In fact, Greyhound ownership tends to become addictive. Many people who start with only one soon find themselves sharing their homes with two or even three.

What is it about Greyhounds that earns them such devoted admirers? I believe it is their unswerving devotion, combined with an uncanny ability to keep their human families constantly amused. Whatever the reason, these devoted companions deserve owners who are willing to meet their special needs.

Greyhounds do have some specific requirements, but none are so different that prospective owners should be worried. Greyhounds are strong, not fragile, and have very few genetic problems or inherited diseases. Greyhounds have stable temperaments and are very resilient animals. They take change in stride and are relaxed in most new situations.

COMPANIONSHIP

Greyhounds are happiest when in the company of their favorite humans. They require many hours of attention and want to be near you and participate in your every activity. At times they can make a nuisance of themselves. You may find it nearly impossible to complete any household task without their help. Greyhounds should not be put in a kennel or yard and ignored. They will be miserable. Desire for and dependence upon human contact is the greatest need a Greyhound has and the most important one you will fulfill.

SOCIALIZATION

It is important to socialize your Greyhound and introduce him to as many people as possible. Exposure to children, the elderly, and the physically challenged at an early age will help to ensure a stable temperament as an adult.

Greyhounds are naturally affectionate and trusting. They usually welcome strangers into "their" homes. I have known a few Greyhounds that would be considered watchdogs, in that they gave warning of the approach of a stranger, but they certainly were not aggressive dogs.

A Greyhound's size and deep bark can make him appear intimidating to those not familiar with their even temperaments. You will find that you will have more problems keeping your Greyhound from jumping up on visitors and licking their faces than you will have keeping them from being overly protective.

EXERCISE

Greyhounds love to run. They need to exercise and should have access to a large fenced area several times a week. Greyhounds can be kept in homes and apartments without a fenced yard as long as you are willing to walk them daily and provide safe opportunities for them to run two or three

Companionship ranks high on a Greyhound's list of requirements; Baggy and Heather Bellis-Jones are great friends.

Exercise, which should include regular and frequent long runs, is critical to a Greyhound's good health. Owned by Hanne Böckhaus.

entertain each other for as much as an hour, playing tag or hide-and-seek, leaping and frolicking. Greyhounds love to play with other Greyhounds and will provide you with many hours of entertainment.

If you do not own another Greyhound and one does not live nearby, try to arrange playtime with a friend or neighbor's dog a few times a week. Or get out yourself and take turns chasing each other, playing ball, and tossing a favorite stuffed toy. Remember that exercise is of utmost importance to the Greyhound, especially to the developing body of a young dog. Free running develops bone, muscle, strong ligaments and tendons, tight feet, and good coordination. A puppy that does not receive adequate exercise may have poor muscle and bone development and weaker connective tissue when an adult. As a result, the underexercised Greyhound may be more prone to injury.

times a week. The ideal situation, of course, is to have a large fenced-in yard that your Greyhound can use every day.

If put out by themselves, Greyhounds usually do several laps around the yard, sniff a few places, sample a blade of grass or two, take care of business, and rush back to the door to be let inside. If two or more go out together, they will

Comfort

Greyhounds are creatures of comfort. They pamper themselves and always seek out the softest places in the house to sleep. Even as I wrote

Greyhounds are not shy about adopting comfortable human furniture for their own and may compete with you for every inch of sofa space. "Julia," owned by Maggie Bryson.

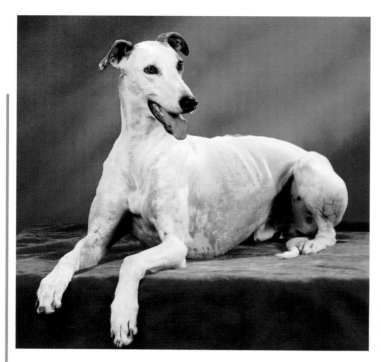

Personality, charm, and a touch of mischievousness have made Greyhounds somewhat of an addiction for many owners.

this, my five-month-old puppy climbed onto the couch, took four throw pillows and arranged them to his liking, pulled the afghan off the back of the couch and laid it out, using his teeth and front feet, on top of the pillows. He then jumped down to the floor and gathered three stuffed animals, a large knucklebone, and his ball. After he placed them all on the couch atop his newly made bed, he settled into his nest and fell fast asleep. This puppy was raised in a kennel, but it has taken him less than one week to discover how to make himself comfortable in my home. There is no need to spoil or indulge your Greyhound; they know how to take care of themselves quite nicely.

If you don't want your Greyhound on the furniture, provide soft beds in rooms you frequent. Greyhounds can be taught to sleep in their own beds as long as they can be near you.

Medical Care

Safe medical care for your Greyhound is extremely important. A Greyhound's unique physical makeup requires that certain precautions be taken in medical treatment. These special health concerns will be discussed at length in a later chapter. In this section I want to stress the necessity of finding a truly knowledgeable veterinarian, one who is familiar with Greyhound treatment, or one who is willing to learn. You may find that both you and your vet will learn together.

Greyhounds are not like many other breeds of dogs in their response to certain drugs. It is important that your vet be aware of Greyhounds' reactions to antibiotics, anesthetics, tranquilizers, sedatives, flea and tick preparations, and house and yard chemicals and sprays.

I recently received a call from a couple

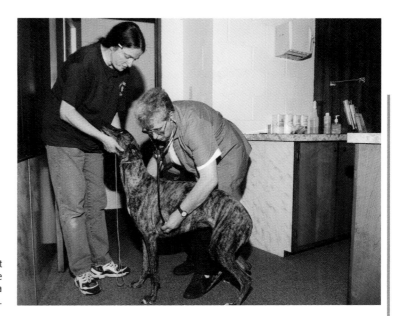

One of the first and most important steps in becoming a responsible Greyhound owner is to find a knowledgeable veterinarian.

looking for a Greyhound puppy. They had been planning this acquisition for quite some time and were well prepared to welcome the little newcomer into their home. The wife had called several veterinarians in their area and located one who was familiar with the precautions necessary when treating Greyhounds. The couple had already filled out the required paperwork for the clinic and had met the staff. They were prepared, well in advance, for any emergency that might occur. A very lucky little puppy went to live with that young couple.

Ch. Gaia the Magician. Owned by Heather Minnich.

Tails

Tails can be a source of frustration to Greyhound owners. These long, wildly wagging appendages bang against walls, cupboards, and furniture, sometimes resulting in broken skin and occasionally broken tails. Be particularly aware of house and car doors. Even though your Greyhound is through a door, his long tail is trailing behind. Be certain that both Greyhound and tail are clear of any door before allowing it to close.

Skin

Greyhound skin is thin and tears easily. We took this into consideration when we fenced in part of our five acres of woods. We wanted to create a safe exercise area for the Greyhounds. We removed most of the smaller trees from the area and cut off the branches of the remaining trees to a height well above the Greyhounds' heads. We check fencing regularly to be certain that there are no loose or protruding wires and no branches caught in the

Ch. Aragon Dark Wind enjoys some fresh air in Colorado. Owned by Helen Hamilton.

chain link. We have been very careful and have not had any serious problems with torn skin, but in spite of the most meticulous precautions, many Greyhounds end up in the vet's office receiving stitches. Often, when a cut or tear occurs, a cause cannot be found. Your Greyhound just comes in and you notice a cut. The best thing you can do is be aware of the potential risk of skin tears and conscientiously try to avoid situations that may cause injury.

Grooming

Greyhounds are naturally clean dogs that require little grooming. Wiping their coats down with a hound glove once a week is usually sufficient to remove dead hair and keep skin in good condition. Baths are seldom necessary. Check ears regularly and clean gently with a soft damp cloth if they get dirty. If you see a dark waxy buildup, have your vet check the ears and prescribe treatment.

Trim nails every two weeks. Long nails catch on things and can cause a Greyhound to break a toe when running. They are also uncomfortable for the dog, and if left untrimmed, can cause feet to break down and splay. Considering the importance of strong, sound feet to an animal that runs as much as a Greyhound, you can understand the necessity of paying close attention to nails and keeping them short. We usually trim nails when the dogs are tired after a day's play; you meet with much less resistance then. Use a well-made clipper that is sharp and only cut a little off at a time. Avoid cutting the quick, as this causes pain and bleeding and will guarantee that the

Ch. Taikatassun Mamba. Owned by Sari Rantenan.

next nail-cutting session will be a battle. Our dogs are so used to having their nails trimmed that they put up little fuss. Two of my show dogs actually jump up on the grooming table when we get out the nail clippers. Whether you are adopting an ex-racer or buying a puppy from a breeder, your Greyhound should be used to having his nails trimmed. Keeping up an established routine will make the nail-trimming session a relaxing experience for both of you.

Bayroad Red Morning Mist takes advantage of a day of surf and sand. Owned by Helen Brox Kalvik. *Photo by Karen Grottjord*

Teeth

Some Greyhounds have naturally white teeth and others seem to have a terrible problem with plaque buildup. I used to think that diet was the culprit, but over the years it has become obvious that some Greyhounds just produce more plaque than others. These dogs will need more attention given to their teeth. Providing large knucklebones, sterilized bones, and high-quality bis-

"Zephyr" retrieving in water. Owned by Linda Colflesh.

cuits to chew will help control tartar buildup. There are special toothpastes and toothbrushes for dogs that help if used regularly; you may also use a damp cloth with a little baking soda to clean teeth. Some Greyhound owners purchase dental tools and work on their dogs' teeth. This prevents their Greyhounds from having to be anesthetized to have their teeth cleaned by a vet. The best time to work on teeth is when the dog is relaxed, lying on the couch next to you with his head in your lap. Do a few teeth at a time and it will not be an unpleasant experience for your Greyhound.

As Greyhounds age, teeth may need more attention. Have your veterinarian check teeth on routine visits. Irritations and infections of the mouth can cause many serious problems and need to be cared for immediately.

Good Manners

It is never too soon to begin teaching your Greyhound appropriate household manners. Even young puppies need to be taught the very basic commands that will make them welcome members of the family. Make learning enjoyable and you and your Greyhound will both relish the time spent on lessons. Use food and lots of praise to encourage your dog. Consistency in training sessions is important, as is repetition. Don't bore your Greyhound, and try to keep training sessions short and fun. Puppies do well with early training because they are so eager to please. They respond immediately to your enthusiasm and praise. Concentrate on a few simple commands. Come, sit, down, stay, and crate are all useful, easily taught behaviors.

Training is not only important for show dogs such as Ch. Schotborgs Earthquake; household pets should also be well-behaved. Owned by Karen Grottjord.

Greyhounds are generally very mild mannered and will get along with other breeds. Hexham Found a Majik Rhythm plays with Keeshond, Majikees Kokomos Vacation. Owned by Joan Malak.

Successful methods for training your Greyhound are discussed in another chapter.

Housebreaking

Whether buying a puppy or rescuing an adult racer, chances are that you will have to housebreak your Greyhound. Greyhounds are one of the easiest breeds to housebreak because they are so naturally clean. Proper use of a crate during this process is a great help and practically guarantees success. A young puppy needs to go outside after every meal, after naptime, and after play. Call your puppy or pick him up and carry him outside. We try to encourage our puppies to scamper after us to the door, if we think they can make it without having an accident. The puppy will soon get the idea and start for the

With the proper training and attention, your Greyhound can be easily housebroken. Am. Can. Ch. Willomoor Mad Hatter waits patiently to return inside. *Photo by Patti Clark*

door whenever he has to go out. Adult Greyhounds respond even more quickly than young puppies when housebreaking. Retired racers have been living in crates and are let out every few hours to eliminate. They also have much larger bladders and can wait for longer periods between trips outside.

THE GREYHOUND IN THE SHOW RING

The first dog show was held at the new Cornmarket at Newcastle-on-Tyre in England on June 28 and 29, 1859. At that time, the purebred dog world was not the same as it is today. There were no kennel clubs, no breed clubs or official standards, no rules and regulations. The English Kennel Club was not formed until 1873; the American Kennel Club was founded in 1884.

There are presently three multi-breed registries in the United States that sanction dog shows and other dog-related events in which Greyhounds may participate.

AMERICAN KENNEL CLUB

The most familiar of these clubs is the American Kennel Club (AKC). The AKC is a nonprofit organization with the primary purpose of registering purebred dogs. The AKC records date back to the late 1800s, and it currently maintains registrations for more than 40 million purebred dogs. The AKC annually registers more than one million dogs in 148 recognized breeds, making it the largest registry in the United States.

The American Kennel Club's other interests include the establishment of the Canine Health Foundation to help promote research into canine health problems; devising and enforcing rules and regulations and licensing activities such as conformation shows, obedience, field, herding, and coursing events; and publishing the monthly *AKC Gazette* and *Events Calendar,* dog books, breed videos, judging guides, and pamphlets related to the above-mentioned activities.

To gain an AKC Champion (Ch.) title, a dog must earn 15 points, including two majors (three to five points each) from two different judges. Points are awarded according to the number of dogs defeated in a breed at each show. Point scales vary in different parts of the country. Check the front of a show catalog for the scale appropriate to that show site.

Dogs that are not champions are entered into one of the following classes: Puppy (6 to 9 months, 9 to 12 months, 12 to 18 months), Novice, Bred by Exhibitor, American Bred, and Open. Classes for dogs are judged first. The winners of each of the classes then compete for Winners Dog (WD). The bitches are judged next, and class winners compete for Winners Bitch (WB). WD and WB are awarded championship points. WD and WB then compete with the Specials (Champions) to determine Best of Breed (BOB), Best of Winners (BOW), and Best Opposite Sex (BOS).

It is possible for the WD or WB to defeat the Specials and be BOB or BOS. If this happens, more points are awarded, again according to the number of dogs defeated. The BOW may also accumulate more points if there were more dogs shown in the opposite sex.

UNITED KENNEL CLUB

The United Kennel Club (UKC) registers more than 250,000 dogs each year, making it the second largest registry in the United States. The UKC was established in 1898 and currently recognizes 286 breeds, having added 74 additional breeds in January 1996. The UKC licenses 8,000 activities each year, and more than 60 percent are working dog events.

The UKC identifies itself as "the registry for people who like to do something with their dog." It sanctions conformation shows, obedience and agility trials, and field and hunting events. The UKC is unique among dog registries in

Ch. Argus of Greywitch in June 1969. Argus became one of the breed's most influential sires.

Owned by Drs. Rudolph and Elsie Neustadt.

Photo by Evelyn Shafer

that it allows the participation of spayed and neutered mixed-breed dogs in performance events, but not conformation shows. *Bloodlines,* the UKC publication, is issued six times a year.

In March 1996 the UKC announced the establishment of a new identity and parentage certification program, "the world's first DNA-based canine registry service." Dog owners collect samples from their own dogs using a kit provided by the club. A DNA-profiled dog will be indicated by the UKC pedigree notation DNA-P TM. Identified dogs whose sires and dams have also been verified will carry VIP TM, VIP standing for Verified Identified Parentage.

STATES KENNEL CLUB

The third registry in the United States that recognizes the Greyhound is the States Kennel Club (SKC). Its stated goal is to be a club "Of the Fancy, By the Fancy, and For the Fancy." It has an open membership to clubs and individuals.

The SKC held its first show in 1987. It recognizes 366 breeds of dogs, more than the other two registries. Many owners, breeders, and clubs of rare breeds in the United States are affiliated with the SKC, thereby affording them the opportunity to exhibit their dogs at all-breed as well as specialty shows. To date, the SKC sanctions conformation shows and obedience trials, but encourages member clubs to hold performance events in conjunction with their shows.

Judges at SKC events have the responsibility of determining whether or not a dog is of championship quality. To attain an SKC Championship, a dog must receive 15 points and three Certificates of Merit (CM) under three different judges. A Certificate of Merit may only be awarded to WD, WB, or BOW during breed judging with competition, or to a dog awarded a Group Placement that did not qualify at the breed level because there was no competition. One of the three CMs must be awarded after a dog reaches 15 months.

The SKC is the only registry in the United States to award an International Championship. A dog must be awarded four International Certificates of Merit (ICM), from four different judges, one of whom resides outside of the United States. One of the ICMs must be awarded after the dog reaches 15 months of age. International Certificates of Merit are awarded only to BOB and BOS winners. At SKC shows the judge is the sole determiner of the quality of the dogs.

The States Kennel Club's magazine is called *The SKC Journal.*

FINDING A SHOW PROSPECT

If the show bug has bitten and you have decided that Greyhounds are the breed for you, then your next step is to acquire a show-quality Greyhound.

Be certain that you are firm in your decision to own a Greyhound. Ideally, you have spent time around adults and youngsters of the breed, have talked with breeders and owners, have attended shows, and have an idea of your ideal Greyhound. Read and reread the standard. Observe dogs at shows. Buy a copy

Ch. Gaia Moon Dance learning to stack at six weeks. Owned by Sue LeMieux, Gaia.

of the AKC Greyhound video and study it. Contact the Greyhound Club of America and subscribe to its newsletter.

If you are ready to purchase a Greyhound but do not know a breeder, the GCA may be able to help. The club has a contact person who can tell you which breeders have puppies or older dogs available.

Very few litters of AKC Greyhounds are born each year. You may want to consider purchasing an older puppy or young adult Greyhound if a baby is not to be found. Sometimes breeders will keep two or three youngsters, very close in quality, to see which matures more to their liking. Their second choice, probably comparable in overall quality, would be a great beginning for your show career. Breeders may also have a young adult champion that they are unable, for one reason or another, to campaign. It could be fun to start in the dog show world by taking a fully trained Greyhound into the ring.

The positive side of purchasing an older puppy or young adult is that you will know what you are getting and will be able to more fully evaluate the quality of the dog as a show prospect. You will bypass some of the work of raising and training a rambunctious puppy, and you will be taking less of a risk if you truly desire a show-quality Greyhound.

The downside of purchasing an older dog is that you will bypass some of the work and fun of raising and training a rambunctious puppy. You will also be taking less of a risk, but missing all of those months of anticipation and anxiety, awaiting the blossoming of your young champion-to-be.

If you decide to purchase a puppy and know what type of Greyhound you like, be prepared to wait for possibly six months to a year or more to get a puppy. Use the time to continue to learn as much as you can about the breed, and spend as much time as possible just being with Greyhounds.

Ch. Woodcreeks Jamaican Sunrise. Owned by Marsha Wartell. *Photo by Luis F. Sosa*

Opposite: Ch. Hewly Hispanic II with handler Sioux Forsyth. *Photo by Ashbey Photography*

CHOOSING A SHOW-QUALITY GREYHOUND PUPPY

When picking a puppy as a show prospect, you will probably want to rely rather heavily on the advice and suggestions of the breeder. Puppies are usually sold somewhere between the ages of 8 to 12 weeks, a good time to look for a show prospect. The breeder will probably stack each puppy and explain the strong and weak

Show training a young future champion takes time and patience.

Do as much research as possible before choosing the "right" show Greyhound. Breeders, handlers, and owners can be a valuable source of advice about show potential.

points of each. Look for a puppy with good rib spring; depth of brisket; overall body length; good front and rear angulation; a clean head; dark eye; small ears; tight, well-knuckled feet; large bone. Choose a friendly, outgoing puppy with no glaring faults. If you are wondering about a specific point, ask. Try to keep the standard in mind when evaluating the litter, but do not choose a puppy who looks like a perfect adult, or one who is tiny, fine boned, or shy. Try not to be too particular about color or sex. Although a flashily marked, parti-color Greyhound will stand out in the show ring, and males are usually larger than bitches, the top-winning Greyhound of all time was a blue brindle bitch.

You should have an opportunity to watch the puppies moving freely in a yard. Look for smooth movement, but remember that puppies can be a little loose at this time. In most cases, you can depend on the breeder to steer you toward the puppy that will best meet your requirements. A breeder does not want any but the very best puppies in the ring representing his or her kennel.

Building Background

It is ideal if the breeder of your puppy will serve as your mentor, helping you through the maze of premium lists, show entries, superintendents, ring procedures, point accumulation, puppy matches, judge selection, necessary equipment, training, grooming, etc.

While your puppy is growing into a champion, you may want to spend some time studying pedigrees and photos of your Greyhound's ancestors. See if you can borrow videos of Greyhound specialties and home videos of other puppy and adult Greyhounds. Learn to recognize correct movement and desirable and undesirable characteristics. Determine what you like and don't like in the breed. Try to observe Greyhounds coursing, open field or lure, so you can better understand the necessary structure of the breed. Stanley D. Petter, Jr., a breeder and exhibitor of show Greyhounds since the 1950s, gives this advice to beginners: "It is by attending the very best shows (Westminster, GCA specialties, and supported entries) and seeing the very best exhibits that the novice learns, the novice hones his eye, gets a sense of appreciation, of quality."

Keep track of your puppy's development by recording height and weight monthly. Describe changes your puppy goes through. These will be invaluable to you if you get another puppy and want to compare the growth patterns of the two. Even though no two puppies are exactly alike or go through the same changes, there will be similarities. By studying puppies as they grow, you will gradually learn to know what to look for in a developing puppy and be more aware of what to expect in the adult Greyhound.

In spite of all the accumulated knowledge and experience a breeder may have, picking puppies is still a risk and always

Seamair the Prophet. "Abraham" is the last Greyhound bred by Blake Froelicher of Seamair Farm.

Owned by Cheryl Reynolds.

Photo by Holloway

an exciting challenge. Breeders and exhibitors of purebred dogs must be risk takers. They thrill to the challenge of picking the very best puppies from a litter and watching them develop into the very best adult show dogs and producers. Gamblers? Yes. The dog show habit can become very addicting.

TRAINING FOR THE SHOW RING

The training of young puppies should begin at an early age. After your puppy has settled into his new home, you can begin training. Ac-

tually, it is relatively easy to train Greyhounds for the conformation ring. They must learn to hold a "stack" and permit a stranger to examine them, to walk and trot on a loose lead, and to "use their ears" or "bait." Training sessions should be short and fun for your puppy. When playing, practice stacking. Periodically open your puppy's mouth to examine the bite and run your hands over the puppy's body. When people visit or you take the puppy somewhere, encourage others to handle the puppy and play with him. Socialization is very important from a young age, so take your puppy with you when you go places. This is the very best way to build self-confidence in your young Greyhound.

Richard Bauer checks to make certain Ch. Suntiger Traveler is ready to be examined by the judge.

Photo by Gail Burnham, Suntiger, courtesy Linda Bell

Train your puppy to bait a couple of times during the day. Feed him bits of hot dog, cheese, or soft dog treats by hand and use a phrase such as "Watch it!" to encourage the puppy to use his ears. It won't take long before those ears will come to attention as soon as you reach for the cookie jar, pull a morsel from your pocket, or whisper, "Watch it!"

Lead breaking is the next step in show training your puppy. Let the puppy wear a lightweight collar for a short time for a few days to get used to the feel of something around his neck. Then attach a lead and encourage the puppy to follow you. Use whatever method is effective with your puppy to get him to move—a squeaky toy, food, another dog, someone calling him. Some Greyhound puppies will fight the lead if you proceed too quickly or force the puppy by pulling him. Go slowly and use plenty of praise. Soon your puppy will be happily trotting by your side.

Practice moving in a large circle going in a counterclockwise direction. Practice going in a straight line and making a triangle with two left turns. Encourage your puppy to keep his head up. Food, praise, and sometimes a gentle pop of the lead with a verbal reminder of "head up," will work well. Move your puppy on a loose show lead that is placed high on the neck just behind the ears.

Hand stacking your Greyhound is the next step in show-ring training. Even a puppy that has been stacked and gone over from a very young age may object to this activity when he is older. Work slowly and calmly, repeating the command "Stand" or "Stand, Stay." The purpose of the stack is to give the judge the opportunity to view and examine your Greyhound, so you want to present your dog looking his very best. A Greyhound has no coat to cover faults, so structural attributes and problems are easily seen.

Stand on your Greyhound's right side, with his head near your right hand. Gently place the front legs so they are directly beneath his shoulders, feet straight ahead, not turned in or out. Repeat, "Stand, Stay." Hold the lead in your right hand and with your left hand reach back and place the rear legs. Take each leg at the stifle, starting with the leg closest to the judge, and place it backward until the hock is perpendicular to the ground.

You want the hock and ground to form a 90-degree angle. Then place the other leg in a similar manner. The rear legs should be set rather far apart. Repeat the "Stand, Stay" command. Return your attention to the front and make certain that the head is held parallel to the ground and the neck looks long and arched at the nape. Work slowly and gently and give much praise each time the stack is held, even for a short time. When your puppy is comfortable and holds a stack fairly well, have friends or family members and then strangers go over the dog. Practice the exact ring procedure, going through all the steps in order: stacking, moving in a circle,

Shows can be held on a number of levels, from local club affairs to international events.

stacking for examination, examination, down and back or triangle, natural stand with ears up when you come back into the judge, circle again. One of my show dogs became so familiar with this pattern that he completed it himself when his handler had dropped his lead.

If a local club holds handling classes, you may want to attend. These classes will give you and your Greyhound a chance to practice in a setting similar to a dog show. It is also a good way to help socialize your Greyhound puppy.

Another good place to practice for the show ring is at a puppy match. Most all-breed clubs hold one or two matches a year. They are conducted like a point show, but no points are awarded.

GROOMING FOR THE SHOW RING

There is not much to grooming a Greyhound for the show ring. Probably the most important aspect of your dog's appearance will be his condition. A Greyhound should not be too thin or too heavy. Ribs should be well covered, muscles should be hard, but not overdeveloped. Coat condition is important, also. A hound glove or chamois cloth used on the coat every day or two will help keep it healthy looking. So will a lot of petting. Ears and teeth should be clean. Nails should be clipped or ground every week or two. Very little trimming is necessary. Most exhibitors remove whiskers, although many opt not to do so. Long hairs on the backs of the thighs and on the flanks to define tuck up are often trimmed. A bath is usually given before a show, and that's all there is.

SHOWING YOUR GREYHOUND

So now you are ready to show your Greyhound. You have entered a local show and have arrived early enough to exercise your dog and get him used to the show site. You will need to find your ring and get the armband that will have your dog's number on it. Ask the ring steward working in the ring for the number; it will have been sent to you along with the judging program. Many handlers get two rubber bands to secure the armband just in case one of them breaks while in the ring. You don't want to have to worry about picking up the armband and trying to show your dog at the same time.

Remember that the judge gets his first impression of your Greyhound when you enter the ring. Pay attention to how you enter and where the ring steward tells you to stand. If you've arrived early enough, it is wise to watch a breed or two before the Greyhounds so you will know this particular judge's ring procedure. Although most judges follow a similar routine, there are enough different methods of judging to make it important to know ahead of time, if at all possible, what will be expected of you and your dog.

When the ring steward calls your class, you will usually be told if the judge wants you to be in catalog order, the dogs with the lowest number entering the ring first, etc. If catalog order is not mentioned, you may want to permit the more experienced handlers to go into the ring ahead of you. This will give you more time to prepare yourself and your dog for judging.

The first thing most judges have you do is set your dog up in line with the other exhibitors. Keep your eye on the judge as you work with your dog to see if procedure may be different. Some judges have you take all of the dogs around the ring first, and then set up for examination. It can be quite embarrassing to look up from your beautifully stacked Greyhound to see all of your fellow exhibitors trotting around the ring with their dogs. Both the judge and the ring steward must check your armband after you enter the ring to check for absences, so if you see one of them staring at you, move your arm around so they can see your number. Usually the judge will stand back in the center of the ring and look at all of the dogs in the class to get a first overall impression. The dogs will then be moved around the ring together and stopped in the place indicated by the judge. Leave plenty of room between you and the handler in front of you so you do not run into each other while going around the ring. After you have stopped, the judge will wait for the first exhibitor in line to set up. The judge will then go over that dog. If you are in a large class and near the end of the line, let your dog relax for awhile, talk to him, play with him, let him know this is a fun thing.

After the judge examines an entry, the handler will be asked to move the dog down and back or in a triangle. The judge is watching front and rear movement. The handler brings the dog back to the judge and lets the dog stand by himself so the judge can see what the dog looks like when it has not been posed by the exhibitor. This is the time when all of that training to bait comes in handy. A dog that baits will stand alertly and expectantly waiting for a piece of liver and will show himself to his best advantage. The judge will then ask the handler to move the dog around

the ring to the end of the line. The judge will be watching to see how the dog moves from the side.

If you are next in line while all of this is going on, you should be stacking your dog and getting ready for the judge. By the time the judge looks at your Greyhound, he should be set up perfectly and be absolutely still. Try to keep your hands off your dog so the judge can get a good look, and stand back out of the way while the judge is examining the dog. Some judges ask you to show them the dog's bite. If you are asked to do this, just open your dog's lips so the judge can see how the teeth meet in front. Follow the judge's instructions. If you do not understand a direction, ask before you begin moving and save yourself from having to do it all over again if you make a mistake. This should not be a problem if you have taken the time to observe how the judge has moved the other dogs. After each dog in the class has been examined and gaited, the judge will want to take a final look at all of the dogs. Reset your dog as you had before and remember to keep your hands out of the way. The judge is comparing the outlines of the dogs and their overall quality. In each class the judge must pick the dogs that most closely resemble the standard. After making the decision, the judge will point to the first, second, third, and fourth place in the class. Again, pay attention to the judge at this point, so you will know if you place. If you have been awarded a placement, take your dog and stand in front of the number marker on the side of the ring. The judge and ring steward will again have to check your armband number to mark the placement in their books. Once the ribbons have been handed out, you may leave the ring.

After all of the classes have been

Ch. Heathero Ariel of the Tempest, CDX, with multiple Group placements.

Owned by Marj and Herman Leider.

Photo by Tom Bruni

Ch. Southwestern Episode Beauty, a classic example of Southwestern Hounds.

Owned by Greg Davis and Roger Owens.

Photo by Rich Bergman

Ch. Greystone's Barcelona, Multiple Group winner and Award of Merit winner at the 1999 GCA Eastern Specialty.

Owned by Kim Fritzler.

Photo by Rich Bergman

Ch. Southwestern Silver Schoone, an elegant young Greyhound champion.

Owned by Roger Owens and Greg Davis.

Photo by Rich Bergman

Ch. Gaia the Magician SC, an accomplished show dog and lure courser.

Owned by Heather Minnich.

Photo by Kernan

Martigra's Played For A Fool, a lovely young Greyhound.

Owned by Marti Bradford, Martigra.

Photo by Pegini Animal Photo

Ch. Heathero African Queen, 1997
Number One Dog in Mexico.

Owned by Penelope Johnson.

Ch. Woodcreeks Jamaica Me Crazy, one
of many champions in a single litter.

Owned by Johnny and Marsha Wartell.

Photo by Missy Yuhl

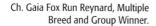

Ch. Gaia Fox Run Reynard, Multiple
Breed and Group Winner.

Owned by Sue LeMieux and David
Hintson.

Photo by Kurtis Photography

Ch. Jets Ravishing Redhead "Nicole" was the 1996 Westminster Best of Breed winner.

Owned by Geri Ann Hendrick.

Photo by Tom Nutting

Ch. Grand Cru Le Montachet, winning Best in Sweepstakes at the 1997 GCA National Specialty.

Owned by Melanie Steel.

Photo by Tom Nutting/A & N Productions

Ch. Andarab Magic Raven, multi-Group placer and Award of Merit winner at 1998 GCA Eastern Specialty.

Owned by Lois Bires.

Photo by B.W. Kernan

Ch. Fox Run Episode Partytime, one of the top-winning Greyhounds in 1998. Owned by Carolyn Phillips. *Photo by Downey Dog Show Photography*

judged in your dog's sex, the winners of each class will be called back into the ring to compete for Winners. It is Winners Dog and Winners Bitch that are

Pat Ide with Ch. Huzzah Tiger Doll. *Photo by Joan Ludwig*

awarded points toward their championships. If you placed second in a class, stay at ringside for the Winners judging, because if the Winners Dog or Bitch was the first place dog in your class, you will have to return to the ring to determine Reserve Winners. When competing for Winners points, the same judging procedure as the classes is usually followed.

If your Greyhound is Winners Dog or Winners Bitch, you will have to return to the ring one more time, with the Specials (Greyhounds who are already Champions), to determine Best of Breed. If there are no Specials entered, Winners Dog and Winners Bitch compete for Best of Breed. In the Specials ring, three ribbons are awarded. Best of Breed goes to the Greyhound that the judge decides is the best Greyhound entry on that day, Best of Winners is awarded to either Winners Dog or Winners Bitch, whichever the judges determines to be the better of the two, and Best of Opposite is awarded to a Greyhound of the opposite sex to that who won BOB.

Helpful Hints

1. A good dog can lose if in poor condition or poorly handled. Conversely, a lesser dog can win if in good condition and well handled.

2. Attitude in the ring is important. A dog that loves to show and is "on," alert, and interested in what is going on has an obvious advantage over a dog that is disinterested, unsure, nervous, or shy. Play with your Greyhound at home when training and at the shows. Build confidence and enthusiasm.

3. A toy or bait may put a sparkle into your Greyhound's eyes in the ring.

4. Talk to your dog while in the ring. Give plenty of praise and reward for a job well done.

5. Do not overtrain or overwork your Greyhound and sour him for the ring.

6. Always move your Greyhound on a loose lead. Even if you want to keep him close to you, keep the lead slack.

7. Stay relaxed. Your feelings can travel right down the lead. A nervous, uptight handler often ends up showing a nervous, uptight Greyhound.

8. Stay positive. Go into the ring with a winning attitude. Don't defeat yourself and your dog before you even enter the ring.

9. Don't get discouraged. If you want to succeed, you will. Seasoned exhibitors often explain to newcomers, "It just takes time. You have to pay your dues."

What About a Handler?

If you are really uncomfortable about showing your own dog or are un-able to do so for some reason, the breeder of your Greyhound may be willing to show for you. Or you may want to employ the services of a professional handler. Handlers have the advantage of having the experience that you may not. They know how to present a dog at its very best. They are familiar with the judges' likes and dislikes in the different breeds and in ring procedures. Many handlers are willing and helpful mentors to their clients. Don't be afraid to try showing yourself if that's what you want to do. Most Greyhounds are owner handled and presented quite nicely in the ring. If you are a bit nervous, just remember that everyone is a novice at one time. Keep at it. Take time at shows to watch the professionals. Have someone videotape you working with your dog. Eventually you and your Greyhound will be seasoned veterans, and even winners, in the show ring.

GREYHOUND SHOW DOGS AND PRODUCERS

Show Dogs

The Greyhound Club of America holds two specialties each year, one on the West Coast and one in the East.

The Eastern Specialty was the original national specialty for the Greyhound Club. The first specialty show was held in 1936 in conjunction with the Morris and Essex Kennel Club Show. The first western show was held in 1968 in Santa Barbara, California. Since 1980 the Western Specialty has been a part of the Western Sighthound Combined Specialties show.

The following is a list of BOB and BOS winners of the two specialties from 1990 through 1998.

		EASTERN	WESTERN
1990	BOB	Ch. Legend's Loch Ness (D)	Ch. My Adventure (D)
	BOS	Ch. Rudel's Red Queen of Wonderland	Ch. Huzzah Mad Hattie (B)
1991	BOB	Ch. Lochinvar Leaps and Bounds (B)	Ch. Wilrick's Le'legante (B)
	BOS	Ch. Arborcrest Skyrac'r O'Kinnear (D)	Ch. Arborcrest Skyrac'r O'Kinnear (D)
1992	BOB	Ch. Lochinvar Leaps and Bounds (B)	Ch. Another Episode Lymelite (B)
	BOS	Ch. Ramachandra Windstorm Cebar (D)	Ch. Hewly Hispanic II (D)
1993	BOB	Hewly Hit The Roof (B)	Ch. Legend's Loch Ness (D)
	BOS	Ch. Hewly Hispanic II (D)	Ch. Abraxas Rocket (B)
1994	BOB	Ch. Sundridge So Be It, JC (D)	Ch. Huzzah Red Alert (D)
	BOS	Ch. Kingsmark Miss Jane Marple (B)	Ch. Willomoor Trick or Treat (B)
1995	BOB	Ch. Shazam's The Journey Begins (D)	Ch. Crestfield Sky's Sunsation, SC (D)
	BOS	Ch. Kingsmark Miss Jane Marple (B)	Ch. Crestfield Camille O'Kinnear (B)
1996	BOB	Ch. Shazam's The Journey Begins (D)	Ch. Helicon Heartstrings (B)
	BOS	Ch. Tadlen Trick Midnite Cruisin (B)	Ch. Jonz Devil Made Me Do It (D)
1997	BOB	Ch. Rockets Elegy (B)	Ch. Gerico's Chasing the Wind (D)
	BOS	Ch. Dakota Go Lightly Dakota Sioux (D)	Ch. Tadlen Trick Midnite Cruisin (B)
1998	BOB	Ch. Sobers Zanthea (B)	Ch. Huzzah Sweet Molly Malone (B)
	BOS	Ch. Greystone's Barcelona (D)	Ch. Hewly Hard Hitter (D)

A new Southern Greyhound Club of America Specialty was held for the first time in Texas in 1998. This new addition permits breeders and exhibitors in all parts of the United States to attend a show in their geographical area.

1998	BOB	Ch. Legacy's Incredible Journey (B)	
	BOS	Ch. Gerico's Chasing the Wind (D)	

It is interesting to note that several of the winners listed above were produced by winners also listed. Ch. Lochinvar Leaps and Bounds was sired by Ch. My Adventure; Hewly Hit The Roof was sired by Ch. Hewly Hispanic II; Ch. Huzzah Red Alert was sired by Ch. Legend's Loch Ness; and Ch. Arborcrest Skyrac'r O'Kinnear was the sire of littermates Ch. Crestfield Sky's Sunsation, SC and Ch. Crestfield Camille O'Kinnear. Ch. Huzzah Mad Hattie, the dam of Ch. Willomoor's Trick or Treat, was the BOB winner at both the Eastern and Western Specialties in 1988. The dam of Ch. Hewly Hispanic II, Ch. Hewly Histrionic, was a three-time BOB winner of the East-ern Specialty, 1985 to 1987. It is also exciting to see that two of the BOB winners had lure coursing titles.

Greyhounds have been considered by some to be a "bitch breed," meaning that the best or top-winning Greyhounds are more often bitches than dogs. The statistics from the GCA specialties might seem to confirm this belief. Of the 56 Eastern Specialty BOB winners, 44 have been bitches, and only 12 were dogs. Of the 31 Western Specialties, 23 BOB winners were bitches and 8 were dogs. As the above stats show, a bitch also won the first Southern Specialty.

Each year in the May-June issue of *Sighthound Review*, the top-winning

Greyhounds are listed, along with the top winners in the other sighthound breeds. Several Greyhounds have made the Top Twenty Sighthound list from 1990 to 1995. In 1990, Ch. Blu-Kale the Hilton Freude was ranked number 16. In 1991, Ch. Legend's Loch Ness was 14, and Ch. Another Episode Speedlite was 17. Ch. Hewly Hispanic II was number 7 in the Sighthound list in 1992, and Ch. Southwestern Episode Holly was 18. Ch. Hewly Hispanic II again appeared as a Top Twenty Sighthound in 1993, this time in fourth place, and Ch. Southwestern Episode Holly was listed number 14. For the third year in a row Hispanic and Holly made the Top Twenty, with Holly in fifth place and Hispanic in seventh in 1994.

Sighthound Review lists the Top Ten placements in Breed and All-Breed competition. The placements are based on the number of dogs defeated at the Breed, Group, and Best in Show levels.

ALL-BREED WINS	BREED WINS
1990	
1. Ch. Blu-Kale the Hilton Freude	Ch. Legend's Loch Ness
2. Ch. Rudel's Red Queen of Wonderland	Ch. Another Episode Speedlite
3. Ch. Another Episode Speedlite	Ch. Blu-Kale the Hilton Freude
4. Ch. Gallant's Late Arrival	Ch. Rudel's Red Queen of Wonderland
5. Ch. Wilrick's Le'legante	Ch. Gallant's Late Arrival
6. Ch. Legend's Loch Ness	Ch. Huzzah Mad Hattie
7. Ch. Kingsmark Moonlight 'N' Roses	Ch. Barbizon Frank de Roberjos
8. Ch. Downsbragh Huzzah Heirloom	Ch. Downsbragh Huzzah Heirloom
9. Ch. Cebar-Iveragh Out of the Blue	Ch. Huzzah Alice Blue
10. Ch. Huzzah Alice Blue	Ch. El Aur Aces High of Elk Run
1991	
1. Ch. Legend's Loch Ness	Ch. Legend's Loch Ness
2. Ch. Another Episode Speedlite	Ch. Sundridge So Be It
3. Ch. Blu-Kale the Hilton Freude	Ch. Wilrick's Le'legante
4. Ch. Rudel's Red Queen of Wonderland	Ch. Another Episode Speedlite
5. Ch. Gallant Somnombula	Ch. Blu-Kale the Hilton Freude
6. Ch. Sundridge So Be It	Ch. Arborcrest Skyracr O'Kinnear
7. Ch. Arborcrest Skyracr O'Kinnear	Ch. Lochinvar Leaps and Bounds
8. Ch. Wilrick's Lelegante	Ch. Lulworth's Garnish Enginuity
9. Ch. Another Episode Lymelite	Ch. Anotherepisode Torchlite
10. Ch. Anotherepisode Torchlite	Ch. Rudel's Red Queen of Wonderland
1992	
1. Ch. Hewly Hispanic II	Ch. Legend's Loch Ness
2. Ch. Southwestern Episode Holly	Ch. Arborcrest Skyracr O'Kinnear
3. Ch. Suden Darlene of Waybroke	Ch. Hewly Hispanic II
4. Ch. Legend's Loch Ness	Ch. Sundridge So Be It
5. Ch. Blu-Kale the Hilton Freude	Ch. Another Episode Lymelite
6. Ch. Another Episode Sunking	Ch. Lochinvar Leaps and Bounds
7. Ch. Arborcrest Skyracr O'Kinnear	Ch. Southwestern Episode Holly
8. Ch. Lulworth Garnish Enginuity	Ch. Blu-Kale the Hilton Freude
9. Ch. Kingsmark Miss Jane Marple	Ch. Kingsmark Miss Jane Marple
10. Ch. Another Episode Speedlite	Ch. Suden Darlene of Waybroke

In 1993 *Sighthound Review* changed their breed system to what they call the "major league system," which is based on the number of dogs defeated by going BOB in a major entry at all-breed and specialty shows.

ALL-BREED WINS	BREED WINS
1993	
1. Ch. Hewly Hispanic II	Ch. Hewly Hispanic II
2. Ch. Southwestern Episode Holly	Ch. Lochinvar Leaps and Bounds
3. Ch. Rocket's Elegy	Hewly Hit The Roof
4. Ch. Kingsmark Miss Jane Marple	Ch. Southwestern Episode Holly
5. Ch. Sundridge So Be It, JC	Ch. Legend's Loch Ness
6. Ch. Suden Darlene Of Waybroke	Ch. Sundridge So Be It, JC
7. Ch. Hewly Hard Hitter	Ch. Willomoor Trick Or Treat
8. Ch. Crestfield Sky's Salute O'Gerico	Ch. Conamor Kirklea Promise
9. Ch. Lochinvar Leaps and Bounds	Ch. Rocket's Elegy
10. Ch. Crestfield Sky's Sunsation	Ch. Kingsmark Miss Jane Marple
1994	
1. Ch. Southwestern Episode Holly	Ch. Southwestern Episode Holly
2. Ch. Hewly Hispanic II	Ch. Sundridge So Be It, JC
3. Ch. Kingsmark Miss Jane Marple	Ch. Hewly Hispanic II
4. Ch. Sundridge So Be It, JC	Ch. Huzzah Red Alert
5. Ch. Suden Darlene of Waybroke	Ch. Abraxas Rockette
6. Ch. Shazam's The Journey Begins	Ch. Artesia Knight of the Sun
7. Ch. Willomoor Trick or Treat	Ch. Shazam's The Journey Begins
8. Ch. Rocket's Elegy	Ch. Tadlen Midnite Cruisin
9. Ch. Southwestern Silver Moon	Ch. Suntiger Tempest Delight
10. Ch. Wilrick's Lucky Shamrock	Ch. El Aur Aces High of Elk Run
1995	
1. Ch. Sundridge So Be It, JC	Ch. Gerico Chasing The Wind
2. Ch. Kingsmark Miss Jane Marple	Ch. Crestfield Sky's Sunsation
3. Ch. Suden Darlene of Waybroke	Ch. Shazam The Journey Begins
4. Ch. Crestfield Sky's Sunsation	Ch. Sundridge So Be It, JC
5. Ch. Gerico Chasing The Wind	Ch. Kingsmark Miss Jane Marple
6. Ch. Hewly Hard Hitter	Ch. Another Episode Skylite
7. Ch. Shazam's The Journey Begins	Ch. Crestfield Sky's Salute O'Gerico
8. Ch. Huzzah Red Alert	Ch. Mrtgr Skyracr Flame of My Heart
9. Ch. Wilrick's Lucky Shamrock	Ch. Conamor Spirit Wind of Quest
10. Ch. Tadlen Midnite Cruisin	Helicon Constant Comment
1996	
1. Ch. Shazam's The Journey Begins	Ch. Shazam's The Journey Begins
2. Ch. Gerico's Chasing the Wind	Ch. Huzzah Red Alert
3. Ch. Huzzah Red Alert	Ch. Gerico's Chasing the Wind
4. Ch. Martigra's Cupid's Beau	Ch. Helicon Heartstrings
5. Ch. Rubicon Ryal Regalia	Ch. Martigra's Cupid's Beau
6. Ch. Martigra's Candy Kisses	Ch. Willomoor Trick Or Treat
7. Ch. Jonz Devil Made Me Do It	Ch. Tadlen Trick Midnite Cruisin
8. Ch. Enginuity Alluring Reflection	Ch. South Western's Silver Moon
9. Ch. Jet's Ravishing Redhead	Ch. Hewly Hard Hitter
10. Ch. Helicon Heartstrings	Ch. Huzzah Blue Mist and Magic

ALL-BREED WINS	BREED WINS
1997	
1. Ch. Shazam's The Journey Begins	Ch. Gerico's Chasing The Wind
2. Ch. Gerico's Chasing The Wind	Ch. Huzzah Red Alert
3. Ch. Gaia Tailor Maid	Ch. Shazam's The Journey Begins
4. Ch. Sobers Zanthea	Ch. Sobers Zanthea
5. Ch. Huzzah Red Alert	Ch. Jonz Devil Made Me Do It
6. Ch. Jonz Devil Made Me Do It	Ch. Talos Honor Grades
7. Ch. Martigra's Candy Kisses	Ch. Martigra's Candy Kisses
8. Ch. Andarab Wild Oats	Ch. Andarab Wild Oats
9. Ch. Huzzah Jumping Jupiter	Ch. Rockets Elegy
10. Ch. Martigra's Cupid's Beau	Ch. Helicon Heartstrings
1998	
1. Ch. Gerico's Chasing The Wind	Ch. Gerico's Chasing The Wind
2. Ch. Lorricbrook Showdown	Ch. Lorricbrook Showdown
3. Ch. Gaia Tailor Maid	Ch. Sobers Zanthea
4. Ch. Shazam's The Journey Begins, JC	Ch. Heirloom Your Wildest Dreams
5. Ch. Fox Run Episode Partytime	Ch. Talos Honor Grades
6. Ch. Sobers Zanthea	Ch. Rockets Caipirinha
7. Ch. Andarab Indigo Bunting	Ch. Huzzah Sweet Molly Malone
8. Ch. Huzzah Sweet Molly Malone	Ch. Gaia Tailor Maid
9. Ch. Jonz Heavenly Body	Ch. Helicon Madrona
10. Ch. Rockets Caipirinha	Ch. Another Episode Bouquet

Producers

Top-winning show dogs do much to determine type and quality desired in a breed, but it is the producers that pass on these traits to future generations. In spite of the fact that AKC Greyhounds are few in number, there have been some outstanding sires and dams in the breed in the United States.

Ch. Suntiger Traveler holds the all-time top Greyhound sire spot with 47 champion get. In 1990, he surpassed the record of Ch. Argus of Greywitch, who is in second place with 33 champions to his credit. Ch. Heathero Really Gallant sired 28 champions, and Ch. and FCh. Midnight Shadow Traveler UDTX, who was the sire of Ch. Suntiger Traveler, sired 27 champions. Ch. Aroi Blue Tiger Blues, Ch. Heathero Really British, and Ch. Shazam's The Journey Begins, JC have sired 26 champions.

Ch. Shalfleet Socialite is the top-producing Greyhound dam. During her years as a brood bitch, she produced 20 champions. Ch. Saga's Electra was the dam of 15 champions, and Ch. Blue Ghost Belphegore produced 14 champions. Ch. Aroi Follow The Sea and Ch. Huzzah Crestfield Calcutta produced 13 champions each.

Ch. Huzzah Tiger Lily, an excellent example of a Huzzah Greyhound.

Owned by Pat Ide.

Photo by Missy Yuhl

Ch. Gallant Somnombula, Best in Show winner, purchased by her owners for only one dollar.

Owned by Jack and Maggie Mitchell.

Photo by Missy Yuhl

Ch. Grey Roc Winged Victory, a multiple all-breed Best in Show and three-time specialty Best of Breed winner.

Owned by Bob Goldstein and Martin Miller.

Photo by Ashbey Photography

Ch. Gold Dust's Tintype, 1992 and 1993 GCA Eastern Specialty winner.

Owned by Bob and Joan Goldstein.

Photo by B. Kernan

Ch. Huzzah Mad Hattie, 1988 Best of Breed Eastern and Western GCA specialties.

Owned by Patti Clark and June Matarazzo.

Photo by Rich Bergman

Ch. Gallant's Late Arrival, 1989 Best of Breed winner GCA Eastern Specialty.

Owned by M. O. and Katie Lawson.

Photo by Booth Photography

Ch. Arborcrest Skyracr O'Kinnear, 1991 Best of Opposite Sex GCA Eastern and Western specialties.

Owned by Sharon Allert.

Am. Can. Ch. Wilrick's L'legante, 1991 Best of Breed GCA Western Specialty.

Owned by William and Patricia Simpson.

Ch. Rudel's Red Queen of Wonderland, 1990 Number One Greyhound Bitch; Top Ten Greyhound Breed and All Breed in 1990 and 1991.

Owned by Elsie Neustadt.

Photo by Chuck Tatham

Am. Can. Ch. Willomoor's Trick or Treat, 1994 Top Ten All Breed.

Owned by Patti Clark, June Matarazzo, and Maida Putterman.

Photo by Ashbey Photography

Ch. Suden Darlene of Waybroke, Top Ten All Breed 1992 through 1995.

Owned by Hubert Thomas and Madison Weeks.

Photo by Ashbey Photography

Ch. Hewly Hispanic II, Number One Greyhound All Breed 1992; Number One Breed and All Breed 1993.

Owned by Judson Streicher and Stanley D. Petter, Jr.

Photo by Booth Photography

Ch. Lulworth Garnish Enginuity, a multiple Group winner.

Owned by Arlene Leibing.

Photo by Booth Photography.

Ch. Rockets Elegy, 1994 Top Ten All Breed; BOB, 1997 GCA Eastern Specialty.

Owned by Mary Trubek.

Photo by B. Kernan

Ch. Sundridge So Be It JC, 1994 Best of Breed GCA Eastern Specialty, 1995 Number One All Breed.

Owned by Sue LeMieux.

Photo by Ashbey Photography

Ch. Huzzah Red Alert, 1994 Best of Breed GCA Western Specialty; Top Ten 1994, 1995, 1996, and 1997.

Photo by Rich Bergman

Ch. Arborcrest Danae CD, SC, a lovely, versitile multi-titled Greyhound.

Owned by Laurel Drew, El-Aur.

Photo by Vicky Cook

Am . and Int. Ch. Hewly Hard Hitter, 1993 and 1995 Top Ten All Breed.

Owned by Joni Lovci.

Photo by Rich Bergman

Ch. Shazam's The Journey Begins, 1994 and 1995 Top Ten All Breed, Number One All Breed 1996 and 1997, Breed 1996.

Owner Kim Fritzler, Jack and Maggie Mitchell.

Photo by Missy Yuhl

Ch. Martigra's Cupid's Beau, 1996 Top Ten both systems.

Owned by Marti Bradford, Martigra.

Photo by Pegini

Int. Am. Nor. Swed. Fin. Dan. Can. Ch. Gaia Sunridge Sunrise, a BIS winner in two countries.

Owned by Sue LeMieux, Espen Engh, and Astrid Knauber.

Photo by Walt

Ch. Gerico's Chasing the Wind, Number One in Breed competition 1995 through 1998.

Owned by Geri Ann Hendrick.

Photo by Rich Bergman

Ch. Rocket's Elegy winning Best of Breed at the 1997 National Specialty.

Owned by Mary Trubek and Susan and Mike Hoffman.

Photo by A&N Productions/Tim and Linda Nutting

Ch. Huzzah Sweet Molly Mallone, 1998 Best of Breed Western Sighthound Combined Specialties.

Owned by Don and Pat Ide.

Photo by Cook

Ch. Andarab Indigo Bunting, a multiple group winner.

Owned by Arlene Leibing.

Photo by Booth Photography

Ch. Legacy's Incredible Journey, Best of Breed First Annual GCA Southern Specialty.

Owned by Ric Metts and Dana Olsen.

Photo by Booth Photography

Ch. Sobers Zanthea, Best of Breed 1998 GCA Eastern Specialty.

Owned by Dr. Elizabeth Hanson and Debbie Butt.

Photo by Bruce Harkins

Ch. Argus of Greywitch, sire of 33 champions.

Owned by Drs. Neustadt.

Photo by W. Bushman

Ch. Shazam the Journey Begins, 15
champion offspring and top-winning
owner-handled Greyhound of all time.

Owned by Kim Fritzler, Shazam.

Photo by Missy Yuhl

Ch. Huzzah the Drumbeat, sire of 18 champions, including
6 specialty winners and 6 group winners.

Owned by Pat Ide.

Ch. Suntiger Traveler, top sire of all time, with 47 champions to his credit. Winner of ten All Breed BIS.

Owned by Linda Bell, Elsie Neustadt, P. Gail Burnham.

Photo by Charles Tatham

Ch. Downsbraugh Huzzah Tango, dam of 7 champions and grand-dam of 16.

Owned by Pat Ide.

Photo by Joan Ludwig

Ch. Legend's Loch Ness, Number One Greyhound Breed 1990, 1991, and 1992. GCA Eastern Specialty BOB 1990.

Owned by Pam Noll and Cindy Dengler.

Ch. Midnight Shadow Traveler UDTX, another top producer of 27 champions.

Owned by P. Gail Burnham

Am. Can. Ch. Gaia Tailor Maid, a BIS winner and top-winning Greyhound bitch All-Breed 1997 and 1998, and her sire, Ch. Jets Heads or Tails. Owned by Laurie Goodell and Judie Treuschel. *Photo by Booth Photography*

Sighthound Review graciously shared their records for top-producing sires, dams, and breeders from 1990 to 1995. The statistics for those years are as follows:

SIRES	DAMS	BREEDERS
	1990	
Ch. Skansen Corbett O'Arborcrest 5	Ch. Cherche Gale Force of Hounslow 4	Ann and Lisa Tater 6
Ch. Suntiger Traveler 4	Ch. Knigsmark Queen Ann's Lace 3	Pat Ide 5
Ch. Barbizon Frank de Roberjos 3	Ch. Shalfleet Socialite 3	James Elmquist 3
Ch. Heathero Really British 3	Ch. Tre Kronor Chewelah 3	Lawrence and Ann Schoolcraft 4
Ch. Kingsmark According To Hoyle 3		James Elmquist 3
	1991	
Ch. Suntiger Traveler 9	Ch. Heathero I Must Be Dreaming 5	P. Gail Burnham 7
Ch. Rich Pickings 7	Ch. Wilrick's L'legante 5	Elizabeth and John Gordon 6
Ch. Heathero British Sun 5	Ch. Shalfleet Socialite 4	Ann and Lisa Tater 6
Ch. Heathero Really British 3	Ch. Quail Roost Trifle Charwin 3	William and Pat Simpson 5
Ch. Huzzah All In Earnest 3	Ch. Suntiger Shadow Hawk 3	Judy Donaldson 3
		Elizabeth and John Gordon 6
		Irmgard Hill 3
		Brenda Adams 5
		Charles Wood 3
		A.G. Zippin 3
	1992	
Ch. Alzanna's Dallas 5	Ch. Kingsmark Jewel In The Crown 5	Ann and Lisa Tater 6
Ch. Kingsmark Scotland Yard 5	Ch. Another Episode Sunlite 4	J. Metzler and L. Transchel 3
Ch. Suntiger Traveler 5	Ch. Heathero I Must Be Dreaming 4	Judy Donaldson 5
Ch. Barbizon Frank de Roberjos 4	Ch. Shalfleet Socialite 3	Sally and Robert Park 3
Ch. Heathero British Sun 4	Ch. Wilrick's L'legante 3	Brenda Adams 4
Ch. Rich Pickings 4		William and Pat Simpson 3
Ch. Heathero Really British 3		Gail Burnham 4
Ch. Heathero Really Gallant 3		
Silverado of Holmby Hills 3		
Ch. Skansen Corbett O'Aborcrest 3		
	1993	
Ch. Barbizon Frank de Roberjos 5	Ch. Another Episode Partylite 4	Ann and Lisa Tater 7
Ch. Arborcrest Skyracr O'Kinnear 4	Ch. Seamair's Regal of Heathero 4	Pat Ide 3
Ch. Sundridge So Be It, JC 4	Ch. Gallant's Late Arrival 3	Cynthis Bellis-Jones 4
Ch. Thonmedia's Main Contender 4	Ch. Huzzah Alice Blue 3	
Ch. Blu-Kale The Hilton Freude 3	Ch. Huzzah Mad Hattie 3	
Ch. Heathero British Sun 3		
Ch. Kilanni Brown Bomber 3		
Ch. Legend's Loch Ness 3		
Ch. Ramachandra Windstorm Cebar 3		
Ch. Rich Pickings 3		
	1994	
Ch. Barbizon Frank de Roberjos 5	Ch. Arborcrest Ceres 3	(Minimum for 1994 was 5)
Ch. Another Episode Firelite 4	Ch. Cebar-Iveragh Out Of The Blue 3	Stanley Petter, Jr. 5
Ch. Hewly Hispanic II 3	Ch. Hewly High Water 3	
Ch. Hubbestad Double Magic, JC 3	Ch. Lochinvar Lacewing 3	
Ch. Ramachandra Wind Storm Cebar 3		
Ch. Rich Pickings 3		
	1995	
Ch. Hubbestad Double Magic, JC 6	Ch. Huzzah Downsbragh Briteside 4	Sue Cassem 6
Ch. Crestfield Sky's Salute O'Gerico 4	Paula from Quest 3	Sharon Allert 4
Ch. Huzzah Let Me Be Frank 4		Pat Ide 6
		Marti Bradford 4
		Ann and Lisa Tater 5
		Geri Ann Etheredge 4

BREEDERS IN NORTH AMERICA

A RICH HERITAGE

Breeders of Greyhounds in this country have been blessed with a rich heritage handed down from the great kennels and breeders of the past. Many of these kennels imported the very best Greyhounds in the world and have left a legacy to which present day breeders can aspire. Several of these kennels are profiled in the first part of this chapter, arranged in chronological order according to the date they first became involved with the breed.

J.B.

Joseph Zane Batten was given his first Greyhound in 1889, when he was only six years old, and he was seldom without one for the next 88 years. He was a charter member of the Greyhound Club of America and served as a judge at the first specialty show in 1923, and as president of the club for many years.

Mrs. Susan Mason of Little Andely's Kennels obtained her foundation stock from Mr. Batten. These were the black litter sisters, Ch. Little Andely's Dark Mist and Little Andely's Dark Appeal, and later the parti-colored littermate Ch. June Beauty. These sisters were sired by Foxden Flamingo out of Bernice, Mr. Batten's favorite bitch.

Two successful breedings out of another favored bitch, Town's Lady, produced three lovely bitches, Ch. Jennepher Blue (by Jungle Blaze) and Ch. Jocelyn Blue and Ch. Just Breezing (by Ch. Boughton Blue Lad). These three bitches were sold to Drs. Elsie and Rudolph Neustadt to provide a foundation for their newly established Rudel Kennels.

Mr. Batten served as a willing mentor to Mrs. Mason, the Rudels, and many other fledging Greyhound breeders. He bred "dogs, not paper," and was quite successful in his own breeding program and in the help and direction he extended to others.

Lansdowne

Ben Lewis, Sr. came to the United States from Wales and settled in Lansdowne, Pennsylvania. He and his son, Ben Lewis, Jr., were well-known, successful breeders and importers of great dogs.

From 1905 to 1925, the Lewises imported or bred more than 20 Greyhound champions. One import, Ch. Lansdowne Liskeard Fortunatus (officially Ch. Rosemont Liskeard Fortunatus), was purchased from Harry Peake (Boveway-Liskeard) of Cornwall. Fortunatus won 17 all-breed Bests in Show.

Ch. Lansdowne Butcher Boy was perhaps the Lewises most influential import. A white and brindle dog, he completed his championship at the age of seven and sired many good Greyhounds. A breeding to Butcher's Queen produced Ch. Master Butcher, who became the foundation dog of Mr. and Mrs. George West's Gamecock-Ewhurst Kennels.

Gamecock-Ewhurst

The Gamecock-Ewhurst prefix was a combination of George West's Gamecock Kennel, established in 1908, and the Ewhurst prefix Dorothy Fowler West had for her Greyhounds. Mr. West exhibited Airedales and Whippets as well as Greyhounds. The Wests' home and kennel were located near Boston, where Mr. West was involved in the formation of Boston's Eastern Dog Club.

Mr. and Mrs. West obtained Ch. Master Butcher from the Lewises as the foundation sire of their line. In 1928, Ch. Gamecock Duke of Wales was whelped, probably the best known of the West's Greyhounds. Duke of Wales was a multiple Best in Show winner and was part of a team (four dogs) that won Best in Show under Judge Harry T. Peters, Sr. at Westminster. Duke of Wales was the sire of several champions.

Mr. and Mrs. West favored Greyhounds that were parti-colored, sound, and that possessed good bone. They insisted on a dark eye and dark pigment. Many early Greyhound breeders based their lines on dogs produced at the Gamecock-Ewhurst kennels. Mr. and Mrs. West were actively involved in showing and breeding Greyhounds for close to 50 years.

Montpelier

Mrs. Marion du Pont Scott loved the hunt and had her own pack, the Montpelier Foxhounds. She also loved the sport of steeplechasing. She was an avid horse breeder and believed strongly in linebreeding. Her Virginia estate, Montpelier, was the ancestral home of President James Madison.

Giralda and Gamecock provided much of Mrs. Scott's foundation stock in Greyhounds. Some of her champions included Ch. Gamecock Daniel Webster and Ch. Montpelier Pibroch, campaigned by the Farrells (Foxden). Two bitches, Boveway Crystal and Ch. Grand Ways, produced several champions sired by Daniel Webster. Mrs. Anderson of Mardormere was the recipient of Mrs. Scott's best Greyhounds when her interest in the breed waned. Grand Ways, bred to Ch. Windholme Blank Check, produced Ch. Magic of Mardormere, probably the best Greyhound to come out of the Mardormere kennel.

Giralda

Geraldine Rockefeller was born in 1882, a daughter of the vice president of Standard Oil and a niece of John D. Rockefeller, Sr. In 1907, she married M. H. Dodge, the president of Remington Arms Company.

The Dodges owned a country home they called Giralda, located in Madison, New Jersey. It was on this 550-acre estate that Mrs. Dodge kenneled as many as 85 different breeds at one time. Mrs. Dodge insisted on the proper care and housing for her dogs. She imported many breeds from the finest foreign stock and helped establish several breeds in the United States. She founded the Morris and Essex Show, which was held from 1927 to 1957 on the polo field of Hartley Farms, Mr. Dodge's estate located two miles from Giralda. Mrs. Dodge was a highly respected judge in North America and Europe.

Geraldine Dodge was interested in Greyhounds for only about ten years, from the early 1930s to 1940s. One dog she imported from Peter George (Parcancady) was Ch. Giralda's White Knight. White Knight was sent to Margaret and William Bagshaw as a foundation dog for their Canyon Crest kennel. Other of Mrs. Dodge's dogs went to Mrs. Scott to help establish the Montpelier Greyhounds.

Mardormere

Mr. and Mrs. Anderson's beautiful kennels, located on their 200-acre Long Island estate, housed as many as 100 dogs at a time, including American Cocker Spaniels, Whippets, and Greyhounds. From the 1930s to 1960, the Andersons were active breeders, importers, and exhibitors.

Percy Roberts, who served as kennel manager for Mardormere, introduced Mrs. Anderson to Greyhounds and Whippets. Ch. Grand Ways from Mrs. du Pont Scott's Montpelier kennels was a foundation bitch for the Mardormere Greyhound line.

Some of Mrs. Anderson's well-known

Ch. Magic of Mardormere, winner of ten All-Breed Bests in Show and three-time winner of Group at Westminster. Owned by Mardormere Kennels.

Greyhounds, successful producers, and show winners included Ch. Yours Truly of Mardormere, Ch. True Elegance of Mardormere, and Ch. Elegant Lady of Mardormere (from one litter sired by Carnlanga Elegance ex Ch. Truly Fair of Mardormere); English import Parcancady Cherry, who produced Ch. Cherry Bounce of Mardormere, Ch. Truly Fair of Mardormere, Ch. Cheryl of Mardormere, Ch. Delight of Mardormere II, and Ch. Nighthawk of Mardormere. The Andersons exhibited only parti-colored Greyhounds. Mrs. Anderson was one of the first Greyhound owners to employ professional handlers to show her dogs. Percy Roberts, Bob Forsyth, and Harry Murphy (Desi Murphy's father) all managed the Mardormere kennels and took winning Greyhounds into the ring.

Mr. Stanley Petter, reminiscing about the great old kennels, recalls that "the most productive breeders, the most successful breeders, not in terms of the show ring, but in terms of producing these gorgeous dogs one litter after another, were Mrs. Mason's kennel, Little Andely's, and Mrs. Anderson's kennel, Mardormere. Those were the two who consistently mixed the two greatest strains available, Parcancady and Carnlanga."

In 1960, Mrs. Anderson gave several of her top Greyhounds—Vanity Fair of Mardormere, Ch. True Elegance of Mardormere, Ch. Elegant Lady of Mardormere, and Ch. Yours Truly of Mardormere—into the safe keeping of Mrs. Virginia du Pont and her Squirrel Run kennels.

Foxden

James and Emilie Farrell returned from their honeymoon in 1934 with two Irish-bred Smooth Fox terriers. These dogs, shown by Percy Roberts, were the beginning of a long line of Smooth Fox Terriers bred and exhibited by Foxden kennels in Connecticut. Foxden also housed Pugs, Lakeland Terriers, Manchester Terriers, Beagles, Whippets, and Greyhounds.

The Farrells' first Greyhound was an English import, Ch. Foxden Snowy, who was never bred.

Mrs. Farrell visited Harry Peter's Windholme kennels, where she was offered any Greyhound in the kennel. She obtained a blue brindle bitch that became Ch. Blue Heron, a great show dog. Blue Heron did much winning, despite her color, during a time when most breeders exhibited only parti-colored Greyhounds.

Foxden Greyhounds—"Happy," "Dart," and "Rocky." –Spring 1949.

During World War II, the Farrells imported Carnlanga Pirate from Jesse Prowse in England. His name was changed to Foxden Flamingo by the Farrells. He became an influential sire and appears in the background of many of today's Greyhounds. Some important Greyhounds in the Foxden kennels include Ch. Boveway Rosy Morn, a top contender imported from Harry Peake (Boveway) in England; Ch. Montpelier Pibroch, bred by Mrs. du Pont Scott; and Eng. Am. Ch. Shalfleet Starlight of Foxden.

The Farrells were actively involved with the GCA, and Foxden served as the host site for the National Specialty quite often over the years.

The Farrells, like Mrs. Anderson of Mardormere, employed professional handlers and kennel managers; over the years they utilized the expertise of Percy Roberts, Bob Nolan, Len Brumby, and Jane (Kamp) and Robert Forsyth.

Windholme

Harry T. Peters, Jr. grew up on Long Island surrounded by dogs. His father, Harry T. Peters, Esq., was quite involved with the Knickerbocker Hunt Set and was Master of Foxhounds of the Meadow Brook Hunt. He also kept Greyhounds.

In 1929, George West (Gamecock-Ewhurst) provided Mr. Peters, Jr. with his foundation stock, Gamecock Dashing Warrior and Gamecock Dancing Witch. Mr. Peters named his kennel Windholme and was active in Greyhounds for more than 50 years.

Mr. Peters imported quite a few English Greyhounds, including Ch. Feminine Wiles of Longue Vue, Ch. Lily of Devoir, Ch. Rose of Boveway, Boveway Beau Brummel, Ch. Picotee of Windholme, and

Stanley D. Petter, Jr. (Hewly) and Harry T. Peter, Jr. (Windholme) at the GCA National Specialty Show at Old Westbury, September 1973.

Ch. Viverdon of Ground Swell. Several of these imports became big winners in the United States and were used successfully in the Windholme breeding program.

Shalfleet Sovereignty, a later English import, was used by the Drs. Neustadt in the development of one of Rudel's main lines.

In the 1950s, Harry Peters, Jr. moved to Virginia, where he became Master of Foxhounds of the Montpelier Hounds. He left his kennel on Long Island in the charge of Henry Hohman and his daughter, Gail Volavka, who continued to breed and exhibit Greyhounds during the 1960s and 1970s.

Little Andely's

Susan Q. and Harding T. Mason's estate and kennel, Little Andely's, was located in New York. Susan grew up around purebred dogs, as her mother was a breeder of Smooth Fox Terriers and Pekingese. Mr. Mason was editor of *Newsweek* magazine for 24 years and then served as editor of the *New Yorker*.

It was in the 1940s when Mrs. Mason met Joseph Batten (J.B.), and through him her love affair with Greyhounds blossomed. Her foundation stock were the littermates Little Andely's Dark Mist and Little Andely's Dark Appeal (Foxden Flamingo ex Bernice). Both bitches proved to be exceptional producers.

Other Greyhounds owned by the Masons included Boughton Bane of Little Andely's, an English import from Bill Boggia's breeding; Ch. Boughton Blue Lad of Little Andely's, bred by Peter George (Parcancady); Ch. Little Andely's Dark Cloud II; Ch. Little Andely's Reflection (Gamecock); and Ch. Boughton Damsel of Little Andely's. She imported Parcancady Lancer, who had sired Ch. Treetops Hawk, but he died a few months after arriving in the States.

Mr. Stanley Petter remembers Mrs. Mason and her Greyhounds: "I would go up on the weekends from the University of Virginia and stay with Susie Mason and her enormous family at that wonderful place. They were generous with their time and their knowledge. I was interested and they wanted to pass the torch. I remember saying to Susie when we were just starting this exercise, we looked at dog after dog after dog and we looked at pictures and I said, 'Susie, I don't know if I'll ever learn anything about Greyhounds,' and she said, 'Yes, you will if you stick with it because you understand horses and you understand architecture. So just train your eye. Learn what they are supposed to look like. Learn balance, symmetry. Learn the standards.'

Ch. Boughton Blue Lad of Little Andely's. Owned by Mrs. Harding T. Mason. *Photo by Evelyn Shafer, courtesy Stanley D. Petter, Jr.*

"The Greyhounds were not in the house, but they were taken out and fiddled with, and they weren't in just runs, they had enormous places to play. They all had benches built up off the concrete. They had huge sleeping quarters. Nobody was cramped. Somebody was with them off and on all day. They had fun."

Mrs. Mason showed some of her own dogs and also employed Nate Levine to handle the Little Andely's Greyhounds. Little Andely's bloodlines provided foundation stock for Kay Morrell's Overrun kennels, and the Neustadt's Rudel Greyhounds.

Canyon Crest

Margaret and William Bagshaw's kennel, Canyon Crest, was located in beautiful Coldwater Canyon, in Southern California. Their first show dogs were Great Danes, but they also exhibited Miniature Pinschers and Whippets.

The Bagshaws became interested in Greyhounds during the 1940s and purchased their first Greyhound, Ch. Giralda's White Knight, from Percy Roberts. They bought other foundation stock from Foxden, Mardormere, and Montpelier kennels.

Some of their important Greyhounds included Ch. Canyon Crest's Hour Glass, Ch. Canyon Crest's How About It, Ch. Canyon Crest's What Of It, Ch. Canyon Crest's Splash, Ch. Canyon Crest's Boomerang, and Ch. Canyon Crest's Coronation, who became the foundation bitch of Stanley Petter's Hewly kennels.

Mr. and Mrs. Bagshaw realized the importance of good handlers, and over the years they employed the services of well-known greats such as Russell Zimmerman, Gus Hill, Harry Sangster, Percy Roberts, and Corky Vroom.

The Bagshaws' thoughtfully linebred Greyhounds were exhibited until the early 1970s.

Pennyworth

Mrs. Margaret (Peggy) Newcombe registered her kennel prefix, Pennyworth, in 1940. She showed American Cockers, Standard Poodles, English Cockers, and West Highland White Terriers, but is best known for her exceptional Whippets.

Mrs. Newcombe imported quite a few good Greyhounds from England in the 1950s. She imported two from Dorothy Whitwell (Seagift)—Eng. Ch. Seagift Parcancady Leader and Ch. Seagift Parcancady Heatherbelle. Other imports included Treetops Raven of Pennyworth, Ch. Seagift Snowfall of Pennyworth, Seagift Swell Dame of Pennyworth, Eng. Ch. Carnlanga Caramel of Pennyworth, and Ch. Treetops Penguin of Pennyworth. Pennyworth Sensation, bred by Ralph Parsons (R.P.), was used as a sire by Mardormere and Downsbragh kennels and was eventually acquired by Stanley Petter, Jr. (Hewly) from Mr. Brainard of Downsbragh Kennels.

Mrs. Newcombe bred only three Greyhound litters. Her most successful litter produced Ch. Pennyworth Peat and Ch. Pennyworth Repeat (Ch. Argus of Greywitch ex Ch. Overrun Thou Swell). Pennyworth Greyhounds won the GCA National Specialty three times: Ch. Seagift Parcancady Heatherbelle in 1951 and 1952, and Ch. Pennyworth Peat in 1970.

Mrs. Newcombe withdrew from the dog show world for a time to raise her children, but is once again an active breeder and exhibitor of Whippets and a well-respected and much sought after judge.

Squirrel Run

The Squirrel Run kennel prefix was registered with the AKC in 1938, when Mr. S. Hallock du Pont began breeding first Labrador Retrievers, then Clumber Spaniels. His wife Virginia (Ginny) bred English Cockers. She and Mrs. Dodge (Giralda) were instrumental in promoting the breed in the United States.

Mr. and Mrs. du Pont acquired their first Greyhounds in the mid 1950s through Mrs. Judy de Casembroot (Treetops), a leading breeder of Cockers and Greyhounds in England. The du Ponts imported Ch. Treetops Blue Gown and Ch. Treetops Flamingo as the foundation stock for their Squirrel Run kennels.

In 1960, Mrs. Anderson, who was phasing out her Greyhounds at Mardormere, sent several of her best dogs to her longtime friend Ginny de Pont. One of these dogs, Ch. Yours Truly of Mardormere, was Best of Breed at the GCA Specialty in 1962. Yours Truly sired the successful stud dog Squirrel Run Squire. Squirrel Run Greyhounds appear in the background of Hewly and Huzzah pedigrees.

Mrs. du Pont served as secretary of the Greyhound Club of America for many years. The du Ponts employed the services of two of the most highly respected handlers in the United States, Anne Rogers Clark and Jane Kamp Forsyth, both of whom are prominent judges in the dog show world today.

Rudel

Drs. Elsie and Rudolph Neustadt, both German psychiatrists, fled their homeland in 1938 and came to the United States. They brought their pet

Ch. Rudel's Reindeer Dancer.
Owned by Dr. Elsie Neustadt.
Photo by Evelyn Shafer

Ch. Rudel's Firefly.
Owned by Drs. Neustadt.
*Photos by William Brown and
Ward's Studio*

Greyhound, a retired racer named Ajax, with them. The first Greyhound obtained by the couple was also a retired racer. They owned five more Greyhounds before they began to seriously breed and show.

In the 1950s, the Neustadts established the Rudel kennels and began to show and breed Greyhounds. They purchased early stock from Mrs. Mason (Little Andely's) and Mr. Batten (J.B.). Three of these dogs were Ch. Jenepher Blue, Ch. Jocelyn Blue, and Ch. Just Breezing. Dr. Neustadt describes Jenepher Blue in her article in the March 1991 *GCA Newsletter's Breeders Forum.* "We felt she was close to our ideal. She did present the characteristics so important for a Greyhound, good head, neck, and shoulders, covering ground with good angulation without being overangulated, well chested, soundness and balance, not often found in a bitch of size. She was not perfect, no dog is. Where one could fault her was that she was somewhat narrow in front, but she was put together properly, presenting a picture of balance and harmony. Her temperament was sweet."

Ch. Jenepher Blue, bred to Little Andely's Well Away, produced Ch. Rudel's Solitaire and Ch. Rudel's Victor. Solitaire won the GCA Specialty in 1959, 1960, and 1961, and was all-breed BIS seven times. Victor was responsible for two bloodlines at Rudel; he produced Rudel's Royal Blue Princess, Ch. Rudel's Reindeer Dorothea, and Ch. Rudel's Firefly (ex Ch. Just Breezing). Blue Princess's owners, Roselle and Theodore Campbell (Greywitch), bred her to Ch. Sobers Orphie. A puppy from this breeding, Ch. Argus of Greywitch, held the title as the top sire Greyhound for many years, with 33 champions to his credit.

Ch. Rudel's Reindeer Dorothea, bred to Shalfleet Sovereignty, produced the BIS bitch, Ch. Rudel's Cupid. Ch. Rudel's Firefly held the honor of being the top-winning Greyhound bitch in the United States for a time. Firefly won the Group at Westminster in 1963, a Specialty Best In Show, 15 all-breed Bests in Show, and was the number one Greyhound from 1962 through 1966.

The Rudel breeding program was based on linebreeding with occasional outcrosses and has produced more than 40 champions.

In an article by Darlene Arden, "The Grande Dame of Greyhounds," which appeared in the February 1995 issue of the *AKC Gazette*, Dr. Elsie Neustadt explains what they look for in a Greyhound when choosing a show prospect. "From the very beginning we both recognized what is the most important thing in a dog: balance." Dr. Neustadt states unequivocally, "It's not important how a dog is made up in pieces, but it is important how that dog is put together. You don't know how good a dog is at a certain age unless you look for that particular balance. Naturally, nothing is perfect, but you always have to consider what is the priority."

Downsbragh

William Brainard, Jr. and his wife Patsy owned and bred dogs from the time they were a young couple. They successfully bred Smooth Fox Terriers, Border Terriers, Labrador Retrievers, Foxhounds, Cocker Spaniels, and Dandie Dinmont Terriers.

In 1959, the Brainards moved to their Virginia estate, where Mr. Brainard served as Master of the Old Dominion Hunt.

Mr. Brainard began breeding and showing Greyhounds in the 1950s. He obtained his foundation stock from Harry Peter's Windholme kennels. He also imported Carnlanga Elegance and Ch. Carnlanga Sceptre from Jesse Prowse.

Three great dogs bred by Mr. Brainard were Ch. Downsbragh Court Jester, Ch. Downsbragh Court Martial, and Ch. Valse, the 1957 National Specialty winner.

Mr. Brainard was a much sought after judge and was very involved with the Greyhound Club of America. He was a student of pedigrees and followed a strict linebreeding program.

Hewly

Stanley D. Petter, Jr. purchased his first Greyhound when he was only 18 and a student at the University of Virginia. But Mr. Petter's involvement with dogs, horses, and other livestock began from birth.

Mr. Petter, known as "Hi" to his many friends, received much of his knowledge about livestock breeding from his grandfather, who bred and owned Saddle Horses, English Springer Spaniels, and Bulldogs, and from his father, who kept sporting dogs. His childhood home was in Paducah, Kentucky.

Mr. Petter literally grew up on horseback and began riding competitively at a young age. This interest in horses led to his choice of careers in Thoroughbreds. He based his Hewly prefix on Hawley, a famous stallion.

Commenting on the Greyhound Club of America in the early days, Mr. Petter observes: "The Greyhound Club of America was not a buddy-buddy or-

Hewly Hirundine.

Owned by Stanley D. Petter, Jr.

Photo by William Brown

Ch. Hewly Harriet.

Owned and bred by Stanley D. Petter, Jr. and handled by Jeanne Millet.

ganization. It was a dog club and there were some very strong wills who were sincerely interested in the betterment of the Greyhound, and they were not necessarily good friends. They were fierce competitors, but they respected each other. The meetings went like clockwork. There was a small group of judges from whom specialty judges were selected and it did not matter that a judge might have passed on the same dogs a year or so ago." He goes on to say: "Everybody, I'm talking about the fifties and sixties when I first was so immersed in it, everybody had the same type in mind. There was no question of sloping pasterns. There was no question of a long foot. There was no question of a flat back, a sloping topline. Everybody had the same goals in mind. Ev-

erybody didn't achieve it in the same perfection. There were so few dogs available then. We were registering sixty-odd dogs a year, counting imports. I can't recall that anyone shipped a bitch from California to New York to be bred, which would have been a good idea. I don't know that any bitches were shipped from the deep south to breed to Foxden Flamingo. Stud dogs were completely regional."

Mr. Petter talks about his first two Greyhounds: "I started really knowing nothing. I had a track dog first. Perfectly gorgeous track dog. This was long before the rescue days. I was up in Nantucket for the summer and I was given this glorious dog. I thought there was something wrong. Surely they wouldn't give me a beautiful dog like that, and I insisted that the man take five dollars and give me a receipt. I showed him and because he was the dog in his breed, he won, and of course, he got nothing in the Group. The judge said, 'Nice going, son,' and I just grinned. Another judge came up to me and said, 'Of course you're never going to win anything with that dog,' and I was horrified. Then he said, 'I have a friend who's having to get rid of a very high-class bitch. Would you like to have her?' I said to a friend, 'Wouldn't it be neat if she were that bitch we saw in *Dog World?*' Well, lo and behold, that's the picture we saw in *Dog World,* the Tauskey picture of Ch. Canyon Crest's Coronation."

Ch. Canyon Crest's Coronation, "Cory," was the foundation bitch for Hewly kennels. When the Army sent Mr. Petter to France in the 1950s, he took Cory with him. Cory became a champion in France in 1957. Mr. Petter comments: "She won big in Paris, which is an honor because there's only one champion of each breed, each sex, a year in France and since the previous year's champion can compete, a champion in France means something. But they must win the Paris show and two Provincial shows." Cory won the breed at a show in Nice "in absentia." "She was entered and the Suez Crisis broke out. All leaves for American personnel were canceled. I called and said I couldn't come. I later got a letter saying 'We're so sorry that you couldn't come, and we understand that you have the best Greyhound in France, so we are awarding you Best of Breed anyway.' Only in France would that happen. The French love beauty."

Upon his return to the states, Stanley Petter and his wife Onnie established extensive stables and the Hewly kennels

at Hurricane Hall in Lexington, Kentucky. Mr. Petter imported several important Greyhounds from England: Eng. Am. Ch. Seagift Parcancady Bluebell, whose littermate Eng. Am. Ch. Parcancady Royaltan also came to Hewly; and Ch. Hewly Red Plume, bred by Ralph Parsons (R.P.). Mr. Petter obtained Pennyworth Sensation, also bred by Mr. Parsons, from Mr. Brainard (Downsbragh).

Some of the successful winners and producers bred at Hewly include Ch. Hewly Hypearion, Hewly Hircine, Ch. Hewly Harriet, Ch. Hewly Headstrong, Ch. Hewly Highbrow, who sired two Best in Show winners, one of whom was Ch. Hewly Histrionic, who won the GCA Eastern Specialty in 1985, 1986, and 1987 under the ownership of the Maytags and handled by Ken Murray.

After more than 40 years in the breed, Mr. Petter continues to breed and show his beloved Greyhounds. A recent multi-all-breed BIS winner handled by Sioux Forsyth, daughter of Bob and Jane Forsyth, was Ch. Hewly Hispanic II. "Nick" was ranked as the Number One Greyhound in all-breed competition in 1992, and all-breed and Best of Breed in 1993, under the ownership of Dennis Sprung. Nick now resides with Mr. Petter. Several breeders in the United States are currently breeding and showing Hewly Greyhounds quite successfully.

Greywitch

Roselle and Theodore Campbell's Greywitch kennels owned some of the top-producing Greyhounds.

In 1965, they purchased their first show Greyhound, a red Swedish import, from Astrid Jonsson (Sobers). The dog,

Ch. Argus of Greywitch held the record of top-producing sire (with 33 champions) until it was broken by Ch. Suntiger Traveler. Owned by Elsie Neustadt. *Photo by Evelyn Shafer*

Ch. Sobers Orphie, produced quite a few champions, including Ch. Argus of Greywitch, Ch. Rob Roy of Greywitch, Ch. Lotus Eater of Greywitch, Ch. Rudel's Rose O'Princess (ex Rudel's Royal Blue Princess), and Ch. Fawnglen's Fascination and Ch. Fawnglen's Oxbow Dispatcher (ex Ch. Fawn Jet), owned by Barbara Danis (Fawnglen).

Ch. Argus of Greywitch held the title of top-producing stud dog in the breed for many years until the record was broken by Ch. Suntiger Traveler. Argus sired 36 champion get.

Clairidge

Claire Kelly and Nancy Kulp were quite active in Greyhounds under the kennel name Clairidge for several years during the 1970s. Both women were actresses.

Ms. Kelly was a motion picture starlet, acting in films in the 1950s and 1960s. Nancy Kulp appeared in films such as "The Three Faces of Eve" and "A Star Is Born" and also appeared on the "Bob Cummings Show" television series and as Jane Hathaway on the "Beverly Hillbillies."

Their first litter, out of Ch. Aroi The Swinger and sired by Ch. Rudel's Reindeer Cupid, produced Ch. Clairidge Courier and Ch. Clairidge Cochise. Cochise was owned by Joni Lovci (Heart Hounds). Shalfleet Spanish Moon, whom they brought back from England, was the dam of their second litter sired by Ch. Argus of Greywitch. There were six champions from this litter—Clairidge Divinity, Clairidge Blue Heaven, Clairidge Starbuck, Clairidge Moon Racer, Clairidge Blue Moon, and Clairidge Angelic. Blue Moon went to

Ch. Clairidge Courier, the 1973 Number Six Greyhound. Owned by Joni Lovci.

Stanley Petter's Hewly kennels, as did Blue Heaven after Anne Bayless's (Seamair) death. Moon Racer and Starbuck were acquired by Seamair, and Angelic became an important dam at Pat Ide's Huzzah kennels.

Ch. Aroi The Swinger was bred again, this time to Ch. Argus of Greywitch. This litter produced five champions: Clairidge Bittersweet, Garbo of Clairidge, What Price Glory, Leeda of Clairidge, and Harlow of Clairidge Arrowsmith. From this litter Pola of Clairidge produced Ch. Anubis Shadowfire and Ch. Jano's Starfire of Anubis.

The last litter born at Clairidge was sired by Ch. Clairidge Starbuck and Ch. Rudel's Reindeer Mimi, obtained after much persuasion from Elsie Neustadt. Three champions resulted from this litter: Clairidge Kitty Hawk, CD; Clairidge Light Fantastic, CDX, TD; and Clairidge I'm Devine. The first two were owned by Patricia Gail Burnham (Suntiger).

Although Clairidge was active for only five years, Ms. Kelly and Ms. Kulp were quite successful, producing top winners and influential producers that have had an important impact on the breed.

Ch. Clairidge Kitty Hawk CD, dam of nine champions. Owned by Stanley D. Petter, Jr.

Greenglen

Mrs. Willard Wright, "Willie" to her friends, has owned Greyhounds since the 1940s and it is only recently, at the age of 80, that she is without one (for the moment). She has also owned, bred, and exhibited Great Danes, Borzoi, Scottish Deerhounds, Salukis, and Italian Greyhounds. Willie, who maintains a joy of life and incredible sense of humor, has many amusing stories to tell.

Mrs. Wright acquired her first Greyhound in 1941, a red brindle bitch named Meg. She remembers Meg:

"I taught riding and could send Meg out to round up the horses and bring them in. During the War, they would go out West and get a load of horses by train. When they arrived in Youngstown, they would be loaded into trucks and taken to the fairgrounds. One time a big white mare took off. All of the other horses went with her and there were horses running all over Youngstown. When we finally gathered them all up several days later, we took them to the fairgrounds where they broke loose again, following the lead of the white mare. I took Meg out and sent her after them. She would haze the white mare every time she tried to run, and she finally cornered the horses in the fairgrounds and held them there until we caught them.

"I was the official photographer for the fair, and between horse races we would entertain the people in the grandstand by releasing Meg at one end of the straightway on the track and time her as she ran to the other end. She could run the straightway in ten seconds."

Mrs. Wright was a good friend of Ralph and Barbara Parsons and used to visit them often. She recalls that they had many great adventures together:

"One time I was traveling with a friend and we all visited the Flyckt-Pedersens (Hubbestad). They wanted me to take a Greyhound home. We left without one, and later they called me at the Parsons's to ask if I wanted one. I said okay, and they met us at the airport with the dog. They brought all kinds of trappings for him, including a passport with his picture on it just like mine. My friend and I purchased duty-free liquor on the plane to bring into the States and we bought too much. You were only allowed so much per passport. So when we arrived in Pittsburgh and went through customs, the official said, 'You have way too much liquor.' So I pulled out the dog's passport and asked if it would count toward our quota. The official laughed and laughed and took that passport and showed it to everyone in the airport."

Mrs. Wright has been very active in Greyhound rescue work and has found homes for more than 20 Greyhounds. One of her rescue dogs is in residence at a nursing home and another is at a school for troubled boys.

Sundridge

James Smith Haring IV permanently registered the Sundridge prefix with the AKC in 1944. His home, Sundridge House, was located in upstate New York. Mr. Haring bred champion English Setters, Smooth Fox Terriers, and had a BIS champion Kerry Blue Terrier.

During the Second World War, Mr. Haring served as one of the original 13 men who trained dogs for the United States K-9 Corps.

Mr. Haring's foundation stock consisted mostly of English bloodlines, ac-

Sundridge Somewhere In Time, with owner James S. Haring IV.

cented heavily with Shalfleet. He imported a few dogs and purchased several imports already in the United States. In the late 1960s, Mr. Haring purchased Shalfleet Eaglelodge Bracken, a red brindle bitch, from Barbara Wilton-Clark (Shalfleet). She was bred to Eng. Ch. Shalfleet Silver Fortune while still in England and imported in whelp to the United States. Eaglelodge Bracken, her litter by Silver Fortune and the bitch, Hathor of Dendera, were the foundation stock of Mr. Haring's tightly bred Greyhound line.

Although Mr. Haring's business obligations prevented him from showing many of his Greyhounds over the years, the Sundridge line did produce several champions. When Mr. Haring became ill in the 1980s, he sold his home in New York and most of his Greyhounds. A bitch from this dispersal became Ch.

Sundridge Society of Khensu. When bred to Ch. Suntiger Traveler, she produced five champions, making her brood bitch of the year for 1989. A litter brother, Sundridge Sunstar of Khensu, owned by Maria Ferguson, was bred to Sundridge Sweet Leila, also owned by Ms. Ferguson. This union produced Ch. Sundridge Solarius Gold Dust and BIS, BISS Ch. Sundridge So Be It, JC, owned by Sue LeMieux (Gaia). So Be It was a BOB winner at Westminster, a multiple Group and all-breed BIS winner, a National Specialty BOB winner, and was ranked as the Number One Greyhound, all-breed, in 1995.

Mr. Haring's last litter out of Sundridge Somewhere In Time and by Suntiger Black Tardis produced a red brindle bitch, Ch. Sundridge Sagitta, who was Best in Sweeps at the 1991 Eastern Specialty. When bred to Ch. Jet's Heads

Or Tails in 1995, Sagitta, owned by Sue LeMieux (Gaia), produced five champion offspring, including two all-breed BIS winners, the Number One Bitch in the United States, two Number One Greyhounds in Canada in 1997 and 1998, and a multi-international champion.

BREEDERS OF TODAY

Today's Greyhound breeders carry on the traditions of the past, producing exceptional representatives of the breed. There has been a strong interest in the Greyhound as a performance animal as well as a show dog and many of today's dogs carry obedience and coursing titles along with their conformation championships. Many of these breeders have written to share their stories. Whenever possible, these have been arranged in chronological order according to the date they first became involved with Greyhounds.

Rockets

Mary Trubek of the Rockets kennel resides in New Jersey and started in Greyhounds in 1968. She writes: "A friend had a Greyhound and I decided to get one as well. Luckily, we found Windholme Kennels and I got a wonderful dog, Windholme Rocket. I have received a lot of advice and help from a Borzoi breeder, Karen Staudt-Cartabona of Majenkir Borzoi, who was a neighbor for many years. We would sit around and talk dogs (sighthounds) and study her pups."

Ch. Windholme Rockets Mardi Gras. Owned by Mary Trubek. *Photo by Ashbey Photography*

Am. Can Ch. Rocket's Anthracite, a multiple Group winner.

Owned by Donald M. Aronson and Paul B. Everitt.

Photo by B. Kernan

Ms. Trubek usually has five adult Greyhounds at one time and breeds a litter about every three years. The main emphasis of her breeding program is to "retain the soundness and functionality of the Windholme dogs with maybe a bit more 'elegance' and also to maintain good health and good temperament." Ms. Trubek is involved with breeding, exhibiting, and coursing activities.

Ms. Trubek has bred 16 champions and has owned 10 herself. Three of her favorites have been Ch. Windholme Rockets Mardi Gras, "a lovely bitch who was not enthusiastic about the show ring," BIS Ch. Rockets Elegy, and Ch. Rockets Midnight Traveler, a classic black bitch owned by Bonnie Violette (Toriani). Two Rockets Greyhounds, Rockets Miss Chief and her son Rockets Agaricus Rex were ASFA field champions. Ch. Rockets Elegy was the Best of Breed winner at the 1997 Greyhound Club of America Eastern Specialty.

Ms. Trubek gets the most pleasure from the success of placing a puppy or grown dog in a home where the humans and the dog each feel they have the better end of the partnership.

Ms. Trubek describes her ideal Greyhound: "A Greyhound should be as graceful as a ballerina and as powerful as Superman; a perfect balance between the two." She is concerned that breeders today "are developing too many 'looks' at various extremes and losing a lot of the functional aspects of the breed." She feels that the breed could be improved with "more open communication between breeders and the education of new fanciers." Ms. Trubek's success can be related to the fact that she concentrates on the conformation in relation to the original purpose of the breed and tries to produce an animal that is functional and at the same time beautiful. Ms. Trubek has been very active in the Greyhound Club of America, serving as the editor of the newsletter and as treasurer, among other positions.

March Hare

Linda Bell of Connecticut saw her first Greyhound in a dog pound in the late 1960s and thought she was the most beautiful dog she had ever seen. She went back the next day to get the dog, who had been adopted only ten minutes before. Still, Ms. Bell knew this was the breed for her and contacted the AKC to try to find a show dog. She was given the name of Elsie Neustadt (Rudel), who invited her to visit, saying she had a Greyhound but didn't know if it was available. Rose of Princess was the dam of that six-month-old puppy.

Dr. Neustadt interviewed Ms. Bell for more than an hour and a half before she was even permitted to see the puppy.

Ms. Bell did obtain the puppy from Rudel, and this purchase led to a life-long friendship between the two women. Ms. Bell wanted a more outgoing temperament in a Greyhound than the Rudel dogs exhibited, so she contacted P. Gail Burnham (Suntiger), whose dogs were multi-titled. She acquired Ch. Suntiger Winter Hawk, a lovely white bitch that she and Dr. Neustadt campaigned for awhile. Winter did quite well in the ring and had multiple group placings.

Eventually, Ms. Bell was ready for another Greyhound and went back to Suntiger for another puppy. Ms. Burnham had two from a litter. Although Ms. Bell had really wanted a bitch, as soon as she saw the red brindle male she fell in love with him immediately. Ms. Bell doesn't usually start showing her Greyhounds until they are about a year and a half old, but Dr. Neustadt wanted to know if she was ever going to start showing the male puppy. When he was about 12 months old, Ms. Bell showed him to Dr. Neustadt, who said he was the very worst puppy that she had ever seen! Ms. Bell said that she could never send him back as she had

Ch. Suntiger Traveler, top-producing sire of all time.

Owned by Linda Bell, Elsie Neustadt, and P. Gail Burnham.

Photo by C. Tatham

fallen in love with him, so Dr. Neustadt said they might as well finish him.

They gave him over into the expert hands of Richard Bauer, the Neustadts' handler, and when the brindle dog was shown the first time to judge Bob Tongren, he won the Breed over Winter and went on to a Group Three. The dog placed every time he was shown and finished at the Bronx Kennel Club show by winning the Breed and a Group One.

Richard Bauer loved the dog, and the dog loved to show. The dog, Ch. Suntiger Traveler, was a winner of ten all-breed Bests in Show and the Number One Greyhound for 1986 and 1987. Ch. Suntiger Traveler eventually became the top Greyhound sire of all time and holds that title to this day.

Ms. Bell sees the Greyhound breed as being in very good shape today. She feels breeders are in a renaissance period, and she likes to see the dogs coming into the United States from overseas. She agrees that the increased interest in performance as well as show titles is a positive direction in which to move.

Huzzah

Pat and Don Ide of California purchased their first Greyhound in 1970 from Georgiana Mueller. Prior to this, Pat had Afghans. She has owned most of the sighthound breeds and several Toy breeds, including Cavaliers, and has also had a French Bulldog, a Lhasa, and a Pointer. There are usually from five to ten adult dogs residing at Huzzah. Mrs. Ide mentions Bill Brainard as one who has given her many years of friendship and support.

Mrs. Ide writes about the foundation of her breeding program. Her comments first appeared in the *GCA Newletter's*

Ch. Aroi Follow The Sea, a BIS, BISS winner and top producer.

Owned by Pat Ide.

Ch. Huzzah Alice Blue, Ch. Huzzah One Moonlit Night, Ch. Downsbragh Huzzah Tango, Ch. Huzzah Downsbragh Briteside. Owned by Pat Ide. *Photo by Rich Bergman.*

Breeders Forum: "My first Greyhound was Ch. Aroi Follow the Sea (Brindie), who was very beautiful and elegant, moved adequately and possessed wonderful type. She was quite successful in the show ring, winning a specialty, a BIS, numerous groups, and the breed at the Garden.

"I bred Brindie to one of the last of Mrs. Du Pont's dogs, Squirrel Run Squire. The subsequent litter was of high quality, containing six group winners, eight champions, and several who became subsequent top producers. Ch. Huzzah the Drumbeat, FCh., is the one I kept for myself.

"Brindie's second litter was sired by Ch. Aroi Battle Royal, a son of the sire of her first litter out of Ch. Aroi Swinging Step. This litter produced six champions, three group winners, and several top producers. I kept a bitch from this litter, Ch. Huzzah The Bounding Main. She was bred once at Huzzah, but the litter, though containing a few really outstanding Greyhounds, was not of the consistent quality that I wanted to breed from. Later, she was bred again by her new owner to Drumbeat and this litter was really smashing. However, most of these did not make it into the show ring for one reason or another.

"I next purchased a bitch from the estate of Ann Bayless (Seamair), Ch. Clairidge Angelic (Ch. Argus of Greywitch ex Ch. Shalfleet Spanish Moon). Angelic was bred to Drumbeat and produced what I consider to be the foundation of Huzzah. Our foundation was not just one Greyhound, it was a combination of Brindie,

Squire, Argus, and Moon. From this combination, we produced nine champions, four specialty winners, four group winners, and three other group placers. Every subsequent litter has been bred from stock going back to the Drumbeat/Angelic breedings, with occasional outcrossings to mostly Shalfleet line, which we already had through Angelic.

"The type that was achieved from the genes of these four relatively unrelated Greyhounds was amazingly uniform and represented what to me is ideal type in a show Greyhound. No one individual was my "ideal," but the general type that was pervasive throughout the litter was just what I had hoped for. This is the type I have strived to maintain as 'Huzzah type.'"

Mrs. Ide usually averages one litter per year and tries to produce functional Greyhounds that are aesthetically pleasing. The more than 100 champions bred at Huzzah have included 10 specialty winners, 36 group winners, and 4 all-breed BIS winners. Of these champions, Mrs. Ide mentions some favorites: Ch. Huzzah the Drumbeat, Ch. Huzzah Tiger Lily, Ch. Huzzah Tigereye, Ch. Huzzah Alice Blue, and Ch. Huzzah Easy Sailing.

Mrs. Ide's goal in breeding has been "to produce Greyhounds that can function as they were intended and to refine their qualities to make them aesthetically pleasing as well. Some of the old coursing dogs were beautiful and some were not. It was only of passing interest to their owners how they looked. How they performed was more important.

"In the show ring how they look is important. In our kennel, it is also important, but only if their beauty is combined with the ability to function as Greyhounds have for thousands of years.

"This goal includes the 'refinement of

a good, useful Greyhound.' I use the term 'refinement' in its literal sense: make free from imperfections, vulgarity, commonness, make more elegant or cultivated; impart polish to. In selecting dogs with which to carry on, I pay careful attention to general balance and symmetry. I have never seen a good working Greyhound—field or track—that lacked these features, but I have seen too many in the show ring that do." Mrs. Ide feels breeders need to be diligent in producing functionally correct Greyhounds of reasonable size, and feels the breed would be improved by testing the dogs' ability to function well and attempting to reduce size to approach the standard.

"Size is of some concern to me also," she continues. "Our standard requires a weight considerably lighter than virtually every current show Greyhound. Some of the smaller bitches might weigh near the top of the limit for dogs, however. Regardless of rationalizations that may be given, this size as stated in the standard is the most desirable for a dog used in the sport of coursing hare, which is the historic activity of the Greyhound and is the reason for his existence these several thousand years. There have been several top winners, past and present, that have managed to be fairly close to the desired size—Champions Magic of Mardormere, Boveway Rosy Morn, Aroi Talk of the Blues, Rudel's Red Queen of Wonderland, and Alzanna's Eugenic Argonaut, to name a few.

"I know of some larger dogs that have much to offer the breed in quality, structure, balance, and type. Nonetheless, I try to keep in mind the desirable size for this breed and attempt to stay reasonably near it. Unfortunately, like the rest of us, I don't always succeed. Nonetheless, extreme size and bulk decreases speed and agility in the field, and this fact cannot be ignored. For thousands of years Greyhounds were bred for the organized sport of coursing. That some were used for other purposes does not change this fact. We would not have this wonderful breed if coursing lords and ladies had not developed and preserved it for so many years. The torch they have handed us is one of preservation of this wonderful breed."

Mrs. Ide is an internationally recognized Hound Group judge. The Ides' current winner is the beautiful red bitch, Ch. Huzzah Sweet Molly Malone. Molly is a specialty and group winner.

Cebar

Cebar Greyhounds are owned by Ellie and Cecil Creech and their daughter Dani Edgerton. Mr. and Mrs. Creech live in Maryland and Dani resides in Ohio. The Creeches got their start in Greyhounds in 1970 when Cecil went out looking for a dog that was of similar style to the Afghans, but without so much grooming. They have been enamored with the Greyhound ever since. Some early breeders who served as mentors to the Creech family were Georgiana Mueller and several of the English breeders, including Frank Brown (Shaunvalley). Between both homes they usually have eight adult Greyhounds. They have bred eight litters in their 27 years in Greyhounds and have bred for healthy, curvy hounds that have a free, easy gait and excellent pet temperament. Cebar has produced 30 champions, and the family has owned 13 champions themselves, which have all been stud puppies, except for their first two Greyhounds and their recent champion, Dogcastle's Xtravagance, co-owned with Robert and Mona Maytag.

The Creeches purchased their first Greyhound, a parti bitch named Ch.

Ch. Firebrand of Aroi, Cebar's foundation bitch.

Owned by Ellie and Cecil Creech.

Photo by Ashbey Photography

Ch. Cebar Iveragh Cold Blue Steel.

Owned by Ellie, Cecil, and Dani Creech.

Firebrand of Aroi, from Georgiana Mueller. In the early 1970s, Ellie and Barbara Henderson went to England—Barbara looking for a Whippet, and Ellie for a Greyhound. They returned with 13-month-old Am. Can. Col. Ch. Shaunvalley Anton, an Eng. Ch. Shalfleet Sir Lancelot son, purchased from Frank Brown. A breeding from this pair produced six champions.

The litter that had the most influence on the Cebar breeding program was one bred by Debbie Littleton (Iveragh), Ch. Greenglen's Blue Image to Ch. Shaunvalley Anton. This was a beautiful litter that produced seven champions. Every bitch bred from this litter produced champions. The Cebar line today is an intermingling of the Lance/Firebrand and Lance/Blue Image breedings with more emphasis on the latter.

A breeding of Am. Can. Ch. Wildwood Winsome of Cebar to Ch. Harbridge Heir Apparent was the next generation away from the Lance/Blue Image breeding. There were four champions in this litter, one of whom was Sherman's father. Sherman, one of Cebar's current winners and producers, Ch. Ramachandra Windstorm Cebar (Ch. Cebar's Artist Proof ex Ch. Ramachandra Sure Shot), goes back to those original breedings on both sides of his pedigree. Ch. Cebar Iveragh Out of the Blue, bred to Sherman, produced five champions who were great-grandchildren and great-great-grandchildren of the Lance/Blue Image pairing.

Dani Edgerton finished Ch. Dogcastle's Xtravagance, a Scandinavian import co-owned with Robert and Mona Maytag. "Chia" was bred to Sherman twice, and youngsters from these breedings have completed their championships. One puppy from the second litter was WB at the 1998 GCA Eastern Specialty and another was Best in Sweeps at that same show.

The Creeches' ideal Greyhound has muscles, curves, an open easy gait, long head and neck, and is happy and adaptable and full of strength and power while still being graceful. The Creeches are all quite active in Greyhound activities. Ellie is an artist who often contributes her work as trophies for the GCA specialty shows; she also judged the Sweeps at the 1995 Western Specialty. Ellie and Dani are both avid collectors of Greyhound art, and Dani is currently editor of the *GCA Newsletter.*

Legends

Pam Noll, who lives in Texas, saw her first Greyhound at a show and was quickly impressed by the breed's easy care and disposition. She bought a lovely bitch from Ann Bayless of Seamair Kennels in California. Although Ms. Noll used to have Afghans, she currently has only Greyhounds. She acknowledges both Pat Ide and Dr. Elsie Neustadt as breeders who have served to inspire her in her breeding program. She is involved with both conformation and coursing. Ms. Noll has one litter every three years or so and emphasizes quality and movement in her hounds. She has owned seven champions over the years, including Ch. Rudel's Ray of Starlight, her foundation bitch and the dam of three all-breed BIS winners; Ch. Legend's Treasure Island; and Ch. Legend's Loch Ness (Ch. Ranesaw Huzzah Raindancer ex Ch. Rudel's Ray of Starlight).

Ch. Rudel's Ray of Starlight is the dam of three all-breed Best in Show winners sired by two different males. Ch. Rudel's Rabbit of Wonderland and Ch. Rudel's Red Queen of Wonderland were sired by top-producing sire, Ch. Suntiger Traveler, and Ch. Legend's Loch Ness, also a two-time national specialty winner, was sired by Ch. Huzzah Let Me Be Frank. Star-

Ch. Rudel's Ray of Starlight, Legend's foundation bitch.

Owned by Pam Noll.

Photo by B. Kernan

light is also the dam of Ch. Wonderlands Mad Hatter, sired by Ch. Suntiger Traveler and Ch. Legends Treasure Island, sired by Ch. Huzzah Let Me Be Frank, two specialty winner dogs. She is also the grandam of Ch. Huzzah Red Alert, the GCA Western Specialty Best of Breed winner for 1994. Ch. Legend's Loch Ness is the sire of eight champions to date.

Ch. Legend's Loch Ness was Pedigree Award winner in 1990, 1991, and 1992. He was top Greyhound in all-breed competition in 1991. He won the Eastern National Specialty in 1990 and the Western in 1993. He is also the sire of the 1994 Western Specialty winner, Ch. Huzzah Red Alert (ex Ch. Huzzah Alice Blue).

Pam's goal for her breeding program is to continue to strive for excellence and "specialty quality" Greyhounds. She sees many excellent Greyhounds today in a variety of bloodlines and feels the breed is in a healthy position for the future. Ms. Noll is an artist and collector and is involved with dog club activities.

Suntiger

Patricia Gail Burnham has had Greyhounds since 1973. She is well known not only as a breeder of top-winning and performing Greyhounds, but also as an author of the obedience book *Playtraining Your Dog* and of countless articles on the breed. Through her writ-

F.Ch. and Ch. California Sunshine Traveler UDT, Versatility Dog Excellent.

Owned by P. Gail Burnham

ing she shares her expertise and vast knowledge with other members of the Greyhound world. Gail tells her story:

"As a teenager I obedience trained working and sporting dogs for myself and my neighbors. After twelve years of Collie hair, I decided that my next dog would be short haired. A friend had a charming Whippet bitch, but I wanted a larger dog. So I set out to obtain a Greyhound without ever having seen one. My first dog came from a shelter. He was a middle-aged brindle dog with a wonderful personality. He taught me about coursing and raised my first show puppies. These grew up to become FCh. and Ch. California Sunshine Traveler UDT, LCM, and FCh. and Ch. Midnight Shadow Traveler UDTX. They were born in 1973 and were from Seamair Kennel. Their names, Sunny and Tiger, gave me the Suntiger kennel name. I started obedience training them when they were three months old. They completed their companion dog titles at seven months and their utility dog titles before they were two years old. Then they went on to finish in breed and lure coursing.

"In 1975 I puppy sat for the last Clairidge litter of Nancy Kulp and Claire Kelly. I eventually took home two puppies: Ch. Clairidge Light Fantastic CDX and Ch. Clairidge Kitty Hawk CD. At that time I was a member of the Santa Barbara Kennel Club and the club later sent me to meet the legendary Barbara Wilton-Clark of Shalfleet Greyhounds at the Los Angeles Airport, in 1978. Two years later she brought me Ch. Shalfleet Stop the World and we toured California as she looked for a stud dog to take back to England. She found and imported Ch. Aroi Sea Hawk of Shalfleet, who would sire the last three Shalfleet litters.

"In 1979, I moved back to Sacramento to care for my parents and there I bred my first litter from Tiger and Kitty Hawk. When Barbara brought me Ch. Shalfleet Stop the World, she was bred to Tiger to produce Ch. Suntiger Traveler. 'Mr. T' went to live with Linda Bell and was shown by Richard Bauer for Elsie Neustadt of Rudel Greyhounds. Mr. T won ten all-breed Bests in Show and was the Number One Greyhound in 1986 and 1987. More importantly, he became the top Greyhound sire of all time. His forty-seven champions included three different best in show winners. Twenty of the champions came from his three litters with Eng. and Am. Ch. Shalfleet Socialite, (owned by the Taters' Another Episode kennels), which made her the top-producing bitch of all time.

"In the meantime I had become interested in the sport of tracking, where a dog is trained to follow a human scent. I started tracking in order to complete Tiger's titles and he became my first Tracking Dog and Tracking Dog Excellent. He was the first sighthound to earn the TDX. But then I went on to put TD's on seven different Greyhounds and a Tracking Dog Excellent on Tiger's daughter, FCh. and Ch. Suntiger No Greater Love. I eventually became a judge for both TD and TDX trials.

"In 1985 I received a letter from Barbara saying that she was going to offer for sale Eng. Chs. Shirley Anne, Shalfleet Socialite, and Shalfleet Stormlight, along with the unfinished Shalfleet Sea Dancer. I got very little sleep that night, waiting until it was a reasonable hour to phone her and make an offer for Shirley Anne. She was the last linebred Shalfleet bitch before the cross to Sea Hawk. I wanted her quite badly even though she was nearly six years old. In 1986, Shirley

Anne was BOB at the GCA's Western Specialty from the Veteran Class. She produced Tiger's last two litters for me, plus a litter by Ch. Suntiger Traveler, co-bred with Mary Trubek and Linda Bell. Nine of her offspring became champions in this country. Meanwhile, back in England, her daughter Shalfleet Sea Dancer finished her English championship and produced very well for Hubbestad, with many of her offspring being imported to this country.

"Annie and Tiger produced Tiger's final litter when he was thirteen. I kept a son and daughter from that litter, Suntiger Star Traveler CD and Ch. Suntiger Sheena CD. Sheena was Best in Sweepstakes at the 1988 Western Specialty and Best of Opposite Sex at the Greyhound Club of Northern California Specialty in 1993. Her brother was High in Trial in 1994 and the Veteran winner in 1994 and 1995 at the Western Specialty.

"I have been extremely fortunate in my experiences with co-breeders Mary Trubek, Linda Bell, John and Beth Ann Gordon, M. J. Barkley, and Kathy Leyba. And Barbara Wilton-Clark was very kind to let me have Stop the World and Shirley Anne.

"I once wrote an article for *Sighthound Review* on preservationist and designer breeders. I am a preservationist breeder. I liked my foundation dogs and would be happy if I could clone them. Instead, I breed older dogs to space out the time between generations. Tiger is starting to fall off the back of six generation pedigrees in parts of the country. At the same time I have his first generation kids living with me. I should be able to cover a twenty-five year span with three generations. I want to dilute the genes from my foundation stock as slowly as possible. So

I breed at long intervals and then cross back on my foundation dogs. By contrast, a designer breeder is breeding toward a goal he has not yet reached. He wants to fit as many generations as possible into a short time because he expects each generation to bring him closer to his ideal."

Ryal

Grant and Sue Cassem have been very successful breeders of Greyhounds for many years. Sue is a sculptor who did the drawings and comments for the illustrated standard chapter in this book. She shares the history of Ryal Greyhounds:

"We started in Greyhounds in 1973 and had our first litter (three puppies) in 1975, sired by Ch. Thadene's Grey Ghost (Ch. Aroi Blue Tiger Blues ex Ch. Solstrand Blythe Spirit) and out of the lovely leased bitch, Ch. Seamair Amulet (Ch. Clairidge Starbuck ex Ch. Seamair Wild Honey). We did not own Amulet, so we took the opportunity to purchase her full younger sister, Seamair Honeygold of Lincoln. Honeygold hated to show, so we bred her to Ch. Saga of Conar Mac Nessa, a Canadian import (Ch. Argus of Greywitch ex Can. Ch. Eaglelodge Laughing Water, imp. UK). We have lost the line out of Amulet, although it is still going in England, Europe, and Sweden through her granddaughter, Ital. Ch. Ryal Macaque, owned by Gilberto Grandi of Della Caveja Greyhounds, in Italy.

"We are now in our sixth generation down from Honeygold (who is on both sides) with our recent litter sired by Ch. Ryal Ramjet (Eng. Am. Ch. Hubbestad Double Magic, JC ex Ch. Ryal Bargain Hunter) out of Ch. Ryal Rumours, JC (Eng. Am. Ch. Hubbestad Double Magic, JC ex Ch. Ryal Chiclette).

Ch. Seamair Amulet, Ryal foundation bitch.

Owned by Ann Bayless.

Photo courtesy of Sue Cassem.

"Throughout the years, we have usually bred to dogs that have carried Shalfleet not too far back in the pedigree, finally culminating in the importation of Eng. Ch. Hubbestad Double Magic (Eng. Ch. Ransley Fortune Seeker ex Eng. Ch. Shalfleet Sea Dancer). For us he accomplished everything we wanted, consistently putting angulated front assemblies, front fill, substance, and sweet sensible temperaments on his pups.

"We have tried to produce a Greyhound that is beautiful and elegant (not too refined or narrow), yet substantial, clean moving on both ends, and having a coordinated, balanced, easy side gait

Ch. Ryal Rumours JC, 1999 GCA Eastern Specialty BOB winner from the Veteran's Class.

Owned by Sue Cassem.

Photo by Allen Photography

that appears effortless, but just eats up the ground."

Lakilanni

Laurie Soutar of Ontario acquired her first Greyhound in 1975, a "consolation prize" to herself when an Afghan bitch she wanted was unavailable. This first acquisition was a prize indeed, as it started Ms. Soutar on a more than 20-year odyssey in the breed. Ms. Soutar is very interested in the Greyhound as a performance animal and has multiple titles on all of her dogs. She feels that a Greyhound needs to be not only beautiful but able to perform its function as a coursing dog.

Ms. Soutar is involved in breeding, conformation, coursing, obedience, therapy work, breed rescue, amateur straight racing, amateur oval track racing, and lure coursing.

Ms. Soutar cites Jacqueline Hagerman of Kilanni Greyhounds as the person who has served as her mentor. She has no other breeds besides Greyhounds and usually keeps 12 to 14 Greyhounds at one time. She breeds once a year and emphasizes function, structure, health,

Ch. Lakilanni Daydream Believer. Owned by Laurie Soutar.

and temperament in her breeding program. Ms. Soutar is truly dedicated to producing a multi-purpose dog.

Some of the Lakilanni Greyhounds that prove that these dogs can "do it all" include:

"Denim" (Ch. Lakilanni Forever in Blue Jeans, FCh. FCHX), who was Number One Greyhound and Number Two All Breed for lurecoursing in Canada, breaking all previous Greyhound records for points in a single season (528), and she was BOS at the Greyhound Club of Canada's National Specialty—all before she was two years old. Denim won Best of Breed (The Fantasy Cup) at the 1996 International Invitational over an entry of 40 of the top coursing Greyhounds in North America—proving the show Greyhound can course if correctly built.

"Barely" (BISS, BIF Am. Can. Ch. Lakilanni The Red Baron FCh. TT, CGC, RTD) exemplifies a dual purpose dog, winning highest honors in both the field and in the show ring.

"Millie" (Ch. Lakilanni Silmarillion FCh.) was the number one straight racing Greyhound in North America for 1995, and was undefeated on the straight track.

"Aurora" (Ch. Lakilanni Aurora Am. Can. FCh. CD, CGC) was number 11 in the United States coursing, is NOTRA (oval track) pointed, has almost completed her open field title, and has qualified for a Grand Course.

"Tolkien" (Ch. Lakilanni Tolkien TT) sired 6 of the top 10 coursing dogs in Canada, and 3 of the top 20 in the United States.

"Arrow" (Ch. Lakilanni Broken Arrow FCh.) finished her championship at seven months of age and is currently in the top ten lists for both lure coursing and straight racing.

Ms. Soutar founded the Greyhound Club of Canada, has been named CKC "Breeder of the Year," and has owned three dogs that earned their international (FCI) championships. Ms. Soutar's goal is to promote and protect the Greyhound, its origin, purpose, and standard, and to encourage and educate newcomers to strive to breed the perfect multipurpose Greyhound. Her ideal Greyhound is elegant, balanced, muscular, and moderate. Ms. Soutar feels the breed could be improved by requiring FCh. and TT prior to awarding a championship, educating breeders about functional structure, encouraging and promoting performance events, and discouraging breeding for extremes.

Andarab

Lois T. Bires of Pennsylvania obtained her first Greyhounds, two males from Willard Wright (Greenglen), more than 20 years ago. She showed one of these for awhile, the male sired by Royser Poner (bred by Ralph Parsons, R.P.), but became truly interested in showing and breeding six years ago. Mrs. Bires attended a show where Dr. Elsie Neustadt had entered Ch. Rudel's Firefly. Mrs. Bires describes Firefly: "She was stunning, and my interest in Greyhounds started with her. Firefly was regal and had a aura of elegance so that it was hard to take your eyes off of her."

Mrs. Bires writes about the Andarab Greyhounds: "My initiation into Greyhounds so many years ago was with the help of Willard Wright. Then about six years ago, the late Nancy MacLean set Calla, a Ch. Barbizon Frank de Roberjos daughter, in front of me and my mind clicked into the dog show mode. Since then I have had a lot of fine help, advice, and conversation from Obie Peck (Lulworth), Sue Cassem (Ryal), and Larry Shaw (Kirklea). Each of the people

Ch. Andarab Sea Lavender.

Owned by Lois T. Bires.

Photo by Booth Photography

Ch. Ryal Ramjet.
Owned by Lois T. Bires.
Photo by Booth Photography

who have helped me have many years of experience in the breed."

Mrs. Bires began showing and breeding Afghans more than 30 years ago. She owned Ch. Alde'Barbe's Tabu, who finished her championship from the puppy classes and went on to become an outstanding producer in the breed.

Mrs. Bires believes that it is more important to breed to type than to breed from pedigrees, and she breeds for type and soundness. She hopes others will find her dogs useful for carrying on the breed.

The Greyhounds now residing at Andarab are as follows: Ch. Conamor Calla of Andarab (by Ch. Barbizon Frank de Roberjos), Ch. Ryal Ramjet (by Eng. Am. Ch. Hubbestad Double Magic), Ch. Kirklea Andarab Autumn Haze (sire closely bred to Eng. Ch. Royal Portrait), and homebreds, Ch. Andarab Wild Oats, Ch. Andarab Sea Lavender, and Ch. Andarab Forget-Me-Not. Her current special, who is doing quite well in breed and group competition, is a black dog, Ch. Andarab Magic Raven.

Mrs. Bires's ideal Greyhound possesses elegance and soundness without coarseness or weediness. She feels there is a lot of variety in type in the breed today, but feels that this gives future breeders a variation in the gene pool. She feels that one area that needs improving is movement, and she thinks emphasis should be on structure and not on eye or coat color: "For me a Greyhound should be an elegant dog with enough substance and body to have stamina in the field, with graceful side movement and soundness coming and going."

Marquis Hounds

Susan Obert of Marquis Hounds started showing dogs in the late 1970s. She started with Afghan Hounds, and she has owned, bred, and shown many wonderful and champion Afghans. Ms. Obert firmly believes in breeding the best in quality, not quantity.

Ms. Obert had always admired Greyhounds at shows and tried to watch them whenever there was an entry. She

Ch. Shamboo's Unruly of Quest.

Owned by Sue Obert.

Photo by Earl Graham Studios

is attracted to all sighthounds, and she finds them very different from many of the other breeds she has known in her experience showing, grooming, or training. Ms. Obert's search for a Greyhound resulted in finding a bitch, Ch. Shamboos Unruly Of Quest, who was specialed for a time. Ms. Obert then acquired her daughter, Coggshalls Morning Dove, finished her championship, and bred her to Ch. Artesia Gin and Jaguar, a Ch. Rich Pickings son she also owned.

Ms. Obert kept four champion get from this breeding and plans to go on from there. She also owns several other champion Greyhounds that she intends to use in her breeding program. Ms. Obert believes that this is not a breed for all people and has kept her breeding to a minimum. She likes to think that the dogs she breeds will be loved and understood first and shown second. Her goal is to preserve the breed at its best and help educate anyone who is owned or wants to be owned by a Greyhound.

Hounds of Delight

Mary Jeanette (M. J.) Barkley of Colorado has had Greyhounds since 1974. Her first Greyhound was an adopted ex-racer, and when that dog died Ms. Barkley purchased her first show Greyhound. Although Ms. Barkley does not consider herself a breeder (she has had two litters in 20 years), she feels that it is important to breed for balance, good movement, and intelligence. She has bred three champions and owned four: Ch. El Aur Talk About Delight, Ch. Holmby Hills Firefly Delight, Ch. Suntiger Desert Rose, and Ch. Suntiger Black Magic. She shows in conformation and obedience, does therapy work with her dogs, and takes them swimming and camping.

Ms. Barkley feels a Greyhound should be well balanced in body and movement and intelligent with a good personality. She believes the importation of Greyhounds from other countries is one good way to improve and expand the gene pool in the United States.

Aryals' Freedom Flight.
Owned by M. J. Barkley.

Golightly

Stacy Pober, whose home is in New York, got her start in Greyhounds in 1982. Ms. Pober tells how she first became attracted to the breed: "I had been lure coursing with another breed of dog. I was impressed with the Greyhounds, both in their speed and consistent running ability, and in their mild and stable temperaments."

Ms. Pober has received help and guidance from P. Gail Burnham (Suntiger). "Gail was a source of inspiration with her multi-titled hounds, and she was always generous with advice and help." Janis Hill, a Scottish Deerhound breeder, taught Ms. Pober about sighthound conformation and movement and helped to give her perspective.

Ms. Pober seldom breeds her dogs, but usually has four or five Greyhounds.

She looks for soundness in all things in her Greyhounds: "sound temperaments, sound gait at a trot and a gallop." She tries to produce dogs that can excel in multiple fields of endeavor—coursing, showing, and obedience.

Ms. Pober has bred four show champions, three ASFA lure coursing champions, two AKC lure coursing champions (these two are AKC dual champions), and three CD title holders. She has owned six show champions and four ASFA coursing champions.

The Golightly Greyhounds are performance oriented and participate in conformation, lure coursing, open field coursing, and obedience. Ms. Pober shares some of her dogs' successes:

Ch. Morley's Sue, FCh., CD, LCM2 (Tiger Lily) finished her field championship, lure courser of merit, and companion dog titles in the same 12-month pe-

Ch. Golightly Dakota Sioux SC and Ch. Golightly Ado Annie JC.

Owned by Stacy Pober.

Photo by Rich Bergman

riod. She is one of the few dogs in the breed to hold the Versatility Certificate Excellent from the GCA. She was the number-one lure coursing Greyhound in the country in her youth and stayed in the top four for three successive years. She is a five-time Best in Field winner, winner of the Grand Prix Challenge Cup and the New England Cup, and she is the mother of two dual champions who are also CD degree holders.

Dual Ch. Can. Ch. Golightly Really Rosie, SC, FCh. Am./Can. CD, CGC (Rosie) is the first AKC dual champion in the breed. She is a winner of four Bests in Field, has a GCA Versatility Certificate, and is NOFCA pointed.

Dual Ch. Golightly Runaround Sue CD, SC, CGC (Suki)—is a Best in Field winner, dam of champions, NOFCA pointed, and has qualified for the GCA Versatility Certificate.

Ms. Pober hopes to produce other dogs that can hold their own in the show ring and on the coursing field. Her ideal Greyhound is sweet in expression but strong in build, with curves of muscle and sinew conveying the picture of power and speed that becomes evident when the dog is put to the test and shows its speed and control. She would like to see more breeders aiming at the "total Greyhound" and trying to produce dogs that excel in more than one arena.

Southwestern Hounds

Southwestern Hounds was established in 1984 by Greg Davis and Roger Owens, who spent several years searching for the ideal Greyhound type. Although the show records and history of the breed played a large role, their final decision was made after seeing the Shalfleet Greyhounds from England. It was upon those Shalfleet lines that Davis and Owens would ultimately base their kennel and breeding program.

Their first greyhound was "Frosty," Ch. Another Episode Frostlite, who was out of Eng. Am. Ch. Shalfleet Socialite by Ch. Suntiger Traveler. Frosty was bred to her uncle, Eng. Am. Ch.

Ch. Southwestern Episode My Man.

Owned by Roger Owens and Greg Davis.

Photo by Allen Photography

Shalfleet Stormlite; this litter produced BIS Ch. Southwestern Episode Holly, a Number One Greyhound with five Bests in Show. It also produced Ch. Southwestern's Silver Moon, who won the Breed at Westminster in 1994; she was also a multiple Award of Merit winner at GCA specialties.

Davis and Owens purchased Frosty's litter sister, Ch. Another Episode Skylite, and bred her to Ch. Alzanna's Dallas. This breeding produced six champions, including Ch. Southwestern Episode Beauty, who garnered three majors in three days at the GCA National Specialty and supported entries.

Davis and Owens then bred Beauty to Ch. Barbizon Frank de Roberjos. This litter is following the tradition of Southwestern Hounds. The first to finish did so with 3 five-point majors in a single weekend, at less than one year of age.

Davis and Owens have been fortunate in having top breeders, top show dogs, and most importantly, cherished family companions.

Wilrick

One of the most prominent Greyhounds of the mid-1980s and early 1990s was the beautiful bitch Multi BIS and BIS Am. Can. Ch. Wilrick's L'legante, "Laly," owned by William R. and Patricia Simpson of Missouri. In L'legante's six-year career, she managed to win some two dozen groups and a multitude of group placements, a remarkable feat considering that she was always owner handled and was shown sparingly due to her owners' careers. She was bred by Barbara Page, DVM, sired by BIS Ch. Alzannas Eugenic's Argonaut and Ch. Lake Prairie's Osage Princess. She was the first Greyhound for the Simpsons, who had owned and shown Doberman Pinschers for many years.

Laly's show career was meteoric in that she finished her American championship in three consecutive shows with 3 five-point majors over Specials and a Group One on her first day as a Special. She finished her Canadian championship in

L'legante's seven champion pups at ten months of age. Bred by Pat and Bill Simpson. *Photo by Downey Photography*

three days, giving her a dual championship before she was 15 months old. She won her first BIS before her second birthday. She was in the top ten in the United States for six years and in the top five in Canada for five years. Her greatest performance came in her only trip to the Western Sighthound Specialty in California in 1991. Not only did she win the Breed at the specialty under the noted Swedish judge Dr. Göran Bodegård, but she also won BOB all three days, the only Greyhound to go undefeated in the Breed at these shows. Her only trip to the Eastern Specialty was also rewarding, as she became the winner of the first Veteran's sweepstakes and earned an Award of Merit from the Veteran's Class.

The day Laly retired in 1991, after the Western Specialty, she was number one in breed points. She was shown on a very limited basis, in Veteran's Classes, from which she still won Breeds, Group placements, and a Group One.

Valued primarily for her companionship as a family member, Laly has also proven her worth as a producer. Bred only one time, she produced 9 champions out of a litter of 11. The sire of her only litter was the very sound Ch. Heathero British Sun, owned by Bob and Shari Mason (Blu-Kale) of Oklahoma. This litter made her number one in the breed, tied for first in the Hound Group, and tied for number four all-breeds for the number of champion get in 1991. All of her pups were owner handled to their championships and several are group winners with many group placements.

The Simpsons take great pride in Laly's influence upon the breed and especially the interest in Greyhounds that helped place more than 30 Greyhounds in loving homes.

Willomoor

Willowmoor Greyhounds came into being quite by accident. June Matarazzo had been breeding Afghans under the name Willomoor for more than 25 years and had owned several

Huzzah Greyhounds, including the specialty winner Ch. Huzzah in Pursuit of Happiness, co-owned with Dennis and Susan Sprung. Patti Clark had shown Dobermans and Shepherds in the obedience ring for about ten years. Clark and Matarazzo met when they each bought a pet-related business from one owner, Clark purchasing a boarding kennel and Matarazzo a grooming shop. Matarazzo was having some training-related problems and brought Huzzah and All That Jazz ("Mona") to the kennel for some behavior modification and show training. Patti and Mona were the perfect combination and were in the show ring after about three months, winning a group placement the second time out. Mona finished quickly and went on to place in the group many more times in her career. With patience, wit, and some criticism, Matarazzo instructed Clark on the fine art of owner handling, and a partnership emerged. As

thanks for finishing Mona, Matarrazo made Clark co-owner, and every Greyhound of theirs since has been co-owned or co-bred.

The pair next purchased Ch. Huzzah Mad Hattie, a leggy, well-angled red brindle bitch, who started her specials career by going BOB at Westminster Kennel Club. Hattie won the Eastern and Western GCA Specialties that year (1988) and was a multi-Group winner and the foundation of the Willomoor Kennel.

Ch. Downsbragh Huzzah Holystone, "Ian," was their next West Coast purchase, a typey blue brindle male who finished with breeds from the classes over specials to get his majors. While very pretty, Ian was not the ticket for Hattie puppies.

Hattie was bred to the Am. Can. Ch. Thonmedia Main Contender, owned by Maida Puterman of Canada, and produced a lovely litter of red brindles and red brindle parti-colored pups

Can Ch. Willomoor Thonemedia Warlock.

Owned by Maida and James Putterman.

Photo by Alex Smith

Am. Can. Ch. Willomoor Jack O'Lantern and Am. Can. Willomoor Trick or Treat. Owned by Patti Clark and June Matarazzo. *Photo by Alex Smith*

with very little brindling. These puppies went to the Eastern Specialty in 1992 and did some wonderful winning that weekend. Am. Can. Ch. Willomoor Trick or Treat, "Trixie," started things off by winning the sweepstakes. Trixie's career has included a BOS at the Western GCA Specialty, a Group One, and many other Group placements. Her brother, Am. Can. Ch. Willomoor Jack O'Lantern, "Manny," won the Bred-by-Exibitor Class and went on to compete for Winners Dog at the specialty. Ch. Willomoor Ghostbuster, a littermate shown in the 9- to 12-month Puppy Class went on to win Winners Dog, and Hattie won an Award of Merit and Brood Bitch for the year.

Manny has gone on to be a Group-placing dog and the top Greyhound in Canada in 1994. He and Trixie won BOB and BOS from the classes at the Ontario Sighthound Specialty. Another brindle male from the litter, Can. Ch. Willomoor Thonmedia Warlock, is a BIS dog in Canada.

In the kennel's second breeding, Hattie was bred to Ch. Legend's Loch Ness, and their puppies are scattered all over the country.

Willomoor Divine Madness from the above mentioned litter was bred to the Australian import, Ch. Jonz Devil Made Me Do It. Several puppies from that litter have finished their championships, including Ch. Willomoor Double Feature, who was WD, BOW at the 1998 GCA Eastern Specialty, and went on to receive an Award of Merit.

Matarazzo and Clark believe that they should support show puppy buyers with as much help as possible, including the actual handling and picking of shows if that is what an owner wants. They also try to stay in touch on a regular basis with both pet and show owners.

Fox Run

Cindy Bellis-Jones has had Greyhounds since 1988, but she has admired them since 1974. Cindy had grown up around dogs, and her father raised Shetland Sheepdogs. She feels that he has been her greatest inspiration in dogs, as she always admired how he cared for and bred his Shelties.

Mrs. Bellis-Jones bought her first Whippet in the 1970s, and she and her husband Hugh, who is from Wales, purchased another one in 1979 from English breeder Dr. G. C. Usher, who was secretary of a whippet club in the United Kingdom. Mrs. Bellis-Jones purchased her first Greyhound, Ch. Another Episode Partylite (Ch. Suntiger Traveler ex Ch. Shalfleet Socialite), from Ann and Lisa Tater and finished her championship in very limited showing. She then obtained another puppy from the Taters,

who grew up to be Ch. Another Episode Sunny Day.

In 1992, Mrs. Bellis-Jones bred Partylite to Ch. Sundridge So Be It, JC. The five puppies from this litter that were shown all completed their championships at a very young age, making Partylite the Number One Brood Bitch in Greyhounds for 1993. From a second litter (by Ch. Alzanna's Dallas) co-bred with the Taters, Mrs. Bellis-Jones has a lovely blue bitch, Another Episode Hunting Party, who won the Breed over Specials and a Group Four the first time she was shown in the puppy class.

Mrs. Bellis-Jones, who breeds only rarely, is involved with many other animals. She does wild animal rehabilitation work and has Thoroughbred horses and Llamas. Mrs. Bellis-Jones, who is treasurer of the Blue Grass Coursing Club, says that she could never be without a Greyhound. She has found no

Ch. Another Episode Partylite.

Owned by Cindy Bellis-Jones.

Photo by Baines Photography

other dog to be as enjoyable a companion. She admires a combination of elegance and soundness and correct structure in her ideal Greyhound.

Enginuity

Arlene Liebing purchased her first Greyhound from Mary Ellen (Obie) Peck (Lulworth). Her daughter Alissa was working as a vet tech and fell in love with the look and personality of Obie's dogs when they were brought into the vet's office. It took two years of waiting for a litter, and in 1989, Ms. Liebing bought a puppy that became Ch. Lulworth's Garnish Enginuity, "Parsley." Parsley was shown by Norma Gibson and Alissa for three years and was ranked as the Number Two Greyhound Bitch each of those years. She was a multiple group winner.

Ms. Liebing then purchased a puppy who finished quickly, Ch. Conamor Quite Frankly. Ms. Liebing's first litter by Ch. Conamor Quite Frankly and Ch.

Lulworth's Garnish Enginuity has given her Ch. Enginuity Alluring Reflection, who is already a multiple group-placing Greyhound. Ms. Liebing wants to maintain the quality she now has in her dogs and hopes that Greyhound breeders will always be able to see the quality in other dogs and will breed to produce the very best Greyhounds.

Skyracr and Gerico

Sharon Allert (Skyracr) and Geri Ann Etheredge (Gerico), both of Texas, have formed a partnership in the last few years that is producing and campaigning some of the top-winning Greyhounds in the United States today. Ms. Allert writes about their partnership, breeding program, and Greyhounds:

"I started with a Scottish Deerhound. I still love and own Deerhounds, but I did not really have much success until I got our first Greyhound, Ch. Arborcrest Skyracr O'Kinnear. Geri Ann, whose Greyhounds go back to the Quest lines,

Ch. Jet's the Boy Next Door.

Owned by Sharon Allert.

Photo by Rich Bergman

Ch. Mrtgr. Skyracr Flame O' My Heart.
Owned by Sharon Allert and Charlotte Fielder.

Photo by Tom Bruni

contacted me about breeding Ch. Quest Paige Touched Me to Skyracr. At that time there were still a couple of puppies available from what turned out to be Skyracr's only litter. This litter was co-bred with Charlotte Fielder, whose mother, Martha Fielder, handled Skyracr through his short but successful show career. Geri Ann decided to buy one of the puppies from the litter, Ch. Crestfield Sky's Salute O'Gerico "JR." Geri Ann's dreams of a Paige/Skyracr litter never materialized due to Skyracr's accidental death in 1993 at the age of three and a half years.

"We kept in close touch and discovered we shared common ideas and goals and an admiration for several of the Scandinavian Greyhounds and their breeders. Shortly after losing Skyracr, we found that Espen Engh (Jet's) had a litter on the way that was very tightly linebred on the Scandinavian lines in which we were interested. Espen agreed to consider us as a home for a puppy if there was one good enough to suit our needs. The subsequent litter was all males. We felt one of them would be a very positive addition to our plans; therefore, we became the proud owners of our first import, Ch. Jet's The Boy Next Door, "Cruise." Shortly after Cruise was imported, I moved to Texas.

"Geri Ann still wanted a bitch and we both wanted to bring in more of the Scandinavian bloodlines to further implement our vision of the future. Shortly before the 1994 Western Specialty, Espen let us know he had bred Hildur (Ch. Jet's Headed Like A Snake) and offered us a puppy. After negotiations, two bitches from the litter were imported, Ch. Jet's Ravishing Redhead (Nichole) and Ch. Jet's Heading For The Top (Lacey).

"Neither Geri Ann nor I have been involved in Greyhounds a great length of time, but we are proud of our success. Skyracr received recognition at every specialty he attended. He was Winners Dog, Best Opposite in Sweeps, and Best

Puppy at the Western Specialty in 1990. In 1991, he was BOS at the Eastern National, the Western National, and the Northern California Specialty. In 1992, he won an Award of Merit and the Stud Dog Class at the Western. He closed out his specialty career with a BOB at the Northern California Specialty.

Two of Skyracr's litter have been specialty BOB winners—JR won the Northern California Specialty in 1993; his litter sister Ch. Crestfield Camille went BOS; and Ch. Crestfield Sky's Sunsation (Sam) won the 1995 Western Specialty, with litter sister Camille again earning BOS. JR's daughter, Ch. Mrtgr Skyracr Flame O'My Heart, won an Award of Merit at the 1995 Eastern Specialty. Ch. Gerico's Chasing the Wind (Chase), a son of JR and Paige, was the Number One Greyhound (breed competition) in 1995 and 1997. He has since won multiple all-breed BIS and Specialty BIS and was ranked as the Number One Greyhound, breed and all breed competition in 1998. In addition, Cruise was Best of Winners and Best in Sweeps at the 1994 Western, and Nichole earned an Award of Merit at the Eastern Specialty in 1995 and BOB at the Westminster Kennel Club show.

"We are very pleased with the results of our breeding program to date, and have spent a lot of time discussing and planning for the future. We feel fortunate to have access to the animals and bloodlines we currently have and blessed to have had the success and support we have received."

Sporting Fields

The Sporting Fields Kennel, owned by Mr. and Mrs. James E. Butt, was first registered in the 1940s. In the late 1960s, they acquired their first Whippets and quickly became one of the best-known, most successful breeders and exhibitors of this diminutive sighthound breed. From the 1970s through the present, Sporting Fields Whippets have consistently won top honors in the dog show world. Some of these much-admired winners and producers include Ch. Sporting Fields Clansman, Ch. Sporting Fields Strider, and Ch. Sporting Fields Kinsman, who was shown to the number one spot by the Butt's daughter, Debbie.

Debbie and her three daughters continued with the Sporting Fields Whippets, and in the 1990s added Greyhounds to the kennel. Debbie purchased the six-month-old blue brindle bitch, Heirloom Denim and Diamonds, who was Best in Sweeps in the Western Sighthound Combined Specialties; she finished her championship and in 1995 was bred to Ch. Sundridge So Be It, JC, producing seven champion offspring. Debbie then imported a blue fawn bitch, Ch. Sobers Zanthea, from Astrid Jonsson and Bitte Ahrens (Sobers) of Sweden. "Sandy," co-owned with Dr. Elizabeth Hanson, won Best of Breed at the 1998 GCA Eastern Specialty. Debbie and Dr. Hanson have recently imported two more Sobers Greyhound puppies.

Shazam

Jack and Maggie Mitchell had always wanted a Greyhound, but they weren't sure they were ready when their daughter Karen Childs, who has Giant Schnauzers, located a red bitch for them. "Darcy" had come from the Gallant Kennels and had been in five different homes. Mr. Mitchell fell in love with her as soon as he saw her.

Darcy was conditioned and socialized for nine months. Mr. Mitchell started showing Darcy, BIS Ch. Gallant Somnombula, in April of 1990, and she finished on May 19, 1990, with five majors. Mr. Mitchell was advised to special Darcy, and for the next three years, he and Darcy enjoyed the show ring, winning groups and an all-breed BIS in Salt Lake City.

Mr. Mitchell later bred Darcy to Ch. Jet's The Voyage Out. From this litter came BIS, BISS Ch. Shazam's The Journey Begins; Ch. Shazam's Journey In Starlight, a group winner; and Ch. Shazam's Journey To Abraxas, who was Best in Sweeps at the GCA Western Specialty.

Windrock

The Shazam story continues with Kim and Colin Fritzler of Colorado, who co-own Bubba (Ch. Shazam's The Journey Begins) and Zephyr (Ch. Shazam's Journey In Starlight) with the Mitchells. Both of these Greyhounds reside with Kim Fritzler, and it is she who has handled Bubba in his meteoric career in the show ring.

Mrs. Fritzler was familiar with Greyhounds since her days as an art student at the University of Wyoming, where a Greyhound that was used as a subject for the art students lived with her. Kim showed horses, Afghans, and English Springer Spaniels for years and says that it is with them that she learned to lose graciously. But since she acquired Shazam's The Journey Begins from the Mitchells, Mrs. Fritzler has not had much practice in losing.

Ch. Shazam's The Journey Begins JC is a multiple BIS and SBIS winner. His seven all-breed Bests in Show and six Specialty Bests make him the top-winning owner/handled Greyhound of all time. Bubba was the 1997 Westminster BOB winner and was the Number One Greyhound in all breed competition in 1996 and 1997.

Bubba's record is all the more amazing when one realizes that he was seldom shown more than 30 times in any year that he was campaigned. Mrs. Fritzler hopes to finish his field championship and at least a CD obedience title.

Several breeders have recognized Bubba's quality and have bred to him in the last few years. Twenty-eight of these offspring have completed their championships, with many more nearing their titles. Ch. Shazam's The Journey Begins is now one of the top-producing sires in the breed and will leave his mark in the breed for many generations to come.

The Fritzlers have chosen a young blue brindle dog to be his sire's successor. Ch. Greystone's Barcelona was awarded Best of Opposite Sex and an Award of Merit at the 1998 GCA Eastern Specialty.

Gaia

Gaia Greyhounds of Ohio came into being when Sue LeMieux purchased her first Greyhound from Maria Ferguson in New York. Although she had shown and bred Collies in the late 1960s and had been involved in obedience as an exhibitor and trainer, she left the dog show world for 20 years to raise her three children and pursue her career.

Ms. LeMieux met her first Greyhound in a Florida antique shop in 1988 and promptly fell in love: "It happened when she looked up at me with those gorgeous, trusting eyes." She went back to visit the lovely brindle bitch, an ex-racer, several times during her stay in Florida and came back to Ohio knowing that this was the breed she wanted.

After many months of searching, Ms. LeMieux happened to see an ad in a *Dog World* magazine and soon drove to upstate New York to see 2 six-month-old Greyhound puppies.

She chose, or rather he chose her, a white and red brindle male, and as they drove home she thought, "So be it, this must be the dog for me," which is how the parti-colored Greyhound, who was to become BIS BISS Ch. Sundridge So Be It JC received his name.

Ms. LeMieux took an eight-month-old "Pepi" to a fun match, accompanying her daughter who was practicing for an obedience degree on her Golden Retriever. Hounds were being judged by Cindy Kelly, and she awarded the Greyhound the Breed and a Group Two. After the show, Ms. Kelly commented on

the excellent quality of the dog and volunteered to handle Pepi for Ms. LeMieux, and a partnership was struck that day.

Ch. Sundridge So Be It finished his championship quickly and they decided to start his specials career. "Pepi" placed high in the rankings each year he was shown. He was Number One Greyhound in all-breed competition and Number Four in breed standings in 1995, in spite of his untimely death aboard an airplane in August of that year.

Ch. Sundridge So Be It JC was BOB at Westminster in 1992, BOB at the GCA Eastern National Specialty in 1994, and won an Award of Merit at the Western Specialty in 1994 and 1995. He was a multiple group and an all-breed Best In Show winner. Pepi loved to course; he obtained his Junior Courser title and had two legs toward his Senior Courser and several Field Championship points. He was the first Greyhound with an AKC coursing title to win an all-breed BIS.

Ch. Sundridge So Be It JC, 1995 Number One Greyhound All Breed.

Owned by Sue LeMieux.

Photo by Kurtis Photography

Ch. Sundridge Sagitta at seven months.

Owned by Sue LeMieux.

Photo by Booth Photography

So Be It sired 14 champions from three litters out of three different bitches. Five champions were from his first litter out of Ch. Another Episode Partylite. His second litter out of Sundridge Sparta produced three champions, a GCA Sweeps winner, and three get with lure coursing titles. Pepi's last litter out of Ch. Heirloom's Denim and Diamonds produced one Canadian and six American champions.

A 1995 Gaia litter sired by Ch. Jet's Heads Or Tails out of Ch. Sundridge Sagitta produced five champions. All of these have proven themselves worthy in the show ring with GCA Sweeps BOB and BOS wins, multi BIS and Group wins and placements: top-ranked BIS Am. Can. Ch. Gaia Tailor Maid; Am. Can. Ch. Gaia Dee's No Plain Jayne, Number One Greyhound in Canada in 1997; Am. Can. Ch. Gaia

Dee's Split Decision, Number Two Greyhound in Canada in 1997; Am. Can. Ch. Gaia Sunridge Serenade, Number One Greyhound in Canada in 1998; and Multi BIS Int. Am. Nor. Swed. Fin. Dan. Can. Ch. Gaia Sunridge Sunrise.

Ms. LeMieux's ideal Greyhound is balanced, powerful, well muscled, and beautiful to look at. Correct structure is a must, as it results in effortless movement at a trot and at a gallop and enables the Greyhound to do the job for which it was intended.

Medina

Hounds of Medina are owned and loved by Laurie and Walt Goodell. The couple learned about sighthounds from their first dog, an Afghan, Thunder Bays Thauney O Medina.

The Afghan wasn't the greatest in conformation, but Mrs. Goodell managed to put a point on him, plus his CD. She also owned a group winner, Ch. Janna's Armageddon, a fabulous red, raw-boned hound. Later she acquired Ch. Applause Midnight Lace Medina CD FCh., "Sissy," who finished quickly. Sissy had a fabulous temperament and great conformation, but "she would walk all over a dog show, get on everyone else's tables, and try to steal food. It got her into lots of trouble."

It was during one of the Goodells' trips with Sissy that they saw Ch. Huzzah Tiger Eye, and they knew that they had to have a Greyhound. Although there were lots of wonderful Greyhounds, none caught their eye. They finally saw a picture of Ch. Jet's Headed Like A Snake in an issue of the *Sighthound Review.* After making contact with Kari Nylén and Espen Engh, they were informed that there was a litter due out of Int. Ch. Jet's Texas Ranger and Int. Jet's A Clockwork Orange. Kari picked their Greyhound, who has since become Ch. Jet's Movado, a white and brindle, very powerful male.

In 1994, Mrs. Goodell went to Skokloster in Sweden and saw some of the best sighthounds she had ever seen, including some of the dogs that were part of her dog's past. While visiting Kari Nylen, she saw the Hildur and Topper puppies and picked a red and white male that was to become Ch. Jet's Heads or Tails. The Goodells have since acquired "Emily," an adorable puppy by Tailor out of Ch. Sundridge Sagitta. Emily grew up to be BISD Am. Can. Ch. Gaia Tailor Maid.

Am. Can. Ch. Gaia Tailor Maid winning an All-Breed Best in Show at 18 months.

Owned by Laurie Goodell and Judie Treuschel.

Photo by Booth Photography

El-Aur

Laurel E. Drew started the El-Aur Greyhound Kennels in the 1970s (the kennel name is a variation on the spelling of her first name). Her first Greyhound, Sheikh, was actually obtained in 1967—a rescue from a dog pound.

She began training Sheikh for obedience when she couldn't catch him if he was running, and she was soon hooked on Greyhounds. By the time she began showing Sheikh toward his CD (1969/70), she knew she wanted a show dog.

In the fall of 1970, Ms. Drew purchased her first show Greyhound from Georgiana Mueller of Aroi Greyhounds. Frolic of Aroi, a lovely white and black brindle bitch, earned 12 points, including one major, two legs on her CDX, and

was fully trained for tracking when she died unexpectedly after presenting Ms. Drew with a litter.

One of Frolic's sons, Parker (Ch. El-Aur Aztec, CDX, TC, FCh.) became one of the first Greyhounds to be presented with the UCA's versatility title. He was the first Greyhound to earn the TD (Tracking Degree), just as Sheikh had been the first to earn the UD (Utility Dog) in obedience. Ms. Drew believes very strongly that a Greyhound must prove itself in at least two fields of endeavor if it is to be bred.

Frolic's litter was the first of eight or ten that Ms. Drew has bred in 30 years of Greyhounds. Of those, she bred one all-champion litter from Ch. My Adventure and Aroi Talk A Blue Streak, which included three group placing (two group winners) dogs.

Ch. El-Aur Remember Roylatan. Owned by Laurel Drew. *Photo by Photos Today*

Ch. El-Aur Summer Breeze. Owned by Laurel Drew.

She has also bred other group placers, several obedience titled dogs, and quite a few lure coursers. El-Aur Greyhounds have been competing in lure coursing since the 1970s, and many have also gone free hunting in the open field.

The bloodlines of El-Aur Greyhounds go back strongly on Aroi, Royaltan, and Ch. My Adventure. Some of the famous old dogs in these lines include Ch. Aroi Blue Tiger Blues, Eng. Am. Ch. Seagift Parcancady Royaltan, Eng. Ch. Treetops Hawk, and Int. Nor. Swed. Ch. Psykotic.

Heart Hounds

Joni Lovci has owned Greyhounds for more than 25 years, most recently under the "Heart" name. In 1993, Ms. Lovci campaigned Ch. An-

Ch. Another Episode Twilite (left), owned by Joni Lovci, and Ch. Another Episode Limelite (right), owned by Chester Wilson, Bill Glover, and Ann Tater.

other Episode Twilite, a Ch. Shalfleet Socialite daughter bred by Anne Tater. Ms. Lovci believes the main function of her hounds is that of companions and show dogs. More recently, Ch. Hewly Hard Hitter, a Ch. Hewly Hispanic II son bred by Stanley D. Petter, Jr. and co-owned with Heather Spak, had been a multiple group winner and top ten Greyhound for 1993 through 1995. In 1996, Ch. Helicon Heartstrings, co-owned and bred by Heather Spak, won the Western GCA Specialty. The Sweepstakes was won by another of Ms. Lovci's hounds, Huzzah Wild at Heart, who went on to earn three 5-point majors during the week of the specialty to become a cham-

pion at nine months of age. She is a daughter of Ch. Shazam the Journey Begins out of Ch. Huzzah Dowsbragh Briteside, bred by Pat Ide.

Grand Cru

After owning and showing Weimaraners in conformation and field for 15 years, Melanie and Jack Steele were introduced to Greyhounds when one of their handlers was showing a top Greyhound. Mrs. Steele fell in love with Ch. Hewly Hispanic II, and she mentioned to the handler her possible interest in the breed if a Greyhound from the same lines became available. Two

Ch. Grand Cru Gevery Chambertin. Owned by Melanie Steele. *Photo by Sheryl Bartel*

weeks later, Helicon Lighthearted, "Belle," arrived.

GrandCru Kennels was founded in 1994. Because Mr. Steele's other passion is wine, all of their dogs are destined to carry the name of wines from a specific region designated by the litter.

Belle's first litter, the Burgandy litter, was born in July 1995. This exceptional litter produced nine beautiful puppies that went to homes across the country. Seven finished their championships before the age of 18 months, with some winning group placements and specialty sweepstakes. The sire of their first litter was Ch. Rich Pickings, a British import from the Ralph Parsons Kennel. Rich Pickings is owned by Brenda Adams of Artesia and Irmgard Hill of Quail Roost.

The Steeles have thoroughly enjoyed sharing their lives with these Greyhounds and look forward to continuing the breed as the Burgunday litter puppies continue in the show ring and go on to produce litters of their own.

WORDS OF WISDOM

After reading about so many successful breeders and the philosophies of their breeding programs, it may be of interest to read a few comments about the breeding of Greyhounds.

Some words of wisdom from Sue Cassem concerning the breeding of Greyhounds appeared in the March 1991 issue of the *GCA Newsletter*. They appear in abbreviated form below.

"Sometimes how you start in a breed is the result of circumstances, availability of quality animals, timing, and luck. How you proceed from there will determine success or failure."

She continues with some pointers "discovered through observation, experience and a lot of trial and error":

1. Start out with a top-quality bitch. If the first one isn't good enough, be realistic and get another.

2. It's great to have a breeding plan, but be prepared to alter it if necessary.

3. Have a goal in mind. Breeding is no use if you don't have a goal.

4. Assess your stock honestly. You can't correct (or keep) what you can't see.

5. Go to the specialties and look, look, look. Get a feel for the breed.

6. Go slow and learn, learn, learn. Don't get loaded down with dogs that aren't worth breeding or leave you no room to breed further.

7. Make every litter count.

8. Try your hardest to genetically screen your stock, especially if you offer a dog at stud.

9. The breed as a whole is more important than any individual dog. If an animal has a severe problem, love it or place it, but don't breed it.

10. Don't breed anything mediocre.

11. It's easiest to breed for—and get—good heads, good feet, good rears.

12. It's hardest to get and keep good front assemblies and topline. Bad tails (carried high and/or curled) are difficult to breed out and can come back to haunt you.

13. Know what you want to improve on when breeding your bitch and don't keep any puppy that is not an improvement in that area.

14. Try not to breed to a dog you have not seen in the flesh.

15. Study your litter from the very first day. If you are very astute, you can pick up movement faults in very young puppies.

16. Know your pedigrees—not that so-and-so produced Ch. Greatness, but what the dog/bitch itself possessed and could produce in the way of faults and virtues.

17. I find that, for the most part, pups at six weeks will reflect what they will be as adults.

18. The best moving puppies exhibit it very early. They are the ones always trotting because it's comfortable for them.

HISTORIC ENGLISH BREEDERS

The Greyhound kennels of England, both past and present, have had an immeasurable effect upon the quality of the breed throughout the world. Almost all of the great old Greyhound kennels in the United States obtained their foundation stock from English breeders.

Breeders in England have always had an eye for a good Greyhound, and they have produced magnificent specimens of the breed. Today, English breeders carry on the old tradition, producing beautiful, sound, correct Greyhounds that continue to maintain and improve the breed. This chapter highlights some of the historic Greyhound kennels and their impact on the early Greyhound kennels in the United States.

CARNLANGA

Jesse Prowse's Carnlanga Kennel was located in Cornwall, an area that was home to many great Greyhounds and kennels. Mr. Prowse obtained the bitch Trye Again as the foundation bitch for Carnlanga. Trye Again bred to Jack Searle's Venton Bruce and produced Miss Jason and Pip; Trye Again also produced Great Scott.

Pip bred to True Form produced the first champion bred at Carnlanga, from a litter whelped in 1933. The dog, Int. Eng. Ch. Jason of Harrowins, was owned by Mrs. D. J. Machetti. Pip also produced King Kong and Carnlanga Flip. Jason was an ancestor of the great stud dog, Ch. Treetops Hawk.

Probably the two most successful Carnlanga litters were by Carnlanga Conqueror (Carnlanga Chough ex Carnlanga Pixie) out of Carnlanga Pat. These two produced many offspring who were to contribute to the success of other kennels, such as Peggy Newcombe's Pennyworth in the United States and Ralph Parsons's R.P. in England. Some of the progeny include Eng. Am. Ch. Carnlanga Caramel of Pennyworth, Eng. Ch. Carnlanga Prelude, and Carnlanga Topaz, who was the dam of Eng. Am. Ch. Seagift Parcancady Bluebell and Eng. Am. Ch. Seagift Parcancady Royaltan. Mrs. Dorothy Whitwell (Seagift) exported Blue-bell to the United States to Stanley Petter's Hewly Kennels. Royaltan also ended up in the United States in the possession of Mr. James Kern Dick (Royaltan).

One of the Carnlanga dogs, Carnlanga Pirate, was purchased by Mr. and Mrs. Farrell (Foxden) and was shipped to the United States, where he was shown and bred under the name Foxden Flamingo. Interestingly, the Greyhound head study that is part of the Greyhound Club of America's beautiful logo is that of Foxden Flamingo.

Another important Carnlanga export to the United States, to William Brainard (Downsbragh), was Carnlanga Elegance, who sired Ch. True Elegance of Mardormere, Ch. Yours Truly of Mardormere, and Ch. Elegant Lady of Mardormere for Mr. and Mrs. Anderson. Am. Ch. Carnlanga Sceptre, from Carnlanga's last litter, whelped in 1957, came to the United States and was used by Mr. Brainard and Georgianna Mueller (Aroi).

PARCANCADY

Although Peter George was unable to read or write, he was a master breeder who knew his Grey-hounds. His expertise in the breed earned him the nickname of the Wiz-ard. Mr. George could often be seen walking his dogs; he encouraged people he met to pet and play with his dogs, and his Greyhounds were well social-ized as a result.

Mr. George bred Bostraze Queen to Butcher's Baron in 1930 to produce his first litter, but he did not register his Parcancady prefix until 1946. Mr.

George kept Parc-An-Cady Girlie. When Girlie was bred to Paul Boy, they pro-duced Eng. Ch. Fair Girl. Eng. Ch. White Snowdrop and Sporting Lad were from Girlie's second litter by Eng. Ch. King of Trevarth; Sporting Lad was used in Jesse Prowse's Carnlanga breeding pro-gram. Girlie was again bred to King of Trevarth, now under the ownership of Jack Phillips (Trevore). A puppy from that litter became Mrs. Dodge's (Giralda) Am Ch. Giralda's White Knight. Knight eventually became one of Mr. and Mrs. Bagshaw's (Canyon Crest) foundation dogs.

Two of Peter George's most important brood bitches were Parcancady Lady and My Queen. Parcancady Lady whelped six litters. Lady's second litter, a repeat of her first to Barnaloft By-stander, produced Ch. Seagift Parcancady Stella, Ch. Seagift Perran Polar Queen, and Ch. Parcancady Banker, all purchased by Mrs. Whitwell (Seagift). A third pairing produced Ch. Parcancady Lily, Ch. Parcancady Heatherbelle, and Ch. Seagift Parcancady Leader. These three were exported to the United States— Heatherbelle and Leader to Pennyworth and Lily to Mardormere. Heatherbelle was BOB at the 1951 and 1952 GCA Specialties.

Three offspring from a 1951 litter by Ch. Seagift Parcancady Leader and Parcancady Daisy made their way to the United States. Eng. Am. Ch. Boughton Damsel of Little Andely's was BOB at the GCA Specialty in 1955. J. Donald Duncan's Ch. Parcancady Cavalier and Ch. Parcancady Magpie both had successful show careers in the United States.

The last litter born at Parcancady in 1953 included two Greyhounds who became very influential in American bloodlines: Eng. Am. Ch. Seagift Parcancady Bluebell, imported by Stanley Petter (Hewly), and Eng. Am. Ch. Seagift Parcancady Royaltan, eventually owned by Mr. Dick (Royalton).

BOUGHTON

Mr. A. G. (Bill) Boggia was a highly successful breeder of Greyhounds and Smooth Fox Terriers. His kennel was active from the 1930s through the 1950s. Mrs. Mason purchased Eng. Am. Ch. Boughton Blue Lad of Little Andely's from Mr. Boggia and used him successfully in her breeding program. During World War II, Mr. Boggia made his living by locating and exporting quality Greyhounds. He had an excellent eye for a good dog and was much in demand as a judge.

BOVEWAY

Mr. Harry Peake, Jr., also of Cornwall, showed his first dog when he was only eight years old. His father had shown and bred Greyhounds and Great Danes since 1886.

Mr. Peake had other breeds and produced many top winners. A Pointer, Ch. Nancolleth Markable, that was exported to Mrs. Dodge (Giralda) was BIS at Westminster in 1932. Mr. Peake also exported quite a few Greyhounds to the United States. Several of them went to Mr. Ben Lewis (Lansdowne). A top winner in this country was Ch. Boveway Rosy Morn, imported by Mr. and Mrs. Farrell of Foxden.

SEAGIFT

Dorothy Renwick Whitwell came from a long line of dog breeders and exhibitors and became involved with purebred dogs in 1925. Mrs. Whitwell and her husband had English and Irish Setters as well as coursing Greyhounds. Ch. Leading Lady was an early champion owned by Mrs. Whitwell.

Shortly after World War II, Mrs. Whitwell obtained three Greyhounds that were bred by Peter George (Parcancady). They were Ch. Seagift Parcancady Stella, Ch. Seagift Perran Polar Queen, and Ch. Parcancady Banker. These acquisitions began a 40-year association with Peter George. Mrs. Whitwell made up almost 20 Greyhound champions and exported many of these dogs to other countries, where they had a profound influence on the breed. Several of these, previously mentioned, came to the United States. Dorothy Whitwell's keen eye for a quality dog made her a successful breeder and popular judge.

TREETOPS

Mrs. Judy de Casembroot owned her first Greyhound in the mid-1940s. In association with her friend Miss Bobbie Greenish, she bred and exhibited some of the top-winning (English) Cocker Spaniels and Greyhounds in England.

Mrs. de Casembroot's foundation bitch was Flicka of Canfield. She was purchased from Mr. Bennetto (Canfield), another Greyhound man from Cornwall. Flicka was bred to Ch. Parcancady Lancer,

Eng. Ch. Treetops Hawk. Owned by Judy de Cassembroot.

Ch. Parcancady Heatherbelle. Owned by Peter George.

Ch. Hewly Red Plume. Bred by Ralph Parsons; owned by Stanely D. Petter, Jr. *Photo by Evelyn Shafer*

Eng. Ch. Shaunvalley Cavalier. *Photo courtesy Ellie Creech*

Eng. Ch. Shalfleet Sir Lancelot.
Photo courtesy P. Gail Burnham

Ch. Shalfleet Stop the World.

Photo courtesy P. Gail Burnham

owned by Mr. Boggia (Boughton). This litter, born in 1950, contained the red brindle Ch. Treetops Hawk, one of the top sires in the breed. During his lifetime he accumulated 16 CCs and was BIS seven times. Bred to his half-sister, Treetops Penelope of Canfield, the pair produced Ch. Treetops Golden Falcon, who was BIS at Crufts in 1956.

Hawk was used extensively as a sire, producing at least 30 champions, and he has had a tremendous influence on the breed—not just in England, but in the United States, Canada, Scandinavia, and South America. His name appears numerous times in the ancestry of most Greyhounds around the world. Some of the well-known Greyhound champions

Eng. Ch. Shalfleet Stop That Tiger.

Photo courtesy P. Gail Burnham

Ch. Shaunvalley Anton and Ch. Cebar Megan. Owned by Ellie Creech, Cebar.

Eng. Ch. Royal Portrait.

Owned by Ralph Parsons.

Eng. Am. Ch. Hubbestad-Double Magic.

Photo by Carlin and Camera

S. N. Ch. Hubbestad Midnight Madness.

Owned by Iris Carlsson, Sweden.

Photo by Karen K. Grottjord

sired by Hawk include Ch. Seagift Parcancady Royaltan, Ch. Treetops Rising Pheasant, Ch. Seagift Parcancady Bluebell, Ch. Treetops Flamingo, Ch. Treetops Raven of Pennyworth, Ch. Hewly Red Plume, and of course, Golden Falcon, whelped in 1954. Golden Falcon was a white and blue brindle dog, who sired several champions before being sold to Pakistan. Ch. Treetops Ringdove, sired by Falcon, became the foundation bitch of Barbara (Odell) Wilton-Clark's famous Shalfleet Kennels.

Mrs. de Casembroot based her breeding program on linebreeding and was extremely successful, breeding 14 Greyhound litters between 1951 and 1957. She was an international judge and served as president of the Greyhound Club.

A nine-month-old Flyalong puppy, already with a Best Puppy in Show.

Owned by Peter and Mair Jones, Flyalong.

SHALFLEET

Mrs. Barbara Wilton-Clark was one of the most influential Greyhound breeders of all time. From 1961 to 1982, 24 Greyhound litters were born at her Shalfleet Kennel. Many of these dogs found their way overseas, with more than 20 coming to the United States.

Ch. Treetops Ringdove was the foundation bitch of Shalfleet. In 1961, she was bred to Shalfleet Wicked William, a Hawk son (ex Parcancady Larky), and produced, among others, Eng. Ch. Shalfleet Scandal and Shalfleet Sovereign. Sovereign was imported to the United States as an older dog, and in his one litter there he sired Ch. Aroi The Swinger and Ch. Aroi Toast of the Town.

Ringdove was bred to Wicked William a second time in 1962. This repeat breeding produced Shalfleet Soverignty, who was imported to the United States by Harry T. Peters, Jr. (Windholme). Soverignty sired 11 champions, including the Drs. Neustadts' Ch. Rudels Reindeer Cupid.

The third Shalfleet litter was born in 1963, sired by Ch. Shalfleet Scandal ex Ch. Charm of Chellheath. From this litter came the BIS winning United States import, Eng. Am. Ch. Shalfleet Starlight of Foxden, owned by Mr. and Mrs. Farrell (Foxden). A BIS winner in England before being exported, many believe Starlight to be one of the greatest Greyhounds of all time.

Mrs. Wilton-Clark's fourth litter, by Ch. Seagift Sheriff ex Ch. Shalfleet Spanish Moon, included the parti bitch, Shalfleet Silver Moon. Silver Moon was bred six times from 1969 to 1975. From the two breedings to Hortondale Treetops Mighty Grand came Eng. Ch. Shalfleet Silver Fortune, Eng. Ch. Shalfleet Sir Lancelot, and Eng. Ch. Shalfleet Spode. All three dogs played an important part in Shalfleet's breeding program. Shalfleet Eaglelodge Bracken (Eaglelodge Rain Harvest ex Shaunvalley Carrousel) was bred twice to Silver Fortune. The first litter included Rita Bartlett's (Ransley) beautiful Shalfleet Shimmering. Bracken was exported in whelp with the second litter to Jim Haring in the United States, providing him with the foundation for his Sundridge Kennel.

Sir Lancelot sired five litters for Shalfleet; Spode whelped two litters. Bred together in 1978, they produced Eng. Am Ch. Shalfleet Shirley Ann, who was eventually exported to P. Gail Burnham (Suntiger) in the United States.

Eng. Ch. Shalfleet Swing High (Ch. Seagift Sheriff ex Shalfleet Enchantment) was another bitch used extensively by Mrs. Wilton-Clark. She produced four litters, two by Sir Lancelot and two by Ch. Shalfleet Sporting Knight. Two of Shalfleet's top-winning Greyhounds were Ch. Shalfleet Sarah Frazer (Ch. Starbolt Cetus ex Ch. Shalfleet Spode) and Ch. Shalfleet Spotlight (Ch. Starbolt Cetus ex Ch. Shalfleet Silver Moon). Shalfleet's last two litters, whelped in 1982, were sired by an American import, Ch. Aroi Sea Hawk of Shalfleet.

Barbara Wilton-Clark eventually disbanded her Shalfleet kennels and moved to the Canary Islands, a dream fulfilled. But she has left the Greyhound world a great gift through all of the beautiful Shalfleet Greyhounds that are in the pedigrees of so many dogs today.

R.P.

Ralph Parsons's history with Greyhounds harkens back to his grandfather and father, who both kept the breed. Mr. Parsons was a regular at local dog shows from a very early age and established his own line as an adult. Eventually all of his dogs were named with his own initials, R.P.

Parsons's first Greyhound was Firefly, who was bred to Jesse Prowse's Carnlanga Monitor. The bitch he kept from this litter was Kaysa Girly, who was bred to Carnlanga Venture. This litter produced Rolf's Prudence. His next breeding was to Ch. Treetops Hawk.

Some of Mr. Parsons's top-winning Greyhounds include Eng. Ch. Rebukys Poth; Eng. Ch. Rych Psycador, a BIS winner; Ch. Ro Poth; Ch. Relentless Pursuit; Ch. Rising Peak; and Eng. Ch. Royal Portrait, perhaps his best known and the breed record holder for number of CCs won in England. Royal Portrait was the top Greyhound in England for four years from 1988 to 1991. R.P. Greyhounds continued their winning ways in 1995. Ch. Rare Porcelain of Springflite was a BIS winner, defeating 10,000 dogs. She was the top CC winner in England in 1995. R.P.–bred Greyhounds have been exported to breeders worldwide and appear as foundation stock in many well-known kennels

Mr. Parsons's death in 1995 ended a lifelong commitment to breeding some of the very best Greyhounds. His goal was to improve the breed, litter after lit-ter, generation after generation. Happily, Ralph Parsons's daughter, Kay Chapman, has followed in her father's footsteps and continues with the R.P. line under her kennel name, Kernow.

Other Breeders

Some other English kennels of the past, not profiled above, are Barmaud, Mr. Barker; Barnaloft, Barney Stevens; Barum, Mr. Abbott; Butcher, James Berryman; Canfield, Mr. Bennetto; Crosswolla, Angela Sturgess; Harrowin, Mrs. D. J. Marchetti; Primley, Mr. H. Whitley; Trevore, Jack Phillips; Venton, Jack Phillips; Venton, Jack Searle; and Viverdon, Mathew Bros.

There are many active Greyhound breeders in England today, where dogs continue to have an international impact on the breed. Some of the present-day Greyhound kennels include Baldrey, Michael and Jackie White; Branwen, Cynthia Boissevain; Crosswolla, Mrs. V. White; Exhurst, Mr. F. Willey; Flyalong, Peter and Mair Jones; Gayside, Brenda and Jim Rowe; Hubbestad, Geir and Gerd Flyckt-Pederson; Kernow, Kay Chapman; Lyntails, Terry and Lyn Clark; Northwells, Mrs. J. B. Bayliss; Ransley, Rita and Paul Bartlett; Rondelin, Edna Hibbs; Seeswift, Rita and Ian Bond; Shaunvalley, Frank Brown; Solstrand, Dagmar (Kenis) Pordham; Sulamim, Janet and Vikki McBride; Wenonah, Daphne Gilpin; Windspiel, Bob and Elaine Newsham; and Xandaleer, Pat and David Alexander.

Greyhound Breeders in Other Countries

The Scandinavian Countries

The Greyhounds produced in Scandinavian countries today are some of the most majestic Greyhounds found anywhere in the world. For the most part they are large, elegant, upstanding, well-balanced dogs, covering a lot of ground when standing and moving. Scandinavian Greyhounds are known for their substance, body and bone, deep briskets, and front fill. They are well muscled, strong, and powerful. Many breeders in the United States have been attracted to these great dogs, and quite a few have been imported in recent years. Scandinavian breeders are also extending their own gene pool by importing Greyhounds from other countries.

Sweden

Greyhounds have been bred steadily in Sweden since the 1950s. Several breeders have been very successful with their breeding programs and have produced some outstanding specimens.

Guld

Mrs. Ann Gustafsson's Guld Greyhounds have been a dominant influence in the breed in Sweden for several decades. Her foundation bitch was Int. Ch. Guld (bred by Bo Bengtson and Dr. Bodegård) from whence came her now famous prefix.

Mrs. Gustafsson follows a carefully planned linebreeding program, utilizing outcrosses when necessary to complement her line. She has an incredible eye for a good Greyhound and is very particular about the puppies she chooses, insisting on top quality and soundness in her breeding stock.

There have been more than 100 Greyhound champions produced at Gulds. Many Guld dogs have been best in show winners. Mrs. Gustafsson's Greyhounds have had an international impact on the breed, in European countries and the United States. Some of Mrs. Gustafsson's recent winners and producers include Int. Ch. Guld's Tawny Topstar; Int. Ch. Guld's Billy the Kid, sired by Tawny Topstar; and BIS winning Int. Ch. Guld's Rare Rachel. Rachel is a liver brindle, a color uncommon in Greyhounds and often quite controversial among Greyhound breeders and exhibitors.

DR. GÖRAN BODEGÅRD

Dr. Bodegård has had Greyhounds since the 1960s, and has bred some of the all-time greats in the breed. His dogs have had a worldwide influence. Some of the well-known Greyhounds co-owned and co-bred by Dr. Bodegård and Bo Bengtson include Int. Ch. Guld, Int. Ch. Piruett, Int. Ch. Psychotic, Ch. Krinolin, Ch. Markurell, and Ch. Magna Charta.

Int. Ch. Guld was produced in Dr. Bodegård's and Bo Bengtson's first litter. Int. Ch. Piruett, a Guld granddaughter, bred to a Guld son, produced Int. Ch. Psychotic, one of the breed's greatest sires. Bred to a full sister of Piruett, Psychotic produced Ch. Markurell.

Ch. Markurell has made his presence known in the United States by producing two dogs that became influential sires there. The two, out of Int. Ch. Guld's Heroine Honey, were Ch. My Adventure, owned by Nathan and Gloria Reese (Holmby Hills), and Ch. Hero Kingsmark, owned by Judy Donaldson (Kingsmark). Int. Ch. Honey Classic Liberty Light, the

BOB winner at the 1991 Swedish Greyhound Club Show, was also sired by Markurell and Heroine Honey.

BOHEM

Although best known for Whippets (initially in Sweden, now in the United States), the first Bohem champions were Afghans, and an involvement in Greyhounds, though of very short duration, had worldwide consequences. In 1966, Bo Bengtson was working with his Whippet imports, but he was watching Greyhounds, and together with Göran Bodegård, decided it would be a good idea to combine the two then most successful lines in Scandinavia: Jidjis and Sobers.

To that end, the red bitch Sobers Nugget was leased and sent to be bred to the famous Ch. Gullfreds Frack a la Fredrik, a multiple BIS winning Jidjis descendant. Since he would not comply, Nugget was instead bred to an unshown dog, Whispering, of similar breeding and quality. The resultant litter, co-bred by Bo Bengtson and Göran Bodegård, included several champions and one legendary bitch, Ch. Guld, whose many champion offspring have carried her name in pedigrees all over the world.

From Guld's first litter, Ch. Gulds Black & White Lady was shown by Bohem with great success and later became the first imported Greyhound ever to become a champion in England. (She was shown to her English title by Terry Thorn, now England's top allrounder judge.) Coming back to Sweden, Lady won the Greyhound specialty at Skokloster and became recognized as a top dam, both through offspring co-bred by Bengtson and Bodegård, and from several Group-winning champions bred solely by Bohem.

Since moving to the United States, Bo Bengtson has not been active in Greyhounds (although he judged them at Westminster in 1982) but retains a strong interest in the breed, as founder of *Sighthound Review* magazine (now owned by Jim and Cathy Gaidos), as publisher of *Dogs in Review,* and as an international judge.

SOBERS

The Sobers Greyhounds of Astrid Jonsson, assisted now by her granddaughter, Bitte Ahrens, have had a far-reaching impact on the breed. Sobers' foundation bitch, Ch. Sobers Blue Isis, whelped in 1958, was bred to another blue, a Ch. Treetops Hawk son, Ch. Treetops Queen's Beast. Two bitches from this litter were both bred to another Hawk son, Ch. Treetops Rising Pheasant, and produced eight more champions, including Ch. Sobers Orphie. A Sobers-bred bitch, Ch. Sobers Nova, was the foundation bitch of Dagmar (Kenis) Pordham's Solstrand kennel. A Sobers Greyhound, Int. Ch. Sobers Lakey, sired one of the top-winning BIS dogs in Finland in the 1960s, Int. Ch. Black Diamond of Pink Sunshine.

In recent years, Sobers has imported from Solstrand. The bitch, Int. Swe. Nor. Ch. Trecarne Amber of Solstrand became a multiple BIS winner. She was the top-winning Greyhound in Sweden in 1990 and 1991. She was BIS at the Swedish Greyhound Club Specialty, Skokloster, in 1991 and 1992. Sobers has been successfully breeding and exhibiting Greyhounds for almost 40 years.

NOBLEGREY

Asa Lindahl's Noblegrey Greyhounds have made quite an impression on the show scene in Sweden in recent years. Since Ms. Lindahl was a child she had dogs of different breeds, but only Greyhounds since 1984; her first was Swe. Ch. Gulds Sweet Shirley.

In 1993 and 1995, Kennel Noblegrey was the number one Greyhound breeder in Sweden (number two in 1992 and 1994). In 1995, Scarlet Pimpernel, Scarlet Paddington, and Silver Dollar topped the male list in Sweden. In 1993, Silver Sterling was the best bitch. Kennel Noblegrey takes pride in its own design—elegant dogs with good substance and nice temperament.

Noblegrey's first litter, in 1988, by Swe. Ch. Gulds Terrible Tyfon (Nor. Ch. Shalfleet Signalight ex Gulds Neat Najad) out of Swe. Ch. Gulds Sweet Shirley, produced three champions: Swe. Ch. Noblegrey Blue Fawn Shadow, Swe. Nor. Ch. Noblegrey Dark Baronesse (exp. Norway), and Int. Swe. Nor. Ch. Noblegrey Sweetheart (exp. Norway). The second litter, whelped in 1990, was sired by Fran Chi Red Hawk (son of Markurell) out of Swe. Ch. Gulds Sweet Shirley. From this litter came Swe. Ch. Noblegrey Silver Coin, Swe. Nor. Ch. Noblegrey Silver Dollar, Swe. Ch. Noblegrey Silver Penny, and Int. Swe. Nor. Ch. Nordic Winner 1995 Noblegrey Silver Sterling. The third litter at Noblegrey was by Am. Can. Int. Nord. Ch. Gallant Major Motion ex Swe. Ch. Gulds Sweet Shirley. This litter produced Swe. Ch. Noblegrey April Joker, Noblegrey April Illusion (exp. Norway), Swe. Ch. Noblegrey April Love, Noblegrey April Sandstorm (2 CC exp. Finland), and Noblegrey April Weather (exp. Russia). The last litter was born in 1994. The sire was Swe. Ch. Telegram Kenny Kiwi and the dam was Int. Swe. Nor. Ch. Nordic Winner 1995 Noblegrey Silver Sterling.

Norway

The Norwegian Greyhound Club was founded in 1952, and today there are close to 130 members. The club publishes the magazine, *Greyhounden* (The Greyhound), an excellent publication that contains valuable information for breeders everywhere.

Although Greyhounds in Norway are a relatively small breed in numbers, they do much winning at the best in show and group levels. Several Norwegian breeders have produced outstanding Greyhounds that have been, and continue to be, extremely influential in the breed around the world.

JET'S

The Jet's Greyhounds, owned by Kari Nylen and Espen Engh, have produced 73 homebred champions and have exported dogs to every corner of the world. The Jet's have won championship bests in show with 17 individual Greyhounds, as well as 18 times BOB at the Norwegian and Swedish Greyhound specialties.

Kari Nylen bought her first Greyhound as a teenager in 1955. This dog, of part show and part coursing breeding, was to be the start of a lifelong association with the breed.

The foundation sire of Jet's, Int. Nord. Ch. Jet Commander, an elegant brindle dog, was acquired in 1966 and was owned by Kari's son Espen Engh. Commander, whose pedigree could be traced back to several Treetops-Carnlanga crosses through his R.P. sire and mother's sire, was an upstanding and elegant brindle dog and a particularly strong character. He was successfully shown to his championship in the late 1960s in Norway, Sweden, and Denmark.

In the early 1970s, two important imports were made by Jet's: the white and blue brindle male Int. Nord. Ch. Gayside Solomon Grundy, from Brenda Rowe; and Int. Nord. Ch. Gulds Choice Cimone, from Ann Gustavsson. Two litters by Commander out of Cimone produced a string of top winners, including Int. Nord. Ch. Jet's Elegant Negress, Int. Nord. Ch. Jet's Estelle Nicolette, Nord. Ch. Jet's Evening Nocturne, Int. Nord. Ch. Jet's Stardust, Int. Nord. Ch. Jet's White Christmas, Int. Nord. Ch. Jet's Night and Day, and Jet's Double Trouble. Negress was top Greyhound in Norway in 1976, and Stardust from 1980 to 1982.

Elegant Negress was bred to the Swedish Int. Ch. Psychotic and produced the white and brindle bitch, Int. Nord. Ch. Jet's Pink Panther. Pink Panther is considered by her breeders to be the very best they ever bred. Pink Panther was rarely beaten in the breed during her show career and won best in show at large international championship shows in both Norway and Sweden; she is the only sighthound ever to win BOB four times at the Nordic Winner shows.

Pink Panther, bred to four different dogs, produced Int. Nord. Ch. Jet's Kerrs Pink, Ch. Jet's Pink Floyd, Ch. Jet's Leopards Bane, Ch. Jet's Wild Cat, Int. Nord. Ch. White Elephant, Int. Nord. Ch. Jet's Coco Chanel, and Jet's Estee Lauder. Coco Chanel, the top Greyhound in 1989, won BOB at the Norwegian Greyhound Club show under Ralph Parsons as well as three times BOB at the famous Swedish Skokloster show.

Another influential import in the early 1980s was Int. Nord. Am. Ch. Gallant Major Motion, bred by the late Don Ginter and Lee Mayfield. He came to Jet's through England and became a sire of note in Scandinavia. "Jeff" was the

Multi BIS Int. Ch. Gaia Sunridge Sunrise. Owned by Sue LeMieux, Espen Engh, and Astrid Knauber.
Photo by Bitte Ahrens (Sobers)

Int. Ch. Gulds Country Queen. Owned by Hanne Böckhaus, Kennel Eikica, Denmark.

S. Ch. Gulds Sweet Shirley. Owned by Asa Lindahl, Noblegrey, Sweden.

Five of Silver Sterling's puppies at nine months old: Scarlet Pastiche, Scarlet Paddington, Scarlet Palette, Scarlet Pearl, and Scarlet Pimpernel. Owned by Asa Lindahl, Sweden.

Best in Show winner Bayroad Red Gazelle with her mother, N. S. Ch. Schotsborg Earthquake.

Owned by Karen Grottjord, Bayroad, Norway.

N. S. Ch. Schotborgs Earthquake. Owned by Karen Grottjord, Bayroad, Norway.

Int. Ch. Eikica Freestyle Freddie, 1996 Greyhound of the Year (Denmark) and 1996 Sighthound of the Year (Denmark). Owned by Hanne Böckhaus, Kennel Eikica, Denmark.

Van Roslau Hounds. Owned by Laurent and Roos Vandeburie, Belgium.

Bakara's Ilona and BIS It. Int. Ch. Bakara's Amanda. Owned by Cecil Duflos, France.

Italian Ch. Ryal Macaque. Owned by Gilberto Grandi, Della Caveja.

Ch. Huzzah the Voyageur. Owned by John Palmer, Jonz, Australia. *Photo by Michael M. Trafford*

Ch. Jonz Heaven Can Wait. Owned by John Palmer, Jonz, Australia.

Int. Ch. Taikatassun Mamba. Owned by Sari Rantanen, Rantalaukan, Finland.

Ch. Sobers Zanthea and seven-month-old Sobers Cyrano, handled by breeder Bitte Ahrens of Sweden. Owned by Dr. Elizabeth Hanson and Debbie Butt. *Photo by Ashbey Photography*

Int. Ch. Jet's Headed Like A Snake.

Owned by Kari Nylen and Espen Engh, Jet's, Norway.

Int. Ch. Jet's the Sting, Finland's top-winning Greyhound of all time.

Mr. Vandeburie (right) in 1943 with brother and sisters and the Greyhound Finette. Courtesy Laurent and Roos Vandeburie, Van Roslau, Belgium.

Ch. Jet's Coco Chanel. Owned by Kari Nylen and Espen Engh, Jet's, Norway.

Int. Ch. Noble Aid de Camp.
Owned by Hanne Böckhaus, Kennel
Eikica, Denmark.

Nordic Winner Dog Show, Stockholm, 1995. Owned by Kennel Noblegrey, Åsa Linclahl. *Photo by Wilhelm Dufwa*

sire of Panther's fourth and final litter, producing among others Int. Ch. Jet's Washington Post, Ch. Jet's Texas Ranger, and Int. Ch. Jet's Virginia Woolf, all of them multiple champion producers. Jeff retained his qualities until very late in life and won BOB at the Norwegian Greyhound Club's 40th Anniversary show at the age of ten under Pat Ide of the American Huzzah Kennels.

Kerrs Pink was bred to Int. Ch. Dogcastle Peacock to produce a string of champions, including Int. Ch. Jet's A Clockwork Orange and Int. Ch. Jet's For Your Eyes Only, who was the top Greyhound from 1990 to 1991. Bred to Coco Chanel, he produced one of the Jet's most admired winners, Int. Nor. Swe. Fin. Dan. Ch. Jet's Headed Like A Snake. At only 14 months of age, "Hildur" won BIS at Skokloster over almost one thousand sighthounds, and BOB at both Norwegian

and Swedish Greyhound Club shows. She was top Greyhound from 1993 to 1994.

Jet's puppies have been exported all over the world. The white/brindle Am. Ch. Jet's The Voyage Out (Int. Ch. White Elephant ex Int. Ch. J. Virginia Woolf) was the first United States export. He is the sire of BIS, SBIS Ch. Shazam The Journey Begins. Am. Ch. Jet's Ravishing Redhead (Int. Ch. Gulds Tawny Topstar ex Int. Jet's Headed Like A Snake) was BOB at the 1996 Westminster Kennel Club show. Littermates Ch. Jet's Heads or Tails, Ch. Jet's Heading For The Top, and Ch. Jet's Movado have also won their AKC titles.

Both Kari Nylen and Espen Engh are international judges of Greyhounds and other sighthound breeds. But breeding takes first priority over both exhibiting and judging. Currently all the Jet's litters are born and raised with Espen and his partner Age Gjetnes, who must also be credited with much of the kennel's recent success.

SHOWLINE

Showline Greyhounds, owned by Cecile and Knut Fr. Blütecher, has owned and produced some excellent Greyhounds since their beginning in 1971, including Ch. Solstrand Deep Blues of Showline. They owned BIS, SBIS Int. Ch. Honey Classic Liberty Light, who was BIS at Skokloster in 1989. Several of her puppies have done exceptionally well in the show ring: Nor. Swe. Ch. Showline Summer Light was BOB at the Norwegian Greyhound Club's 40th Anniversary Specialty in 1992. Her brother, Nor. Swe. Ch. Showline Summer Chase, won the dog CC at the same event. Another littermate, Showline Summer Pheasant, was exported to Robin Barry in the United States, where he completed his American championship at the age of 14 months.

DOGCASTLE

Dogcastle Kennel is owned by Ingebjorg Stenhaugen, who has had some top-winning Greyhounds, along with winners in other breeds. Two of her dogs were Ch. Dogcastle Panda With A Feather and Ch. Dogcastle Peacock, who was the top sighthound in Scandinavia in 1987 and 1988. These two were sent to Mr. and Mrs. Nathan Reese (Holmby Hills) to campaign to their titles in the United States.

BAYROAD

Karen Kvassheim Grottjord of Bayroad Greyhounds is carefully planning her breeding program and has a clear idea of where she is going with her line. She is also the editor of *Greyhounden*, the Norwegian Greyhound Club's magazine.

She currently has two Greyhound bitches at home. One of them is three-year-old Nor. Swe. Ch. Schotborgs Earthquake (Nor. Swe. Ch. A Son of Pryveth and Int. Nor. Ch. Dogcastle's Queen Victoria). Ertha had a litter of nine puppies by Swe. Ch. Sobers Santaro (Int. Nor. Swe. Ch. Gulds Tawny Topstar and Int. Nor. Swe. Ch. Trecarne Amber of Solstrand). The puppies have several group winnings and best in show placements in puppy classes. Dogs cannot participate in "adult" classes in Norway until they are nine months old.

Ertha was bred to Swe. Nor. Ch. Hubbestad Midnight Madness (Rondelin Marching Home ex Shalfleet Sea Dancer) in the spring of 1996.

FINLAND

Greyhounds have been shown in Finland since the 1960s. There is a complete separation of show and racing Greyhounds in Finland, but all Greyhounds are registered with the Finnish Kennel Club, which was established in 1971.

There are not a great number of Greyhounds in Finland. In fact, from 1984 to 1987, there were no litters of show Greyhounds registered. Understandably, many of the top-winning Greyhounds in recent years have been imports.

One of these imports was Int. Swe. Fin. Dk. Est. Ch. SFW 1990 7 1993 Jet's the Sting (Int. Scand. Am. Ch. Dogcastle Peacock ex Int. Scand. Ch. Jet's Kerrs Pink). Sting was top Greyhound in Finland from 1989 to 1993, and was ranked as top Sighthound in 1990. Int. Scand. Ch. SFW 1987 & 1989 Guld's Pablo Piccolo was the top Greyhound winner from 1986 to 1988.

TAIKATASSUN

Taikatassun Hounds, owned by Mrs. Jaana Laatto-Huvinen, has been breeding Greyhounds successfully for several years. Her first litter, in 1990, by Swe. Fin. Ch. SFW 1991 Jet's Texas Ranger and Swe. Fin. 7 Swe. Ch. Jet's Leopards Bane, produced puppies who did well in the show ring and on the coursing field.

Her second litter, whelped in 1992 by Int. Swe. Fin. Dk. Est. Ch. Jet's The Sting ex Swe. Fin. & Est. Ch. EUJW 1991, ESTW 1993 Jet's Mrs. Dalloway, produced five champions. One of these is Int. Fin. Nor. Est. Ch. Taikatassun Mamba, owned by Sari Rantanen of Rantalaukan Greyhounds.

RANTALAUKAN

Although Int. Fin. Nor. Est. Ch. Taikatassun Mamba is Sari Rantanen's, of Rantalaukan Greyhounds, first Greyhound, she is not new to sighthounds, having owned and bred Afghans for 15 years.

Mamba, who is now shown 10 to 12 times a year, started her show career at nine months of age, when she was Best of Winners and received her first CC. In 1994, Mamba was beaten only once, otherwise she was always BOB or BOS. She became the top Greyhound in 1994 in Finland. Most of all, Mamba is a wonderful friend to the Rantanen family.

DENMARK

EIKICA

Kennel Eikica in Denmark is owned by Hanne Böckhaus, who has been a devoted Greyhound owner and breeder for the past 12 years. She has bred almost 100 Greyhounds, mostly show bloodlines and a single litter of racing bloodline. Quite a few Eikica Greyhounds have done very well in the show ring: world winners 1992, 1994, 1995; several international champions—Danish, Luxembourg, Swedish, Norwegian, Belgian, etc. She is also interested in obedience training and attends agility and lure coursing, as well as track racing.

Hanne Böckhaus's foundation dogs mostly originated from Sweden and Norway. After owning and racing two good-looking dogs of Irish bloodlines, she fell in love with the show-type Grey.

Eikica Greyhounds has been the home of many outstanding dogs that have been owned or bred by Hanne Böckhaus. Among these are Int. Dk. Bel. Ch. KGh. V. 1988, Belgian Winner 1989 Noble Aide De Camp; Int. Dk. L. KLB. Ch. Eikica Tricky Tracey, a white and chocolate liver-colored dog; Int. Dk. L E. Swe. Nor. Nord Ch. Eikica Yankee Doodle Dandy, Sighthound of the Year 1991, KLG. Ch. Vice World Winner 1992, Europa Winner 1992, World Winner 1994; Int. Dk. L. E. Bel. PL. Ch. Eikica Yatzy Winner, KLG Ch. World Winner 1992, Poland Winner 1992 & 1993, Copenhagen Winner 1992 & 1993, Belgian Winner 1994; Int. Dk, L. KLB Ch. World Winner 1994 Swe. Ch. Sighthound of the Year 1993 Eikica Affected Alicia; Int. Dk. L. Swe. Ch. Eikica Bailey the Bookie, Greyhound of the Year 1994, World Winner 1995, Belgian Winner 1995, Copenhagen Winner 1995.

Another breeder of show Greyhounds in Denmark is Mrs. Lisbet Knak Madsen, who had a litter in 1994 by Kingsmark Freudian Slip out of Multi Ch. Eikica Zoe of Zealand. Out of this litter, Lisbet kept Noble Prize, a white/red male, and Maharanee, a white/creme bitch.

Mrs. Annette Nielsen, prefix Always Allmighty, had a litter of eight white/red and white/black pups by Multi Ch. Jet's For Your Eyes Only (owned by Eikica), out of Eikica Zara Zoffi of Zealand.

BELGIUM

There are only a few show Greyhounds in Belgium. The top Greyhound kennel is van Roslau, owned by Laurent and Roos Vandeburie.

VAN ROSLAU

Van Roslau has a long history in the breed, with parents who also bred Greyhounds. Although the Vandeburies breed only one litter a year, they have produced many Greyhounds who have become champions throughout Europe.

The Vandeburies have imported several Greyhounds—among them, Kingsmark Love Song from the United States and Ch. Gayside Royal Pardon from Kay Chapman, bred by Brenda and Jim Rowe of England. They have bred 20 champions and have owned 33.

Van Roslau Greyhounds have achieved much success in the show ring. One multi winner, Ch. Jessica van Roslau, was a Belgium, Holland, and international champion and was the number one Greyhound in Belgium for a number of years. Some other van Roslau Greyhounds of note are Multi. Ch. Larky van Roslau, Multi Ch. Rainbows van Roslau, Int. Ch. Ismael van Roslau, WW Ch. Rebirth van Roslau, WW Ch. Jenna van Roslau, WW Ch. Love-Song van Roslau, and Multi and World Ch. 1995 Gayside Royal Pardon.

Laurent and Roos plan to continue breeding good Greyhounds with proper structure and elegance. Besides breeding and exhibiting Greyhounds, the Vandeburies are also active in the Belgium Kennel Club, are handlers and trainers, and tattoo puppies of all breeds.

FRANCE

There are some very dedicated breeders producing excellent Greyhounds in France. Several of the kennels of note are Bakara's, owned by Cecile Duflos; Mrs. Belgherbi's Ad Honores; and Just Charming Greyhounds, owned by Claire Beladina.

BAKARA'S

Cecile Duflos' foundation bitch was Ch. Romane, who was shown in Italy and Spain and finished her championships quickly. She produced four champions in her first litter in 1985 by Ch. Rondelin Mohawk of Solstrand: BIS Ch. Bakara's Alexia, BIS Ch. Bakara's Amanda, Ch. Bakara's Arthur, and BIS Ch. Bakara's Astrella. Bred again to Mohawk in 1988, Mrs. Duflos kept BIS Ch. Bakara's Daphnis, who became a world champion in 1992. From her third litter, out of Amanda, Mrs. Duflos kept Bakara's Elisa. Elisa was bred to her uncle Ch. Bakara's Arthur in 1993. From this litter, she kept Bakara's Flora, who at only 16 months old won a specialty BOB in Italy.

ITALY

There are several active breeders and exhibitors of show Greyhounds in Italy. Among these are Gilberto Grandi of Della Caveja Greyhounds; Gilberto Santarelli of Ofelia Kennels; Stefano Montefiori; and Sylvia Rosolen and Piero Chiesa; and Pio Galli and Giorgio Minelli of Attimo Fuggente.

Mr. Grandi, who is also a renowned judge, has produced many champions. Some of his more recent winners include Ital. Int. Club Ch. Lollpop Della Caveja, Ital. Int. Ch. Lancelot Della Caveja, Ital. Ch. Momentomagico Della Caveja, and Eur. J. Ital. Ch. Olivia Della Caveja, who is owned by Solstrand Kennels.

Mr. Montefiori bred Ital. Int. Eur. World Ch. Leopoldo, sired by Ch. Rondelin Mohawk of Solstrand; Ital. Ch. Igrayne, Ital. Int. Eur. Ch. Claretta, sired by Ital. Ch. Momentomagico Della Caveja, who was BOB at the 1993 European Champion Show; Ital. Ch. Dotto; and Ital. Ch. Pisolo.

Ofelia Kennels produced two champions: Ital. Ch. Ofelia Caterina and Ital. Ch. Ofelia Filidor.

AUSTRALIA

The first Greyhounds arrived in Australia in the 1700s, in the company of Captain James Cook's expedition, which resulted in the English discovery of the continent. No descendants of these two dogs, owned by Mr. Joseph Banks, remain. Coursing became a popular sport during the 1800s, and Greyhounds were imported from England and Ireland to participate in coursing events in Australia. Greyhound kennels include: Xilone, Kristine and Greg Coralluzzo; Jonz, John Palmer; Elwick, Gail Wilde; Dansn, Wayne Douglas; Bayan, Dennis and Chris McGreewj; Quam, Colleen and Adam Khoury.

XILONE

One of the top-winning Greyhounds in Australia has been Aus. Ch. Xilone Down Memory Lane, sired by Int. Ch. Huzzah the Voyageur ex Aus. Ch. Branwen Hedda (British import). Down Memory Lane won many all-breed bests in show and was a best hound winner. Mr. and Mrs. Coralluzzo, of Victoria, imported Aus. Ch. Branwen Hedda, sired by Eng. Ch. Solstrand Double Diamond ex Int. Ch. Padneyhill Phylida. Hedda holds the title as top-producing brood bitch in Australia, with many BIS and group winning offspring.

JONZ

Mr. John Palmer of Jonz Kennels, New South Wales, started in Greyhounds in 1985, when he imported Am. Aus. Ch. Huzzah Phantom Lake Romance and Aus. Ch. Huzzah the Voyageur from Pat Ide in the United States. Although he only breeds one or two litters per year, he has produced 17 champions and has owned 22. Some of his particular favorites are Ch. Jonz Dressed To Kill (now in the United States), Am. Aus. Ch. Phantom Lake Romance, and Am. Aus. Ch. Gallant Western Reunion. Phantom Lake Romance was top hound in Australia for two years, with multiple BIS wins. Aus. Ch. Huzzah The Voyageur is the top-producing sire in the breed with more than 20 champions to his credit.

Mr. Palmer's ideal Greyhound has a long, lean classic head, is sure footed, with long flowing lines and a beautiful sweep of hindquarters.

Besides breeding and exhibiting his own dogs, Mr. Palmer is also a handler and is licensed to judge the Hound and Sporting Groups.

CARING FOR A GREYHOUND

NUTRITION

Nutrition affects every aspect of your Greyhound's life. Good nutrition is absolutely necessary for optimum growth, development, and maintenance. But what constitutes proper nutrition is one of the most hotly debated issues related to dog care.

How many feedings a day? What about supplements? Is self-regulated feeding preferred? Which dog food is best? What kinds of meat or additives should be fed? Should I try an all-natural diet?

For every question there are many answers.

Although there are certain basic requirements in a Greyhound's diet at every stage of development, there are many correct ways to feed your dog. Owners have to determine what works best for them and for each of their individual Greyhounds. A puppy has different food requirements than an adult dog. A bitch in whelp or one nursing a litter may need to have her diet adjusted. Greyhounds that are being shown,

coursed, or raced frequently will have increased dietary needs. A diehard couch potato will probably need less food than a more active dog. An aging Greyhound with early signs of kidney dysfunction may require a special diet.

Your own personal schedule and lifestyle will also affect the way you feed your Greyhound. Are you home all day? Would you enjoy cooking and mixing special foods that make up a completely balanced diet? Are you at work for eight hours every day? Is there someone who can exercise your Greyhound when you are away from home? Does your dog have free access to an exercise yard?

All of these considerations, and probably many others, will influence the choices you make in developing a sound nutritional program for your Greyhound.

Feeding Your Greyhound Puppy

Greyhound puppies usually begin receiving supplemental feedings somewhere between the ages of three and four weeks. Puppies are up and around by then, though still a bit wobbly on their feet. Their tiny nails and new teeth are sharp, and nursing becomes a bit uncomfortable for the dam. Although some Greyhound bitches may refuse to feed their puppies after three or four weeks, many will continue to nurse their babies until they are six to eight weeks old.

Some breeders begin weaning by using a puppy replacement formula mixed with baby rice cereal. Meat and soaked kibble are gradually added to this mixture until the puppies, at six weeks, are eating moistened puppy kibble and meat three to four times a day. Powdered lamb and kid replacer, cottage cheese, yogurt, sour cream, and goat's milk are calcium-rich foods that breeders may use in place of puppy formula during the weaning process. One of the above is often added to the kibble and meat throughout the puppy's first year. Fresh water should be provided as the puppies nurse less frequently. Be certain all puppies are drinking well, usually by six weeks of age, before weaning completely.

The trend today seems to be away from the old weaning formulas using milk replacer and baby cereal. More and more breeders are using kibble and meat soaked until soft or mixed in a blender to wean their litters. They feel this method is one less change in a young puppy's diet and results in fewer problems with loose stools and digestive upsets.

The most important consideration when feeding your Greyhound puppy is the quality of the kibble and meat. Large, fast-growing Greyhound puppies need the correct balance of vitamins, minerals, protein, and fat to allow for optimum growth. Choose a premium brand puppy kibble, preferably one with no artificial dyes, and use a high-quality canned dog food. Small amounts of other additives mentioned above, and maybe even some fresh chopped or shredded vegetables, may be included. None of these additives should exceed 10 to 20 percent of the total amount fed.

Recent studies in the area of canine or-

Good nutrition, in the form of milk replacer and cereal or blended, soaked kibble and meat, may be used to wean puppies. Bred by Laurie Soutar.

As puppies grow older, a high-quality soaked kibble should be gradually introduced.

thopedics have revealed two interesting and very important findings related to the nutrition of young, fast-growing dogs.

The first is that dietary supplementation of puppies already receiving a complete diet can be detrimental to proper bone growth and development. Oversupplementation of calcium, phosphorus, magnesium, and vitamin A can be as harmful to a puppy's bone formation as inadequacies of these nutrients. The current recommendation is to use a high-quality, nutritionally complete food and avoid vitamin and mineral supplements unless prescribed by a veterinarian for a specific condition.

The second finding is that overfeeding a fast-developing Greyhound puppy can have a negative effect on skeletal growth. Many bone defects occur during the canine adolescent growth period, prior to closure of the growth plates. Excessive weight at this age can cause unnecessary strain on bones and joints. That fat, healthy-looking puppy who gobbles his food with gusto may not turn out to be as structurally sound as his slimmer sibling with a less voracious appetite.

It appears that optimum skeletal growth and development is accomplished by avoiding excessive nutrients and food intake and providing puppies with a simple, well-balanced diet.

Feeding Your Adult Greyhound

The goal when feeding an adult Greyhound is the same as when feeding growing puppies—to meet nutritional needs with a complete, well-balanced diet. In most instances, when choosing a commercially prepared dog food you "get what you pay for." The fact is that the ingredients that make up a high-quality, nutritionally sound food are more expensive than those found in low-cost brands.

When choosing a food for your Greyhound, follow the same suggestions for choosing your own healthy foods. Learn to read labels and compare ingredients. Look at the percentages of protein, fat, and fiber, then determine their sources. Feathers, hair, and hooves are mostly pure protein, but none of these are easily digested. Look for foods that have meat or meat by-products listed first or second on their labels. Choose foods that have natural preservatives and do not contain red dyes.

Choosing a complete, balanced, high-quality diet for your Greyhound should eliminate the need to supplement with vitamins and minerals. Dogs need a correct

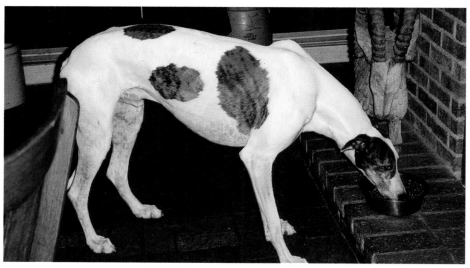

Consider whether a self-feeding method or a more scheduled form of feeding best suits the needs of your Greyhound.

balance of nutrients. Supplementing commercially prepared, nutritionally complete foods may upset this balance. A truly good diet should need no supplementation. There are quite a few good, and several excellent, dog foods on the market. Your search for the best food for your Greyhound may become one of trial and error. The brand you choose will depend on your dog's nutritional needs, likes and dislikes, activity level, and health status.

When deciding how often and how much to feed your Greyhound, study your dog's attitude toward food. Some dogs live for mealtime and seem to think of nothing but eating. Others are finicky eaters with a ho-hum attitude toward meals. Some Greyhounds are slow eaters, and others devour their food as soon as it is set before them. Your Greyhound's personality and eating habits will partially determine the feeding method you choose.

Greyhound owners use a variety of feeding methods that each maintain good body weight and sufficient nutrient intake. Some feed twice daily, dividing the food into two equal parts so as not to overload

the stomach. They feel this method cuts down on the susceptibility to bloat. Some soak the food until the kibble swells, some just add warm water. Meat, and sometimes vegetables and cottage cheese, are added to one or both of these meals.

Other owners, especially those whose Greyhounds are slow or picky eaters, choose to self-feed, leaving fresh dry kibble out all day so the dogs can eat as much as they like, whenever they like. This method also ensures that only a small amount of food is in the stomach at one time.

Another popular method is to combine the above two, giving dry food in the morning, permitting the Greyhounds to free feed all day, then feeding an evening meal of soaked kibble and meat. Giving biscuits in the morning and a full meal in the evening is a variation of this last feeding program.

No matter what regimen you choose, have fresh cool water available to your Greyhound at all times. And for health's sake, thoroughly wash food and water pans each day.

Feeding Your Senior Greyhound

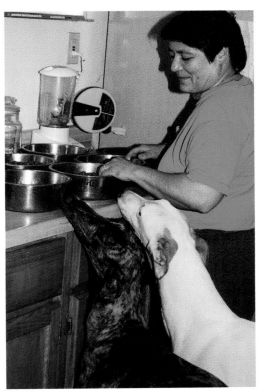

Good nutrition continues to be critical for adult dogs; choose a premium dog food that supplies your Greyhound with all of the vitamins, minerals, and protein he needs.

The age at which Greyhounds reach senior status is much later than most breeds of similar size. It is not unusual for Greyhounds to live 13 or 14 years, and so they may not be considered seniors until their tenth or eleventh birthday. They often stay very active throughout their lives, and the only telltale sign of aging is a graying of the face.

In most cases, a senior Greyhound has the same nutritional needs as a younger adult dog. It is not necessary to choose a dog food formulated to meet the needs of senior dogs with specific health problems, such as diminished renal function, unless the problems are actually present.

One necessary modification in feeding the senior Greyhound may be to decrease the amount of fat consumed. Energy expenditure and activity level of older dogs begins to diminish with age. It is important to maintain good condition in the older Greyhound and guard

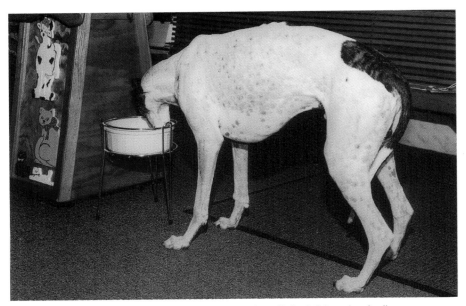

Many breeders recommend elevating a Greyhound's food dishes when feeding.

267

against obesity. Encouraging continued activity within reasonable limits and reducing fat and calorie intake, if necessary, will maintain good body weight.

An opposite problem associated with aging is loss of weight. Keep a close eye on your Greyhound's teeth. Dental and periodontal disease can lessen the desire to eat. Loss of the senses of sight and smell can affect eating habits, as can any general infection or subclinical disease.

It is not always easy to recognize illness in an older dog who is less active and sleeps much of the time. Take notice of even the smallest changes in behavior, sleep patterns, bowel and bladder control, and physical condition. It was easy to tell when your young "wild child" was having an off day. But changes in an older dog are more subtle. Train yourself to stay alert to any signs that may signal trouble.

Many dog food manufacturers advertise their dog food for seniors as having reduced protein content. But evidence shows that older dogs can tolerate the same protein levels as younger ones, unless the food you are using contains extremely high levels of protein. Protein intake needs to be restricted only if a dog exhibits clinical signs of liver or kidney disease. Phosphorous may then have to be restricted as well.

The question of whether to use a vitamin and mineral supplement for your older Greyhound may arise. Again, the answer remains the same. As long as your Greyhound is consuming adequate amounts of a well-balanced diet, no nutritional supplements should be necessary. If, however, the immune system is compromised for any reason in the older dog, some supplementation may be advised.

The senior Greyhound will thrive best when kept on a familiar schedule, fed and exercised regularly, and protected from stressful situations. Since older dogs can more easily become dehydrated, make certain that fresh water is available at all times, and encourage sufficient fluid consumption.

Providing proper nutrition for your Greyhound will certainly be an important consideration throughout your dog's life, but it does not need to be a difficult task. Consider your dog's needs and your schedule and feed accordingly.

INJURIES

One of the foremost concerns of Greyhound owners and breeders is finding a veterinarian who is familiar with the special needs and concerns of Greyhound patients. In the past, the search for a knowledgeable, qualified veterinarian could be extremely frustrating, and the most an owner could hope for was to locate someone who was familiar with some of the other more numerous sighthound breeds, or a person who was willing to listen and learn.

Today, with more and more Greyhounds living in homes as family pets, it is usually a much easier task, even in rural areas, to find a vet who has several Greyhound clients. Adoption agencies and breeders have done a good job of educating new Greyhound owners about the special concerns of caring for their Greyhounds. Several excellent books are available that contain valuable health information for Greyhound owners and veterinarians.

The best time to find a vet who is familiar with Greyhound care is before you bring a Greyhound home. If you are lucky enough to live in area where there are several veterinarians, make an appointment with them, visit their clinics,

Regular visits to the veterinarian for checkups and inoculations—as opposed to those for emergencies and illness—can prevent problems before they arise.

interview them about their experience working with Greyhounds. If there are no vets in your area that are aware of the special needs of some sighthound breeds, then choose one who is extremely conscientious in caring for each individual animal and who is willing to do some research into suitable medications, treatments, and anesthetics appropriate to Greyhounds. The choice in veterinarian could well mean the difference between life and death for your Greyhound—he or she must be someone you like and trust, and who values the life of your dog as much as you do.

It is a good idea to take your Greyhound to visit the vet before any seri-ous problems arise. Set up an appointment for a general checkup and keep the visit fun. Be sensitive to your dog's responses to this new experience and reassure him whenever necessary. This visit will also give you an opportunity to observe the veterinarian and staff in action and give you a feel for their overall attitude toward animal care.

Assessing Your Greyhound's Health

For the most part, Greyhounds are hardy and long-lived, with few genetic problems compared to many other breeds. The standard does not call for any physical alterations such as tail docking or ear cropping. Greyhounds are pretty much as you see them.

The breed's short coat enables owners to easily assess physical condition. Any weight gain or loss is easily observed. Skin problems are readily apparent.

Take some time each week to go over your Greyhound, checking for problems that may have arisen. You will find that it won't take long to train your eye to do a quick examination every time you look at your Greyhound. Look for signs of lameness and abnormal body postures. An arched back and cramping abdominal muscles could indicate abdominal pain. A head held to the side is a characteristic of a dog with an irritated or infected ear. A drooping head may mean that your Greyhound is not feeling well.

Be attentive to your Greyhound's overall attitude. An active, outgoing dog that suddenly becomes quiet and lethargic may be ill. A change in pulse rate may indicate health problems (you may take your Greyhound's pulse by placing your fingers on the inside of the upper foreleg and pressing gently). Normal resting pulse for a dog ranges from 60 to 120

beats per minute. An abnormal pulse rate, accompanied by other signs of distress, could signify a serious health problem.

A dog's normal temperature may be anywhere between 99.5 to 102.2 degrees Fahrenheit. When in an excited state or immediately after exercise, a dog's temperature may temporarily be as high as 103.5 degrees Fahrenheit. A dog's temperature is taken rectally. Insert the lubricated tip of a rectal thermometer gently into the rectum and hold it in place for two or three minutes.

Examining the Head

When doing a physical exam of your Greyhound, begin with the head. Check eyes for redness, cloudiness, or drainage. The whites of the eyes (scleras) should not be yellow or reddened. Inspect ears for discharge, foul odor, or black or brown waxy buildup in the ear canal. Watch for signs of ear trouble such as scratching or head shaking. Because a

Greyhound's ears are open to the air, they seldom experience any ear problems.

Greyhounds seem to be prone to tartar buildup on their teeth, which, if left unattended, can eventually lead to gum disease and tooth loss. Tartar can be controlled by regular brushing with a toothpaste made especially for dogs, as well as scaling and cleaning by your vet once or twice a year. Many Greyhound owners learn to use dental tools to scale their own dog's teeth. The best time to do this is often when a dog is tired at the end of a day. Some veterinarians clean Greyhounds' teeth without anesthetizing the dogs; instead, they give them something to make them a little drowsy. A Greyhound's gums and mucous membranes of the mouth should be pink and moist. Pale, dry gums and membranes may be signs of anemia or dehydration. If your Greyhound has sustained an injury, whitish gums may indicate shock.

A Greyhound's nose should be moist and cool, but may be dry when sleeping

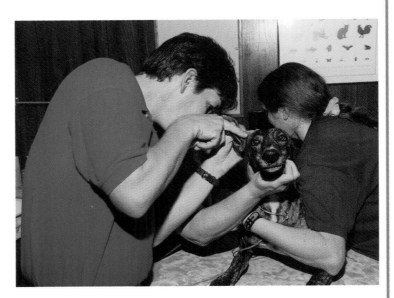

An ear examination is an important part of any veterinarian checkup.

Photo by Mark Scioto Photo

Left: Ch. Suntiger Sheena CD, owned by P. Gail Burnham, shows all signs of good health.

or when exercising in warm weather. A chronically dry and warm nose could indicate illness.

Examining the Body

Even though most injuries are readily apparent on a Greyhound, it is possible to miss something. A cut or skin tear can be more easily missed on a brindle dog than on a solid or parti-color.

Use both hands, beginning at the head, and move them over your dog's entire body. Feel for any lumps or bumps. If you find something you think may be questionable, check to see if the same mass or bulge appears on the other side of the dog. If it does, chances are it is normal muscle or bone. Lumps can be signs of swollen lymph nodes, cysts, abscesses, hernias, injuries, insect stings, bruises, or cancer. Abnormal lumps should be reported to your vet if they do not disappear in a day or two. Evaluate your Greyhound's coat and skin. The hair should be sleek and shiny, the skin free of scaliness or flakiness. Some Greyhounds lose hair on hips, elbows, points on their hocks, and on the tips of their tails. Daily applications of Horseman's Dream Cream, Bag Balm, A and D Ointment, or some other similar softening agent can help in these areas. Look closely for fleas and ticks, especially the tiny deer ticks that carry Lyme disease; they are so small, they can be easily missed. In fact, if you live in an area where Lyme disease is prevalent, it may be a good idea to get in the habit of checking for these ticks every time your Greyhound comes in from outside during warm weather; again, external parasites will not be as noticeable on a brindle Greyhound, so use special care. Check with your vet about vaccinating against Lyme disease.

Examining Legs and Tail

Many injuries that occur in Greyhounds involve legs, feet, and tails, so pay close attention to these body parts. Actually, considering how much running, jumping, twisting, and turning Greyhounds do when they exercise and play, it is surprising that more leg and feet injuries do not occur. If your dog is limping or refusing to put weight on a leg, you will know that something is not right. Run your hand carefully over the leg to see if you can locate an injury. Check between the pads of the foot for thorns or cuts. Look for swelling or bruising at the sight of an injury. Notice the toes. Are any of them flat? This could mean a break in one of the small bones. Is there a cut that requires stitches? If you can find no reason for the lameness and your Greyhound shows no other signs of distress, allow time for rest and see if the dog is still limping. If lameness continues, it should be checked by a veterinarian.

Long Greyhound tails wag constantly and often quite vigorously, making them susceptible to injury. Skin on tails can break open or tear easily. A Greyhound's whip-like tail can even break when hit against a wall, piece of furniture, or the corner of a refrigerator. They can bang against a tree or fence when a Greyhound passes too closely when running. Many tails accidentally get caught in doors—house doors as well as car doors. Make it a habit to watch and be certain your Greyhound's tail is out of danger before closing any door. A tail at rest can be raised in excitement or anticipation in a split second, so always leave plenty of extra space between a closing door and your Greyhound's tail.

Treatment of tail injuries will vary with the severity of the injury. If there

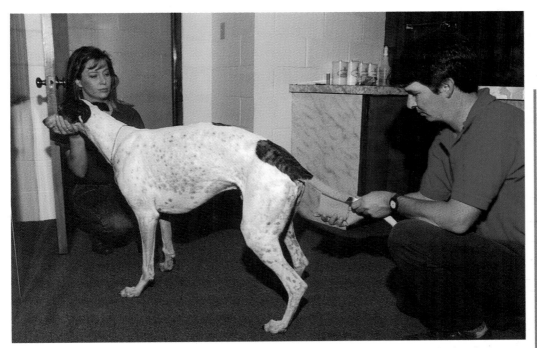

Tail injuries, both breaks and skin tears, are a common concern of Greyhound owners. *Photo by Mark Scioto Photo*

is only a small cut or tear, keep the area clean and allow it to heal by itself. Larger tears and cuts may need stitches. Keep a close eye on the site of an injury and check several times a day for warmth and swelling in the area. These could be signs of infection. Actually, the most serious challenge when caring for tail cuts or tears is preventing them from reopening. A cut that is constantly broken open heals slowly, may become infected, and could result in permanent hair loss at the site of the injury. It may be necessary to wrap the tail to protect it and prevent further injury; your vet can show you how to do this. You need to be certain the dressing is on tightly enough to stay in place, but not so tightly that it interferes with circulation.

A broken tail will need to be set by your veterinarian and will usually be splinted and wrapped for several weeks. Most Greyhounds will leave dressings alone, but some need to be watched constantly. If you are a multi-Greyhound home, you may have to isolate your injured companion from his chums, who may solicitously remove that foreign object wrapped around their friend's injured tail.

First Aid

First aid is immediate care given in the event of sudden illness or injury. First aid is intended to sustain life until medical help is available. Any first aid that you provide for your Greyhound should not replace veterinary care but can greatly improve your dog's chance of recovery or even save your Greyhound's life.

Most first aid procedures are not complicated and rely on common sense and the ability to remain calm in an emergency situation. To be successful, you must work quickly.

The best defense if an emergency should arise is to be prepared. A first aid kit can be assembled and kept on hand. It is a good idea to take this kit with you whenever you travel with your dog. Accidents can happen on the road as well as at home.

A basic first aid kit should contain activated charcoal, muzzle, splint material, adhesive tape, non-stick bandages, sterile gauze pads, antibiotic ointment, oral glucose concentrate, sterile gloves, Betadine, iodine, or hydrogen peroxide, Pepto Bismol, large syringe without needle, blanket, roll of gauze, thermometer, cloth strips, bandages, saline solution, large and small towels, instant cold packs, scissors, tweezers, phone numbers of your veterinarian and the National Animal Poison Control Center.

Another aspect of being prepared for an emergency is to learn to recognize the symptoms exhibited by a dog in extreme distress. Make an immediate assessment of the dog's general condition. Is the dog breathing? Is the breathing rapid, slow, or labored? Is the airway blocked? Is there any blood coming from the nose or mouth? Is there severe bleeding from an open wound?

If severe bleeding is not stopped immediately, irreversible shock and death can occur. Most bleeding can be stopped by applying firm, steady pressure to a wound until clotting takes place. Use supplies from the first aid kit to make a pressure bandage. If a cut is so severe that bleeding will not stop with just the application of pressure, you may need to use a tourniquet, placed between the injury and the heart.

Check the dog's heart rate and pulse. The heartbeat can be felt midway along the chest wall through the ribs. A Greyhound's heartbeat is easily seen through the ribcage. Another way to check pulse rate is by pressing your fingers lightly on the underside of the

Owners should have a first aid kit on hand at all times, even when on outdoor excursions. Owned by M. J. Barkley.

When it's necessary to check for bone or internal injuries, a vet may decide that an X-ray is in order. *Photo by Mark Scioto Photo*

Greyhound's thigh. If you do not find a pulse or heartbeat, it is time to take action.

When breathing has stopped, it is absolutely necessary to quickly re-establish respiration. Check for any objects that may be blocking the airway. Place your dog on his side. Carefully remove any foreign object with a finger if you can reach it. Several abdominal thrusts, applying sudden pressure to the abdomen at the edge of the sternum, may be necessary if you cannot manually dislodge the object. This may work the object up into the throat where you can reach it or it may be expelled completely.

If you have an open airway and there is an absence of respiration, you will want to perform artificial respiration. With the dog on his side, extend the neck, hold the muzzle closed, and place your mouth over the dog's nose. Slowly blow air into the dog's nose until you see his chest expand. A Greyhound should receive 12 to 15 breaths per minute.

If your dog has not responded to artificial respiration and you cannot find a heartbeat or pulse, you will have to start CPR. Place both hands, one on top of the other, over the heart behind the elbow where the chest wall is widest. Compress the chest one to three inches with a firm downward movement. Compression should be rapid, approximately 80 times per minute. Check for a heartbeat every 30 to 60 seconds. If you are alone and need to do both artificial ventilation and CPR, give two quick breaths every 15 compressions. When two people are available to work on the dog, a breath should be given every three to five compressions. If you are able to resuscitate your Greyhound, transport him to your veterinarian immediately.

Shock

Any severe injury or illness can precipitate a state of shock. Signs of shock include low blood pressure, a rapid weak pulse, pale gums, cool extremities, low rectal temperature, general depression, and lack of response. Shock can lead to death and needs to be treated quickly. Wrap your Greyhound in blankets or plastic to retain heat and increase body temperature. Keep the head slightly lower than the rest of the body. Stop any bleeding. Keep your dog calm and get to a veterinarian. Shock will be treated at the clinic with intravenous fluids.

Broken Bones

The best treatment for a break is to keep your dog as quiet as possible and seek veterinary attention. If improperly applied, a splint or bandage may do more harm than good and should only be used to keep the limb immobilized if it will be quite some time before medical help can be obtained.

Heatstroke (Hyperthermia)

Greyhounds do not tolerate heat as well as people do, so always be on guard against situations that could bring on heatstroke in warm weather. Do not take your dog with you in the car in hot weather unless absolutely necessary. Never leave your dog in a car on a warm sunny day, even if you can leave the windows open. Some Greyhounds will run and play regardless of outside temperature, so allow your Greyhound to exercise only in the morning and evening on very hot days. Keep male Greyhounds away from bitches in season, especially during hot weather; their excitement combined with the heat could cause heatstroke. Another caution concerning heatstroke involves flying your Greyhound. If you must fly during hot weather, fly at night. Choose direct flights whenever possible, even if it means you have to travel some distance by car.

First aid treatment for heatstroke is to lower the body temperature. If you can immerse the dog in cold water, do so. You may use cold, wet towels, wet sponges, ice packs, even a garden hose to cool the dog and lower body temperature. Once the dog's temperature is at or below 103 degrees Fahrenheit, keep the dog in a cool place and continue monitoring the temperature until it returns to normal. A veterinarian should see your dog after heatstroke for

As with other breeds, Greyhounds can have a difficult time coping with hot weather; cold water or play time in a pool may help to keep dogs cool. "Tess" is owned by Donna Arcaro.

follow-up treatment to prevent further complications.

Hypothermia and Frostbite

Despite their lack of hair and body fat, most Greyhounds love cold weather and snow. They seem to become invigorated and will sprint and jump and roll in delight, running with their muzzles buried in the snow, leaping and turning in the cold air.

Greyhound owners delight in watching their hounds cavort in the snow, but some cold weather conditions call for precautions. Very young, old, sick, or injured dogs cannot tolerate cold temperatures and should be outside only long enough to eliminate. If you are going to walk your Greyhound, a warm coat would be as appropriate for your dog as for yourself—and as appreciated. Watch your dog for signs of chilling and return home if the dog appears uncomfortable. If you are going to walk where sidewalks or streets have been salted, you may want to get dog boots or coat foot pads with mineral oil.

Exposure to bitter cold for only a short period of time can cause frostbite, especially on extremities such as the ears, tail, feet, and genitals. Frostbitten skin appears white, gray, or red in color. A dog with frostbite may appear shocky. To treat frostbite, warm the affected tissue by immersing it in water that is just warm to the touch, 100 to 105 degrees Fahrenheit, for 15 to 20 minutes. Lightly dry the area by patting, not rubbing, the skin, as frostbitten skin can slough off.

Hypothermia can occur in a Greyhound left in the cold for too long a time. As long as your dog is active, his body temperature remains high. When he slows down, his temperature will de-

A Greyhound's lean build and thin coat offer little protection from cold and snowy weather conditions. Ch. Willomoor Ghostbuster is owned by Patti Clark and June Matarazzo.

crease. If the dog falls asleep in the cold after a vigorous period of exercise, or even lies down to rest, hypothermia may occur. Signs of hypothermia include drowsiness or lethargy, depressed respiration, uncontrollable shivering, anxious expression. Slowly warm a dog with hypothermia by placing the dog in a tub of warm water or wrapping him in blankets warmed in a clothes dryer. In the case of frostbite or hypothermia, seek veterinary attention as soon as possible.

Burns

If your Greyhound should be severely burned, treat by applying ice cold water to the burned area and transporting the dog to a vet.

Poison

There are many agents in our environment that could poison your Greyhound. Most of these potentially poisonous items are found in every home, so take precautions to keep these products out of reach of your always-curious Greyhound. The best treatment is prevention when it comes to poisons, but accidents can happen, in spite of your best efforts.

Some common household poisons include aspirin, acetaminophen, gasoline, rodent poisons, antifreeze, herbicides, rubbing alcohol, bleach, insecticides, shoe polish, brake fluid, kerosene, soaps, cleaning fluids, mineral spirits, suntan lotion, disinfectants, mothballs, turpentine, drain cleaners, nail polish remover, windshield washer fluid, fungicides, paint, wood preservatives, and ibuprofen.

Warm coats for wintertime—and rain coats for the rainy season—are available to keep Greyhounds as comfortable as possible in inclement weather. Owned by Maggie Bryson.

Many plants and plant parts are also poisonous to your Greyhound. If you'd like to use some of these ornamental plants, do so in areas to which your Greyhound has no access.

Some poisonous plants include Amaryllis Bulbs, Chokeberry, Hydrangea, Peach, Apple Seeds, Daffodil, Iris, Philodendron, Avocado, Delphinium, Japanese Yew, Poison Ivy, Azalea, Dieffenbachia, Laurel, Rhododendron, Bittersweet, English Ivy, Marigold, Rhubarb, Boxwood, Elderberry, Mistletoe, Stinging Nettle, Buttercup, Foxglove, Mushrooms, Tobacco, Caladium, Hemlock, Narcissus, Toadstools, Castor Bean, Holly, Nightshade, Tulip bulbs, Cherry Pits, Hyacinth bulbs, Oleander, Walnut, and Wisteria.

Treatment for poison is specific to the poison ingested, so it is always best if you can identify the agent. The National Animal Poison Control Center can tell you if a substance your Greyhound has ingested is poisonous and can then explain the proper method of treatment.

In most cases of poisoning, the dog should be made to vomit, to rid the body of the ingested toxin. The exception to this rule is if your dog has swallowed a caustic or corrosive substance such as lye, bleach, furniture and floor cleaners, etc. Regurgitation of caustic substances could cause more damage to the stomach and esophagus.

One or two teaspoons of hydrogen peroxide or table salt, or a small dose of ipecac, will usually induce vomiting. Your vet can also give your Greyhound an injection that will cause vomiting. Your goal is to rid the body of a toxic material as soon as possible after ingestion.

If a caustic material has been eaten, give activated charcoal to absorb the poi-

Ch. Wydlewood Winsome of Cebar and her son, Cebar Neil of Barne, out for a brisk stroll. *Photo courtesy Ellie Creech*

son. If you have no charcoal in your first aid supplies, give milk of magnesia. If possible, toast some bread until it is burned, crush it and mix it with the milk of magnesia. This will help to absorb the poison.

Deskunking Recipe

The following recipe may come in handy in the event that your Greyhound decides to chase a skunk instead of a rabbit or squirrel. Bathe your dog with a mixture of one quart of 3 percent hydrogen peroxide, one-quarter cup baking soda, and one teaspoon of liquid soap. Then rinse well.

Transport

Transporting an injured Greyhound must be done carefully. You should move the dog as little as possible so you do not cause further injury. If a dog cannot walk, use a blanket, large towel, rug, plastic sled, or board as a stretcher. If you have two people to help, you can lift and carry your Greyhound to a safe place or a vehicle for transport to the vet's office. If you are alone, you may have to drag the stretcher and dog to the vehicle, then, as carefully as possible, place the dog inside.

Muzzle

Any dog, no matter how gentle, may try to bite in reaction to pain or fear. You may want to muzzle a badly injured dog before attempting first aid or transport.

An adequate muzzle can be made from a long strip of cloth or rolled gauze, a bandage, even pantyhose or a necktie. Bring the middle of the strip under the dog's muzzle and make a half-knot on top. Bring both ends below the muzzle again and make another half knot. Then bring the ends behind the back of the dog's head and ears and tie in an easily released slip-knot or bow. Make certain the restraint is tight enough to prevent it from slipping off, but not so tight that it impedes respiration.

If you are called on to administer first aid to your Greyhound, remember to stay calm and talk soothingly to the animal. Use your head and do not put yourself in danger. Get in touch with your veterinarian as soon as possible. Medical care is usually a necessary follow-up to any emergency situation.

GREYHOUND HEALTH CONCERNS

There are several health concerns that are relative to Greyhounds and some other similar breeds.

Bloat

Bloat—or gastric dilatation or volvulus—is a syndrome that affects mostly large to giant, deep-chested

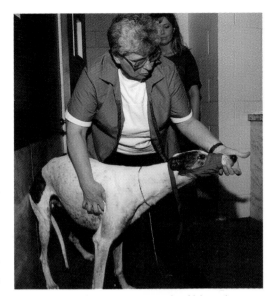

It may sometimes be necessary to muzzle a frightened or injured Greyhound before treatment. *Photo by Mark Scioto Photo*

dogs. Although bloat is not a common problem in Greyhounds, it does occur occasionally, and Greyhound owners should be aware of the symptoms and treatment.

Bloat is caused by gas buildup in the stomach, which causes distention and makes the dog uncomfortable. The gas becomes trapped when, because of a sudden movement or the pressure of the gas, the stomach twists or flips. The dog becomes highly distressed and will pace restlessly. His back may be arched and painful. He may retch but will produce nothing but a little mucus. He will obviously be in pain as the stomach becomes more distended. When the stomach twists, it blocks the flow of blood to the stomach and spleen. Tissue death begins almost immediately. Infection and toxins build up and cause shock, coma, and death—all of which can occur in a matter of two or three hours.

When the first signs of bloat appear, immediately get your Greyhound to your veterinarian. This is an emergency situation, so do not hesitate, even if it is the middle of the night. The veterinarian will first try to relieve pressure by passing a tube into the stomach through the mouth. If the tube does not pass or does not relieve pressure, a large hypodermic needle may be inserted through the abdominal wall into the stomach.

If the stomach has twisted, surgery will be necessary. The stomach will be righted and will usually be sutured to the abdominal wall to prevent volvulus from reoccurring. Surgery has a high success rate if the dog receives medical attention early enough.

Although no one knows for certain why bloat occurs, there are some recommended precautions that can be taken to prevent it.

1. Choose a high-quality dog food that does not contain soy.
2. Self feed or feed two smaller meals a day.
3. Soak food before feeding.
4. Limit exercise one hour before and after eating.
5. Avoid excess water intake before and after exercise and meals.
6. Keep your Greyhound in good physical condition.
7. Give plenty of exercise.
8. Keep your dog well muscled.
9. Maintain ideal weight.

The risk of bloat increases with age, so you may want to monitor your Greyhound more closely as the years pass. Researchers continue to study bloat, looking at genetic and environmental factors that may affect dogs at risk.

Anesthesia

Greyhounds and most other sighthounds are extremely sensitive to anesthesia, and great care must be taken by your veterinarian when it is necessary to anesthetize your dog. Many vets like to avoid general anesthesia whenever possible and use local application to stitch a tear or perform some other minor procedure.

Isoflurane, a fairly new inhaled anesthesia, seems to cause less cardiovascular depression than other FDA-approved inhaled anesthetics. It is the anesthesia of choice for maintenance during surgery.

Short-acting barbiturate drugs such as thiopental (Pentathol R) are not at all well tolerated. Greyhounds have an extremely slow recovery rate from anesthesia if given these drugs; some have even been lost on the operating table. Greyhounds should not be induced with any of the thiobarbiturate drugs.

According to Richard Bednarski, DVM, diplomate in the American College of Veterinary Anesthesiologists and an associate professor in the Department of Veterinary Clinical Sciences at Ohio State University, a safe protocol for administering anesthesia to a Greyhound is to first give a mild premedication injection under the skin or into the muscle 10 to 15 minutes prior to surgery. This is followed by an induction drug, usually Propyfol, or a mixture of diazepam and ketamine, and then the inhalant anesthetic, Isoflurane.

The reason for Greyhounds' heightened sensitivity to anesthetics is not known for certain. It may be due to the lower percentage of body fat per pound carried by Greyhounds and other sighthound breeds. Another factor may be that the drugs are metabolized differently by the liver. A study conducted at Ohio State revealed

Check with your veterinarian about what kind of schedule you'll follow for your Greyhound's vaccinations.

Photo by Mark Scioto Photo

that Greyhounds have a lower liver enzyme activity level, which does affect the rate at which a dog's body rids itself of an anesthetic. It also noted that Greyhounds are more prone to hyperthermia during surgery, which can also affect their response to anesthetics and recovery time following surgery. Whatever the reason, be certain that your veterinarian is aware of the special care necessary when operating on your Greyhound.

Vaccination

There has been much discussion in the veterinary field in recent years about the safety and efficacy of vaccination protocols. Which vaccines should be given? When and how often? Which is better, modified live or killed? Should puppies be vaccinated every two weeks, three weeks, every month? Should all vaccines be given simultaneously, or should they be spread out? Should dogs be immunized against a disease that is not prevalent in your area? Is the quality of all vaccines equal?

Greyhound owners and breeders need to make important decisions regarding vaccination procedures. These are probably best made with your veterinarian, as each dog is different.

The following table outlines the most widely recommended vaccination schedule.

Vaccine Administration	Puppies—Weeks of Age	Booster
Adenovirus	6, 9, 12, 16	Annual
Distemper	6, 9, 12, 16	Annual
Parvovirus (MLV)	6, 9, 12, 16, (20)	Annual
Parainfluenza (Inject)	6, 9, 12, 16	Annual
Coronavirus	9, 12	Annual
Leptospira	9, 12, 16	Annual
Bordatella (Inject)	9, 12	Annual
Bordatella/ Parainfluenza (Intranasal)		Annual *or prior to exposure*
Rabies	12 or 16	1 or 3 years

Although the table recommends only annual boosters for most of the vaccines, many Greyhound owners whose dogs are often exposed to other dogs at shows, training classes, coursing events, etc., prefer to vaccinate twice a year. That decision, again, should be made with your vet.

GREYHOUNDS AND GENETIC DISORDERS

For many years Greyhound owners and breeders prided themselves in having a breed that was free of any genetic health problems: no hip dysplasia, no retinal dysplasia or atrophy, no cardiomyopathy, no panosteitis. Few of these problems surfaced. For the most part, the breed has been genetically sound and free of many of the serious problems that affect other large breeds.

However, today's breeders and owners are not willing to assume that these disorders are absent in Greyhounds. They want to make certain these abnormalities do not get a foothold in the breed. More and more breeders are X-raying their Greyhounds for hip dysplasia before using them in their breeding programs; many are also X-raying elbows. Those breeders are also breeding only to dogs that have good or excellent ratings from the Orthopedic Foundations for Animals (OFA), an organization that evaluates X-rays of dogs' hips and elbows submitted by veterinarians or owners. Consideration is made for the dog's age, breed, etc. The X-rays are evaluated by three veterinary radiologists. If the hips pass, an OFA number is awarded.

Another assessment of hip condition is propounded by researchers at the University of Pennsylvania and International Canine Genetics (PennHIP™/ICG), who believe that hip joint laxity (looseness of the hip joint) can lead to the degenerative joint disease of hip dysplasia. A three-year study revealed that not all dogs with loose hips will later develop hip dysplasia, but hip laxity is necessary for hip dysplasia to occur. Investigators believe the PennHIP™ compression/distraction radiographs can be used as a predictor of future phenotypic development of hip dysplasia.

Few things are more important to a sighthound than eyesight. Imagine your Greyhound running at breakneck speed,

Eyes, as well as hips, can be examined by a veterinarian in order to check for heritable disorders or abnormalities.

Photo by Mark Scioto Photo

playing with his buddies, chasing prey, or following a lure without the aid of perfect vision.

Again, concerned breeders are having their dogs' eyes examined for heritable eye disease by a veterinarian who is a member of the American College of Veterinary Ophthalmologists (ACVO). Puppies can be examined as soon as their eyes are physically mature. Test results are submitted to the Canine Eye Registration Foundation (CERF), a national registry whose goal is to eliminate heritable eye disease in purebred dogs. If a dog is found to be free of eye disease, it is given a CERF registration number.

Hip and eye examinations are important, even necessary, procedures for Greyhounds that are being used in a breeding program. Conscientious breeders want to make certain that new genetic problems do not develop as well as ensure that any existing problems do not go undetected.

Hypothyroidism

Hypothyroidism is a topic that is often discussed among owners and breeders of Greyhounds. A dog that is hypothyroid has decreased thyroid function.

Hypothyroidism is probably the most prevalent endocrine disorder that occurs in dogs. A low to normal thyroid reading seems to be relatively common in Greyhounds. Although most do not show any outward signs of the disorder, it is often discovered when bitches are tested after they fail to conceive following one or two breedings.

Dogs that are hypothyroid may have a dull brittle coat, excessive shedding, and may actually have hairless patches on their bodies. They are more prone to skin problems. They are often lethargic, overweight, and have reproductive problems.

If you or your vet suspect that your Greyhound may be hypothyroid, several blood tests can be run to determine thyroid levels. Thyroid replacement therapy usually produces excellent results.

Parasites

It is important that your Greyhound be kept free of all internal and external parasites. But care must be taken when using chemicals to prevent or rid your dog of these parasites. Some Greyhounds are very sensitive to the chemicals used to keep your dog and your property parasite free.

External Parasites: Some Greyhounds cannot tolerate the chemicals found in many common flea and tick preparations. It is suggested that if you

Internal parasites can be detected in stool and blood samples by your veterinarian. *Photo by Mark Scioto Photo*

want to use a flea collar, choose one with an herbal or all-natural base. Some Greyhounds react to internal flea pills and the chemical that is applied to a dog's skin.

If you need to use a flea or tick product on your Greyhound, choose one that contains pyrethrins. These are natural products made from the chrysanthemum plant. Look for labels that state that a product is safe for kittens and puppies.

The incredible spread of Lyme disease makes it especially important to check your Greyhound for ticks daily if you live in an infested area. Deer ticks that usually spread Lyme disease are very small compared to a normal dog tick and are difficult to spot. It has recently been found that some American Dog Ticks are also carriers of Lyme disease.

There is now a product on the market that appears to be a promising nontoxic way to control fleas on your property. Diatomaceous earth is a powdered mineral product made up of tiny sea skeletons and aquatic algae known as diatoms. On contact with a flea's body this product acts as a drying agent; the tiny sharp particles also cause death if they are ingested. Diatomaceous earth does not cause immediate death, but according to authorities it should work to clear your property of fleas within several weeks.

Internal Parasites: Roundworms, tapeworms, whipworms, hookworms, giardia, coccidia, and heartworms are all parasites that can live within your dog. Again, care must be taken when ridding your Greyhound of any of these parasites.

Prevention is the first line of defense when dealing with internal parasites. Keep your Greyhound's living quarters clean and dry. Keep stools picked up. Have regular stool and blood tests run by your veterinarian to check for the presence of any parasites.

If your Greyhound does have one of the parasites, the following products are considered safe for most Greyhounds:

Roundworms—Strongid-T
Tapeworms—Droncit
Hook, Round, Whip—Panacur
Heartworms—Heartguard.

CARING FOR YOUR AGING GREYHOUND

Greyhound owners are blessed with a large, healthy breed that is relatively free of any serious genetic disorders and lives to a ripe old age. Many Greyhounds live to be 13 or 14 years old, a few even longer.

As your Greyhound ages you will have to make a few adjustments. Changes in routine, care, and feeding may have to be made.

Your elderly Greyhound will naturally slow down a little, sleep more, begin to gray, and lose some sight and hearing acuity. These are all normal changes that accompany aging.

Owners of geriatric dogs must be alert to warning signals of illness and be able to distinguish these from normal signs of aging. Some signals that your Greyhound is not well may be cessation of eating, weight loss, shortness of breath or labored breathing, constant cough, frequent thirst and urination, lameness, chronic diarrhea or vomiting, unpleasant or foul-smelling breath.

Kidney disease, liver disease, heart disease, and cancer are the leading causes of death among older dogs. As dogs age, the kidneys are the organs that experience the most deterioration. Kidney (renal) disease can become quite

With proper care, nutrition, and exercise, a Greyhound should thrive for many healthy and happy years.

advanced before any symptoms appear. For this reason, it is not often diagnosed in its early stages. Early signs may be that your Greyhound drinks and urinates more often. Later symptoms include loss of appetite, vomiting, loss of weight, incontinence, lethargy, constipation and/or diarrhea. Special diets that are lower in phosphorus and salt are often prescribed for the older dog with suspected renal failure; antibiotics and steroids are also used.

Heart disease can mean deterioration of the heart muscle or valves, changes in rhythm, or infection. Cardiac problems may affect all of a dog's other organs. Symptoms of heart disease include coughing, labored breathing, weakness and inability or unwillingness to exercise, and edema of legs and abdomen.

Through the use of appropriate drugs, vitamins and minerals, and diet changes, heart disease can be treated and will help to prolong the life of your dog.

The form of cancer most often seen in dogs is lymphoma; older dogs also develop lumps and tumors. As your Greyhound's age progresses, watch for their development and report them to your vet. Surgery, chemotherapy, and, in some cases, radiation treatments are available to treat cancer in your dog.

Dogs, like people, are living longer, healthier lives. This is because of the availability of better nutrition and medical care, the ability of dog owners to recognize problems when they arise, and their willingness to treat these problems and make the adjustments necessary to live with an older dog.

GATHERING GREYHOUND TREASURES

Collecting Greyhound art can be a fascinating and addictive habit for many who love Greyhounds. Dani Edgerton, Greyhound breeder, editor of the *GCA Newsletter,* and avid collector, is one of those people and an expert on the subject. Drawing on her own experiences, she has put together some history and advice for those interested in collecting.

Greyhound art is just uncommon enough to make the search for collectibles exciting, but available enough not to be discouraging. Once you know where to look, however, you should find plenty to choose from. There are Greyhounds in necklaces, pottery, lamps, and etchings. Greyhounds can be depicted running, standing, sitting, with women, with cats, and with other dogs. They can be seen in hunt scenes and play scenes.

The Greyhound has been a favorite subject of artists and craftsmen for centuries. Greyhounds are featured in Egyptian tombs and on Grecian urns. Through time, Greyhounds have been painted, sculpted, carved, and cast. The smooth flowing lines of the Greyhound have naturally been paired with the Art Nouveau woman, and their fine muscular definition made the Greyhound an excellent subject for 19th-century etchings.

Sculpture is by far the most prevalent art form modeled on the Greyhound. It's possible to find life-size concrete pieces, stunning bronzes, delicate porcelain and tiny pewter objects. Sculptors of worldwide renown, such as Pierre-Jules Mene and Renee Lalique, frequently chose Greyhounds as their subjects. Hundreds of pieces of Staffordshire pottery depicting Greyhounds and their game were manufactured. A variety of carnival chalkware features Greyhounds on the hunt or with their mistresses.

Available Greyhound sculpture ranges in age from several hundred years old to contemporary. A wide span in price makes Greyhound sculpture highly collectible. Wonderful pieces can vary from more than $10,000 for an Art Nouveau bronze to a couple of dollars for a small ceramic or metal hound. There are excellent originals, both antique and contemporary, available, as well as well-produced reproductions.

Greyhounds have been crafted in every type of jewelry imaginable and in every medium. There are many marcacite running Greyhound pins, Art Nouveau necklaces, and Greyhound heads fashioned in silver and gold. Jewelry prices are determined by the medium, age, and uniqueness of the piece. In addition, Greyhound jewelry is an area where custom work is readily available.

Paintings, prints, etchings, and posters featuring Greyhounds are abundant. Nineteenth-century coursing hounds are depicted in hand-colored etchings and restrikes. Many English prints feature Greyhounds because they have always been cherished by royalty as excellent hunters and pets, particularly by Queen Victoria and Prince Albert. There are many contemporary posters available with the Greyhound as their subject, and a few posters from the Art Nouveau/Art Deco eras can be found; sizes vary from small etchings to oversized posters.

Many other paper items, old and new, feature Greyhounds, including classic collectibles such as stamps, cigarette cards, and postcards. You can find and buy notecards, stationery, and greeting cards with Greyhound art depicted. Historical photographs of people and their hounds can be found by the most diligent searchers.

Boxes, tins, clocks, bookends, plates, doorstops, glassware, buttons, hood ornaments, pillows, blankets, vases, and

Antique stores are great places to find such Greyhound treasures as etchings, porcelain sculptures, and pitchers.

The Greyhound figure is one that makes a dramatic photographic subject. Pictured is Ch. Astara's Back in Black. Owned by Jim S. Porcher. *Photo by Joyce Fay*

many other items feature the Greyhound as their subject. You will be surprised at the amount and amazed at the variety of Greyhound pieces you may find.

Greyhound collectibles can be found in many places, some obvious and others not so obvious. Dog show vendors and dog-related catalogs are a prime source for newer items. Antique stores, auctions, galleries, and flea markets are the obvious choices for older, rarer Greyhound art. These places require a good deal of searching, but you are of-

Ohio artist Annie Fitt's depictions of a Greyhound appear in miniature on pins and in paintings.

Greyhound collectibles are out there for those willing to search. The lifesize white Greyhound was originally used for a 1940s department store display.

ten rewarded with a spectacular find. Furniture departments and stores and interior design shops are a great source for new decorator pieces such as Greyhound sculptures and prints.

When it comes to Greyhound collectibles, the old adage "buy only what you like" is particularly true. First, because there is so much to choose from, there is no reason to buy a piece that you do not find beautiful, interesting, or amusing. If the Greyhound isn't lovely or to your liking, leave it, you will find another. And second, while some of the pieces, such as a bronze or oil painting, will increase in value, most have more intrinsic value to you as a Greyhound art collector than they will to an antique dealer or collector. Buy wisely, but buy what you love.

BIBLIOGRAPHY

Arden, Darlene. "The Grande Dame of Greyhounds," *AKC Gazette*. New York: The American Kennel Club, February 1995.

Ash, Edward C., M.R.A.C. *The Practical Dog Book*. London: Hutchinson & Company, Ltd., 1933.

Barnes, Julia. *The Complete Book of Greyhounds*. New York: Howell Book House, 1994.

Blythe, Linda L. DVM, PhD. and others. *Care of the Racing Greyhound*. American Greyhound Council, 1994.

Branigan, Cynthia A. *Adopting the Racing Greyhound*. New York: Howell Book House, 1992.

Bruette, William A. *The Complete Dog Book*. Stewart Kidd Co., USA, 1922.

Burnham, P. Gail. *Play Training Your Dog*. New York: St. Martin's Press, 1980.

Carlson, Delbert G., DVM and Giffin, James M, M.D. *Dog Owners Home Veterinary Handbook*. New York: Howell Book House, 1980.

Clarke, H. Edwards. *The Waterloo Cup*. Surrey, England: Saiga Publishing Co., Ltd., 1978

Cole, Robert. "Trotting Greyhounds," *Sighthound Review*, May-June 1992.

Copold, Steve. "Open Field vs. Park vs. Lure: An In-Depth Look at the Mechanics of Coursing," *The Gazehound*, January-February 1976.

Cox, Major Harding. "Dogs By Well-Known Authorities," 1905. *The Gazehound*, July-August 1972.

Cuccione, Gary. "Footnotes," *The Greyhound Review*, May 1995.

Custer, Elizabeth Bacon. *Boots and Saddles*. New York: Harper & Bros., 1885.

Custer, Elizabeth Bacon. *Following the Guidon*. New York: Harper & Bros., 1890. Reprint, Lincoln, Nebraska: University of Nebraska Press, 1994.

Custer, Elizabeth Bacon. *Tenting on the Plains*, 1887 reprint. Norman Oklahoma, University of Oklahoma Press, 1971.

Dalziel, Hugh. *The Greyhound*. Upcott, Gill. England, 1887. *GCA Newsletter* reprint, 1988.

Genders, Roy. *Greyhounds*. New York: Arco Publishing Co., 1975.

Gresham, Fred. *New Book of the Dog*. London: Leighton, Cassell & Co., 1912.

Greyhound Club, The. *Greyhound Club Handbook, 1989-1993.* Ira and Rita Bond, editors. England, 1993.

Scheele, Ed. *Roots of the Greyhound.* Abilene, Kansas: Greyhound Hall of Fame.

Greyhound Pets of America, editors. *The Retired Racing Greyhound as a Family Pet.* Rochester, New Hampshire: Laser Design.

Holder, C.F. "Coursing with Greyhounds in Southern California," St. Nicholas, Nov. 1889. *The Gazehound,* Vol. XVII No. 1, September-October 1974.

Homer. *Odyssey.* P.F. Collier & Sons, 1909.

Horwitz, Debra, DVM. "Puppies Socialization: Getting Off to a Good Start," *Pedigree Breeders Forum,* November 1994.

King James Version Bible. Archon Books, 1968.

Kramer, Charles L. *Agility Dog Training for All Breeds.* Manhattan, Kansas: Cascade Press, 1987.

Lackey, Sue A. *Greyhounds In America,* Vol. I. Greyhound Club of America, Inc., 1989.

Lennox, Alan. *Greyhounds, The Sporting Breed* Sportman's Press, 1987.

Lyons, McDowell. *The Dog In Action.* New York: Howell Book Co., 1978.

Michel, Kathryn E., DVM, MS. "Feeding The Senior Dog" *Pedigree Breeders Forum.*

Miller, Constance O. *Gazehounds: A Search for Truth.* Wheat Ridge, Colorado: Hofflin Publishing Ltd., 1988.

Mueller, Georgianna. *How to Raise and Train A Greyhound.* T.F.H. Publications, Inc., 1965.

Ovid. *Metamorphoses.* Heritage Book, 1961.

Rolins, Anne. *All About the Greyhound.* Australia: Weldon Publishing, 1982.

Sawyer, Dr. Braxton B. "Study of the Greyhound Standard, Parts I, II, III & IV," *The Gazehound,* May-June, July-August, September-October, November-December, 1973.

Senour, Caro. *Master St. Elmo.* Chicago: Juvenile Book Co., 1904.

Shakespeare, William. *The Complete Works of William Shakespeare.* Scott, Foresman. 1951.

Shaw, FRA Vero. "The Illustrated Book of the Dog," 1879-1881. *GCA Newsletter,* 1991.

Stewart, Martha Morley. *Greyhound Fanny.* Seattle: H. De F. Stewart Controlling Publisher, 1912.

Stonhenge, (Dr. John Henry Walsh). *The Greyhound: The Art of Breeding, Rearing and Training Greyhounds for Public Running.* London: Longman's Greens & Co., 1866.

Strong, James H., STD, LLD. *Strong's Exhaustive Concordance.* Grand Rapids, Missouri: Baker Book House, Co., 1985.

Thurston, Mary E. "The Dogs of Ancient Egypt," *AKC Gazette,* August 1993.

Unger, Merrill F. *Unger's Bible Dictionary,* Chicago: Moody Press, 1979.

Wilcox, Bonnie, DVM, and Walkowicz, Chris. *The Atlas of the Dog Breeds of the World.* Neptune City, New Jersey: T.F.H. Publications, Inc., 1989.

Appendix

Publications

Greyhound Club of America Newsletter

Dani Edgerton, Editor
7115 West Calla Rd.
Canfield, OH 44406
(330) 533-6576 (phone and fax)
GCANews@compuserve.com

Sighthound Review

Jim and Cathy Gaidos
10177 Blue River Hills Rd.
Manhattan, KS 66503
(785) 485-2992 or (785) 485-2096 (fax)
gaidos@jc.net

Canine Collectibles Quarterly

736 N. Western Ave., Suite 314
Lake Forest, IL 60045

Canine Images

1003 Central Ave.
P.O. Box 916
Fort Dodge, IA 50501
(515) 955-1600, (800) 247-2000 hlil@dodgenet.com;
http://www.canineimages.com

Celebrating Greyhounds: The Magazine

The Greyhound Project, Inc.
P.O. Box 173, Holbrook, MA 02343

Celebrating Greyhounds Calendar

The Greyhound Project, Inc.
261 Robbins St.
Milton, MA 02186
(617) 333-6655

The Greyhound Review

National Greyhound Association
P.O. Box 543
Abilene, KS 67410
(913) 263-4600 (phone and fax)

AKC Coursing News

RD 1, Box 1733
Stewartstown, PA 17363

Field Advisory News

American Sighthound
Field Association
P.O. Box 399
Alpaugh, CA 93201

Greyhound Adoption Resource Directory

The Greyhound Project, Inc.
261 Robbins St.
Milton, MA 02186

The Home Stretch

Greyhound Friends, Inc. Newsletter, 167 Saddle Hill Rd.
Hopkinton, MA 01748
http://www.greyhound.org

Hares 'n' Hounds

North American Coursing Association
P.O. Box 507
Upton, WY 82730

Off Track Greyhound

GPA, California Adoption Center
P.O. Box 2433
LaMesa, CA 91943-2433

So You Want To Run Your Sighthound

Denise Como, author
Running Your Sighthound
P.O. Box 137
Cassville, NJ 08527-0137

Complete Book of Coursing

Steve Copold, author
Hoflin Publishing, Inc.
4401 Zephyr St.
Wheat Ridge, CO 80033

Gazehounds: The Search for Truth

Connie Miller, author
Hoflin Publishing, Inc.
4401 Zephyr St.
Wheat Ridge, CO 80033

CATALOGS

Dog Goods, Ltd.

2035 Wabansia
Chicago, IL 60647
(800) 736-6746
Coats, leather collars and leads

The Dog Museum Catalog

1721 South Mason Rd.
St. Louis, MO 63131
(314) 821-DOGS

GAIA Greyhound Greetings

4503 Church Rd.
Urbana, OH 43078-9365
(937) 652-3271
slemieux@ctcn.net
Notecards, tablets, stationery, pins, pendants,

Greyhound books and coloring books

The Glorious Greyhound

P.O. Box 160
Bellingham, MA 02019-0160
(508) 520-4852 or (508) 528-7101(fax).

Collars, jewelry, prints, T-shirts, and chimes

Greyhound Friends Catalogue

Steve Prior
34 Fisher St.
Uxbridge, MA 01596

(508) 278-0359

Greyhound Hall of Fame Catalogue

407 Buckeye
Abilene, KS 67410
(800) 932-7881 (phone) or

(913) 263-1704 (fax)

Homeward Bound:
The Greyhound and Whippet Catalog of Gifts

Greyhound Pets of America
P.O. Box 2433
LaMesa, CA 91943-2433

Calendars, T-shirts, key chains, jewelry, and chimes

National Greyhound Association

P.O. Box 543
Abilene, KS 67410
(913) 263-4660 or
(913) 263-4689 (fax)
http://www.jc.net/greyhd

Dog supplies

Operation Greyhound Catalog

P.O. Box 2058
Lakeside, CA 92040-0922
(619) 525-3161 or
(619) 525-3161 (fax)

OpGrey@aol.com

Ray Ann Enterprises

P.O. Box 2965
Springfield, MO 65801-2695
(417) 869-2555

Afghans, mugs, dishes, sweatshirts

Tails

4708 Utah Ave. North
New Hope, MN 55428-4522

(612) 535-3053

The Voyagers

P.O. Box 378
Deerfield, WI 53531
(800) 352-3762 or (608) 764-8028 Jewelry design,
coats, collars, and accessories

INDEX

CONTRIBUTORS

I'd like to thank all of the people and organizations who have helped make this work possible. Please forgive me if anyone has been left out.

Donald Aronson, NJ; K. Dale Baer, FL; Lois T. Bires, PA; Margaret Bryson, VA; Sharon Allert, TX; M.J. Barkley, CO; Linda Bell, CT; P. Gail Burnham, CA; Sue Cassem, MN; Linda Colflesh, PA; Ellie and Cecile Creech, MD; Dani Edgerton, OH; Patti Clark, CT; Dee Dee Colella, CA; Linda Allen and Anita Dengler, PA; Annie Fitt, OH; Renee Coates, OH; Paul Everitt, NJ; Joan Goldstein, NJ; Beth Anne Gordon, NM; Kim Hamm, KS; Don and Pat Ide, CA; E.F. Hill, NJ; Kim Fritzler, CO; Katie Lawson, IN; Joni Lovci, CA; June Matatrazzo, CT; Jack and Maggie Mitchell, UT; Joan Malak, MI; Pam Noll, TX; Stacy Pober, NY; Barbara Parker, NY; Stanley Petter, Jr., KY; Jim Porcher, NM; John Parker, GA; Ric Routledge, IN; Ann Cantrell, APO; Jini Foster, MA; Brad and Heather Spak, WA; Lorrie Richer, RI; Mr. and Mrs. William Simpson, MS; Bea Smith, OH; David Skeldon, MN; Jerry Sargent, OH; Mary Trubek, NJ; Hubert Thomas, FL; Madison Weeks, FL; Arlene Leibing, OH; Willard Wright, OH; Karen Ackerman, WY; Jan, Steve, and Jackie Casto, OH; Fern White, WY; Laurie and Walt Goodell, MI; Judie Trueschell, MI; Lindsey Strutt, MI; Drs. Donald and Judy Sanders, OH; Michelle Sanders, OH; Cindy Kelly, OH; Laurie Soutar, Canada; Cindy Bellis-Jones, KY; Heath Stimmel, OH; Lynda Meeuws, MI; Donna Arcaro, CA; Jody Spires, OH; Laura Hodder, OH; Stanley Tyree, FL; Mark Reidinger, OH; Greg Davis, KY; Roger Owens, KY; Colin Fritzler, CO; Laurel Drew, NM; Debbie Butt, VA; Bett Hanson, WA; Terri Fletcher, PA, Ric Metts, TX; Paula Hikkinz N. Lohkonza, Finland; Cecile Duflos, France; Gilberto Grandi, Italy; Hanne Bockhaus, Denmark; Laurent and Roos Vanderburie, Belgium; John Parlmer, Australia; Asa Lindahl, Sweden; Kari Nylen and Espen Engh, Norway; Karen Kvassheim Grottjord, Norway; Sari Rantenan, Finland; Peter and Mair Jones, England; Dean Dennis, Canada; Ashbey Photography, Inc., PA; Luc Allen Photography, TX; Alverson Photography, OH; Rich Bergman Photos, CA; Booth Photography, MI; Sue Baines Photo, NC; Pam Ross, Pet Portraits, GA; Kitten Rodwell Photos, CA; Joan Downey Photography, MO; Vicky Fox Photo, CA; Bernard Kernan, NJ; Kurtis Photo; Lloyd Olson Studio, MN; Robert Pearcy, CA; Paul's Studio, MI; Alex Smith Photography, MI; Evelyn Shafer, NY; Charles Tatham Photos, NH; Missy Yuhl, TX; Tom Bruni Photography, CA; Carlin and Camera, NY; Michael M. Trafford, Australia; Foto Per Unden, Sweden; Foto Wilhelm Dufwa, Sweden; Greyhound Club of America; Greyhound Friends, Inc., Louise Coleman, MA; Greyhound Hall of Fame, KS; National Greyhound Association, KS; North American Coursing Association; National Open Field Coursing Association; American Kennel Club; States Kennel Club; United Kennel Club; Ancient World Arts, NY; Sighthound Review, CA; The Ohio State University College of Veterinary Medicine, OH; Urbana Veterinary Clinic, OH.